Chiron, 2012, and the Aquarian Age

The Key and How to Use It

Tom Jacobs

Also by Tom Jacobs

The Soul's Journey I: Astrology, Reincarnation, and Karma with a Medium and Channel

Saturn Returns: Thinking Astrologically

Living Myth: Exploring Archetypal Journeys

Seeing Through Spiritual Eyes: A Memoir of Intuitive Awakening

Channeled Material

Approaching Love

Understanding Loss And Death

Goddess Past, Present, and Future

Conscious Revolution: Tools for 2012 and Beyond

ISBN-13:
978-1470031114

ISBN-10:
1470031116

Cover image courtesy of NASA/JPL-Caltech.

Table of Contents

Preface

This book is a transcription of an 11.5- hour MP3 audio course.[1] My aim in producing the course was to relay the perspective on Chiron shown to me by the Ascended Masters I work with, known as Djehuty, Thoth, and St. Germain, as a teaching to support us in our evolution as humans.

Since this view on Chiron began coming through in early 2008, producing a book to share it widely has felt important. The outline sat on my computer as I completed other projects, never really feeling right to dive into it fully. Then it became clear that an audio course would be a great way to share the information, and it would impart at least some of the vibration the Masters impart to me as they teach me. It began to flow easily when I sat down to articulate all I have been shown about Chiron and its place in our individual and collective evolution. It took the time between first channeling the material to the recording of the audio course in late 2010[2] to put it in practice and then articulate it fully as an astrology teaching.

I am really pleased that the information is now available in book form. Enough of the audio course is channeled to make the 11 hours of MP3s worth hearing. The Masters I work with bring the information through in a particular way, and being exposed to their vibration is important for us as we evolve into having more awareness of our true, spiritual natures. Much benefit can come from the course in its original audio format.

For those who have listened to the audio, this transcription will serve as a handy reference guide. For example, it will be very easy to look up specific house placements or natal aspects here in book form. There is also a wide variety of learning styles among people, and we sometimes need to hear something more than once or encounter it in various formats in order for it to really take root in

---

[1] Available via http://tdjacobs.com/store.html#chiron.
[2] "Chiron, 2012, and the Aquarian Age: The Key and How to Use It" MP3 course, recorded in August and September of 2010, is available at http://www.tdjacobs.com/store.html#chiron.

our consciousness. This is true especially of infor᠁ ᠁᠁ ᠁᠁᠁ lead us into a
new paradigm.

A Note on the Ascended Masters

It is natural that some might wonder about
information that became the course. It is not often that someone publishes an
astrology book based on information from such beings. Those who are familiar
with my work will have come across at least some mention of beings I channel in
his handful of faces, but it is not commonplace to hear about astrologers working
with such beings. I began working with these Masters a few years ago. I had
questions about the nature of soul and how to use astrology to more accurately and
better support humans in our evolution, and I didn't know where to go for
answers. So I asked these questions in meditation, just sort of "put it out there,"
and I began receiving answers.[3] My relationship with them has been evolving
ever since. As to whether this being should be trusted, I will leave you to trust
your instinct and inner radar regarding the vibration behind these teachings. My
own life has been remarkably changed for the better by trusting what feels to me
the vibration of truth that the teachings offer.

Djehuty, Thoth, and St. Germain are three manifestations of the Master and
represent different faces of the same being. This Master is present and
mythologized in all world cultures and has been available to those on this planet as
a resource and guide for as long as there has been anyone on it. According to him,
he has had a hand in human evolution since there were first humans.

But who is this guy, you ask? What does he do? Djehuty is committed to
supporting the unfolding of the divine plan, which is to say the perfection of the
"manifestation experiment." This is how he has explained it to me, using this
phrasing.

"Manifestation experiment" is a way of referring to the fact that all that is in
manifest form represents the will of the Creator energy expressing the desire and
the intention to know itself. In order to do that, it had to separate itself, split off
into pieces and manifest into physical form so that these separate pieces might
encounter, and thereby know, each other. This is what we are doing here; this is
the function of life. We are running around, hanging out with, and bumping into
each other in various ways in order to experience all the possible experiences we

---

[3] For more on these Masters and what I have learned from them, see *The Soul's Journey I:
Astrology, Reincarnation, and Karma with a Medium and Channel.*

can have here, as individuals and with each other and together. As we do this, we naturally forget that we are divine, part of the Source. Forgetting seems part of the human plan/Earth trip but eventually all the parts of Source, all living beings, will understand themselves as parts of the divine (will fully remember) and the experiment will be complete.

In the meantime, we are each engaged in a process of evolution. Each of us is on a particular path that is tailored for us by our soul and our spiritual guidance team. Djehuty, et al. are one source of guidance and support for us as we explore being human as we – individually and ultimately as a collective – perfect the divine plan.

The main human tool during this process of evolution is choice, the expression of free will. We can do whatever we want to do. We can love each other. We can hurt each other. We can be generous. We can steal. We can rescue and protect each other. We can kill. We can choose all manner of behaviors sourced in all manner of motivations.

Djehuty, et al. are committed to providing whatever assistance is needed to us as we evolve, no matter our choices – he recognizes that free will is our greatest asset and a primary tool of our learning. He is famous for not taking sides, not judging what we are up to, but supporting us in our evolution, even when we have hurtful motivations and do things for destructive reasons. For this reason this being is at times thought to be evil, yet this is simply a misunderstanding of his purpose, his commitment. Those assumptions, judgments, and fears reflect the dualistic lens through which humans have been living as long as there have been humans. That lens structures the world in terms of opposites – black and white, light and dark, good and bad, right and wrong. I have encountered students and colleagues who have been taught in very clear terms by various teachers and mentors that Djehuty, et al. are not to be trusted, are evil, and/or should be avoided at all costs. Such an attitude of fear can in fact keep one from doing healthy spiritual work as those teachers and mentors aim to do and teach their students to do, as when we generate fear we create barriers to growth.

I include this note on the Masters for two reasons. First, so that you might know who these beings are. Second, to introduce you to the nondualistic perspective this Master embodies and offers us, as it is a wonderful starting point for teaching you how to see astrology, yourself, others, and the world in terms of energy. This Master's intention is to help you find your way to trusting your instincts and fine-tuning your own motivations so that you might evolve into knowing yourself as part of the divine, which is loving, and this course is in part

intended to be an exposure to these beings as available to us for support and help during that process.

A Note on the Text

It felt important to stay close to the original spoken version while ensuring that the material is clear and makes sense. The natural flow of a person's speech is markedly different than the flow when that person writes. I mention this simply to tell you to expect this book to read a little differently than a book that comes into existence solely via the written word. I have left in some sentence fragments but edited many others out, and there are a number of sentences that would make my mother, our grammar teachers, and our software grammar checkers cringe and/or have a complete and total breakdown. In other words, I have not rewritten the text to make it seem as though originally written. I invite you to flow with the information contained here, encountering it as the transcription that it is.

My thanks go to Barbara Grosvenor for her fine efforts in transcribing the material. Thanks also go to Amy Herring for being a "first listener" to the audio course and providing me helpful feedback on this venture. Finally, thanks also go to Jillian Sheridan for her work to edit this text. Any remaining errors are my own.

T.D.J.
Tucson, Arizona
October 2010

Introduction: 2012 and Where We Are Now

My approach to Chiron begins with it being an energetic sensitizer. To really understand what that means we have to look at how we typically think about energy and our level of consciousness about what energy is, does, is for, and brings us, etc. – what all of that stuff is and how that is changing, given certain conditions of being on Earth right now. So, what I want to talk about is how things are changing.

The first thing is, people hear a lot about 2012, the end of the Mayan Calendar. People hear a lot about that and if you've been listening to me and reading about my work, and following what I'm doing, you'll have seen a lot of talk about 2012, a lot of talk about the energetic changes, and the energetic shifts that are taking place right now.

The ultimate or the end of these shifts is the evolution of consciousness. It's that simple. The Mayan Calendar was formed to track the evolution of consciousness, here on Earth in this plane, in this time-space dimension. It's a series of overlapping cycles that begin at different times and all end at the same time, and that is the end of the Mayan Long Count Calendar. The Mayans have several calendars, but the one we're talking about is the Long Count Calendar, which is the one that stretches over 16 billion years.

Each person has, essentially, the choice on where he or she is going to end up on the consciousness spectrum. This idea of evolution of consciousness has to do with understanding ourselves as spiritual beings, understanding our true natures as spiritual beings. What goes with that is understanding in what ways we are powerful creators, in what ways we create the world around us.

It has always been true that everything is about energy. Everything we can talk about in the physical world boils down to energy. It all begins with energy, but we are now more capable than ever, now with these shifts that are unfolding and that culminate at the end of the Mayan Long Count Calendar (a.k.a. 2012), we are now capable of understanding in what ways we have been creating things all along.

So this is an unprecedented time in the history of this planet and in the particular time-space dimension in which it exists. If you are alive now, you have signed up to experience these shifts. You have opted, at the soul level, to be one of the billions of humans who encounters the challenges inherent in experiencing these shifts and in making the decisions about how you will navigate them. For those who are along for the ride in conscious ways, you are cleaning up your history. You are learning in what way all of your, for example, relationship choices have reflected the needs of your soul. You are learning in what ways all of the difficult dynamics in your life – all of the dense, intense, knotted, and tangled family relationships – have served your evolution and you are acknowledging in what ways they are contributing to your soul's mission, and you're thanking all of the people who have brought you difficult circumstances. So that's kind of the end game. That's kind of the end game strategy that we're talking about.

As we shift our consciousness and we understand in what ways we are powerful, divine, creative beings, we have to go through our history and thank all of the teachers who have participated in our journeys, even if they can't thank us in the same way.

In many ways this journey – this particular chapter of our evolution and our evolution in consciousness – has to do with learning about the importance of love. We talk about everything being energy. There are basically two kinds of ways of using energy: One is opening and generating love and the other is closing and withholding love, or stopping love, or preventing love from being generated or shared.

This is getting into talking about 4ᵗʰ-chakra stuff, the heart center, which is located in the middle of your chest and is a simple circuit. It is either opened or closed or, perhaps more accurately, opening or closing. Every single thing you encounter either makes you open or close to it. You either feel good and you feel welcoming, and you open your energetic field to it, or you don't – you close it. Now, there is a very important teaching with the heart chakra regarding Chiron and I will get into that when we talk about the archetypical journey later in the course, but that's kind of the nutshell to get us started with this.

There are two kinds of responses to these challenges to evolve – evolution being owning our creative power, owning our having created the manifest world around us according to our energy fields. One response is: "Thank you for the education, thank you for the loving support in helping me further my evolution, thank you for reflecting to me what's going on." The other response: "I can't believe this is happening to me, this stinks, the Universe is crazy, God hates me," etc. Because as these shifts intensify, as these lessons intensify, we get challenged with more difficult parts of our life. What's happening is we're being challenged to choose to change our minds about why things have happened to us. When we can understand why it has happened and take responsibility for it, then we move into – we move closer or we move into – that space of being the divine creator that we are, being the portion of divine creative energy that each of us is.

The shifts can look in different ways to different people. Some people say, "Wow, things are speeding up," or "Gosh, I'm having to go through this filmstrip of all of my history, all of my relationship choices, all of my work stuff, all of my emotional stuff from all throughout my life." Some people will see these things manifest in their physical bodies more and that is a result of the energy. Some people will come down with challenging illnesses, for example. With the right viewpoint, these things can be mitigated, reduced, and eliminated, but that's one of the ways things are manifesting and will continue to manifest.

Remember that everything in the physical world is because of energy and then look to why it is happening and then own it; take responsibility for everything. One of the big things about this whole entire shift I'm talking about is going from "Things happen to me" – that perspective that the world is acting on you or other people do things to you – to "I make this happen." Just saying "I make this happen" is not enough. It can lead to self-judgment, self-criticism, and self-hatred for having created painful scenarios, so it's not enough. We have to go several steps further and understand the point of why it is.

And this is why I do the work that I do, helping people understand why the soul has signed up for what it is experiencing, why you are experiencing what you are doing. This whole Chiron teaching that I've been channeling for a couple of years fits into that nicely. You'll soon see why.

Taking responsibility for what's happened to us helps us relieve others of the responsibility for what has happened to us. The way that Chiron has been understood since its discovery and naming when it started entering the astrological mind or astrological vocabulary in 1977, that understanding of woundedness and then what healing is and if for – all of that understanding is essentially an infancy of this archetype. We'll explore more of that in the Myth and Archetype section.

We have understood that other people act on us, as we have so far in our evolution as humans looked at the things that happened to us as having happened from outside forces, that other people make choices that affect us. This shift, this Chironic 2012 shift, is everything about understanding why we have created it and in what ways – every single thing that's happened to us.

When I work with clients deeply on Chiron issues, they learn to take responsibility for what has happened to them. They learn why it has happened.

Taking apart Chiron in a chart is a great exercise, which is what you'll be able to do once you've completed listening to this entire course. Taking that apart is a great exercise in understanding how to not take energy personally.

What happens with Chiron is we get triggered by energy and we take it personally. This way of looking of Chiron that the course covers – and framing it in terms of 2012 with these energetic shifts that are taking place right now – it *is* personal. But it's personal not because the Universe is out to get you; it's not because you are supposed to be in pain and suffering, and it's not that you signed up to suffer. What you signed up to do is to learn how to manage being an energetic being having a physical experience. Every single person signed up to do that. What it comes down to a lot of the time is deciding what our experiences mean. You'll hear that probably four hundred million thousand, billion, trillion times during the course of this whole audio project: What the experiences mean is the key to unraveling all these Chiron issues.

Knowing ourselves as energetic beings having physical experiences, understanding the spiritual truths about living as energetic beings in this physical time-space plane, requires taking a bird's-eye view on what's going on with us. Meditation is very important. Meditation helps you cultivate the capacity to develop an inner space so that you can observe what's happening in your life with a measure of detachment so that you can learn. It actually opens up the space through which you can learn to see why the things are happening the way that they are, and not just experiencing things happening to you.

Because of this – learning that we are divine creative beings having human experiences and going through this shift from "Things happen to me" to "I create my reality" – is a tremendous leap in spiritual maturity. For a lot of people who are being challenged – I mean as a collective – we have never really gone through this. We've had individuals who shine through as exemplars of spiritual development in the past, but we have never as a collective been faced with this opportunity to accept the truth of why things happened and to know ourselves as energetic beings and the powerful divine creators that we are. We've never experienced it.

So, for some people who have been on spiritual paths for a very long time – including this life and other lives, either way – they are finally unlocking the secret, what has seemed the secret tools, the missing ingredients to their processes, and they are able to ease into this process in a certain way. For those of us who are not looking at life through spiritual eyes and for those of us who are not accustomed to this, what we are seeing is the results of what we've been creating intensifying. So I mentioned physical illness earlier. I don't talk about this in order to scare people – believe me, I don't – but as one way that energy manifests and one site of action in which things can intensify, physical illness is one of the ways.

Another way is difficulty in relationships. Relationships that have never worked, that have never supported the spiritual path that a person is on or is being invited to step onto that's waiting for him or her. Economic issues, job issues, issues with authority figures, issues with where love comes from and why. Getting needs met. Self-care. All of these arenas are intensifying for people who have the lessons presented to them, but they're really not sure what to do with them. The vast majority of people do not know what to do with these lessons. The vast majority of people are not prepared to go through this shift.

What that looks like for them is these difficulties will intensify, but they won't understand why it's happening. Now, they're experiencing the transition, but for those of us who have opted to experience the transition in a more conscious way and to have kind of an overt, conscious understanding of what's happening and why, we can move through these historical knots faster. The capacity to move through history, to unravel karma, to process old beliefs in our energy fields and thereby change our lives, is accelerated just as the manifestation of the knots, if we don't do it, is accelerated.

So, it's very important – no matter who you are, no matter what you're doing, no matter what you're up to – to withhold judgment of those who are not choosing to change. Everybody who is shifting will be, for example, surrounded by family members who are not shifting, people who are not understanding that if you make changes, if you choose to understand things differently, if you look at things through your spiritual eyes with a bird's-eye view, that life *will* change, having optimism about advancement and spiritual evolution.

It's very important to withhold judgment of everyone who is not doing it, and also to withhold judgment of the process of anyone who is or is not going through it. Each of us is here on a spiritual journey, whether we're conscious of being spiritual beings or not. Each of us is facing these questions and our souls are benefiting from exploring these possibilities.

So, let's say that you're changing, but other people aren't changing. Just let them be what they are. If they want to take cues from you and learn from you, then great. If you happen to be a practitioner of some kind – of any kind of energetic or spiritual category – and people want to take cues from you then perfect. But just hold in your heart not to judge their process. Also, don't judge *your* process. You're being invited to go through your history and clean up a lot of junk. This is difficult. So don't judge yourself either. Just create a loving space where there's no judgment and learn to create enough detachment so you can observe what's going on and move through it.

This is a lot about these energetic shifts. As you listen to the rest of the course, you'll understand how Chiron fits into this. A lot of what I do with Chiron results from – especially the channeling over the last two-plus years – results from me asking my Guides and Ascended Masters what will happen in 2012. I was starting to hear some things, whenever I hear people say, "Oh, you should be afraid of this." Whether it's implied or explicit I'm always doubtful, because we all have choices about how to respond to things and anytime someone tells me to be afraid of something, I step into it, which is why I do such in-depth work with Pluto, Lucifer, and Lilith as well.

I sat down in meditation, and it was a half-dozen sessions of sitting down with this one question: "What is going to happen in 2012?" And every single response was very direct and very clear, an unfolding picture of how to help people with their Chiron issues. So, the teachings that you're going to hear in the course are channeled, and then I've spent time and energy articulating it in terms of how people already understand Chiron and chart analysis. But the core teachings that you'll be hearing have everything to do with what my Guides and Ascended Masters, specifically Thoth and St Germain have to say about what's going on with Chiron.

At the time, I was thrilled to get this information, but I was also a little disappointed that my question wasn't being answered. And then I had to remember that sometimes you ask a question that isn't answerable. Sometimes your motivation is out of whack and so the answer you'll get from Guides or other spirit beings is either nothing (because if you're operating from fear, they can't understand you) or they can't respond to you if you're not open to hearing the frequency that they work on. Also, sometimes there is no answer to the questions you ask and so what you get is what you "are supposed" to be focusing on instead.

After about a half-dozen of these sessions where I said, "Great, thank you for this Chiron teaching," and I made notes furiously, getting all this stuff down in my notebook, I realized that this is what we should be focusing on: Changing our relationship to energy. Changing our understanding of ourselves. Who do we think we are? When we focus on this idea of being spiritual beings, which is a way of saying energetic beings, having these physical/human experiences, that takes us into really understanding what Chiron is all about. So I'm extremely grateful to my Guides and to Thoth and to St. Germain for bringing a lot of this through and answering these questions.

But when I first looked at all of this and I said, "Well, okay, I asked what was going to happen in 2012, and I received all this stuff about Chiron," I had to deduce, in time, after being a little confused about it, that this shifting of our perspective of energy and our understanding of who we are and how we experience life – which is essentially how we experience energy – that shifting that conception *is* the answer to 2012.

So, the key, when it comes to Chiron – and it's obviously a little bit ironic … you're probably laughing because the glyph for Chiron looks like a key – the key when it comes to Chiron is changing our relationship to energy. Changing the labels we put on energy, changing our capacity to traffic in energy, altering how we relate to emotions, which are energy.

What I eventually articulated (and then had it confirmed with really enthusiastic thumbs-up from all those Guides) is that what is going to happen in 2012 has nothing to do with what might happen in the physical world. Nobody knows that; we don't know that. There's a movie out that plays on all these disaster scenarios: the entire world is crumbling, etc., and people are freaking out. There's all this stuff in the media. This is going to continue to intensify, but that is not where our attention needs to be. Our attention needs to be on how we experience energy, how we experience ourselves as energetic beings.

When I asked, "What's going to happen in 2012?" and the information on Chiron came through as how to heal Chiron issues – doing what I call now "emotional archaeology," digging through these layers, these strata of what's in our energetic field – one way to access it is looking through the emotions that we have experienced in this life and in other lives. So, this also has a lot to do with karma in many people, when Chiron is tied in with Pluto or the nodes or the nodal rulers. So, that's one way to have a prominent Chiron, in other words.

Looking at changing this history, rewriting the history of why things happened – because that frees up you to feel everything that you can feel, which is the end goal – to become fully human at this stage in our evolution is to accept everything about ourselves. So we have to heal shadow stuff, but in any given moment, it has a lot to do – like inhabiting this sense or this full sense of human being, this full sense of being human – has to do with feeling everything we can feel while we learn to manage our energy.

This will sound to many to be outside the scope of astrology, which is okay. I don't have any judgments about that. I think this takes us into "astrology plus," where we learn that astrology is a language of energy, and if you've followed my work and you've read *The Soul's Journey I* and some other of my books, you see that I'm really focused on teaching people to think astrologically, which is thinking in terms of energy, not in terms of specifics and details. When you understand the energy of a chart, then you can really work with people as they live that energy, because the choices they make determine everything.

Again, while this might seem outside the scope of astrology, I can assure you that this kind of thinking is a major part of the future of astrology. For those of us who shift, who evolve, who change, and who alter our understanding of ourselves as energetic beings, we are in a process of evolution, of moving into understanding ourselves as these divine creative beings, understanding in what ways we create the world around us. No other kind of astrology – no kind of astrology, no version, no form, no dialect of this language of energy that does not speak about energy – will remain relevant to people.

My own personal feeling on this – not to get too sidetracked, but it does set the stage for the rest of the course, so it seems relevant – my own personal feeling is that each of us is naturally wired to seek meaning and we each know on some gut level, we each intuitively know, that astrology and other divination arts can tell us who we are and what we're doing here. In one sense, all of these divination tools are ways to go down the path of spirituality, but if we get away from spirituality and start getting in our heads, start doing these divination arts as intellectual pursuits or if we get caught up in the ideas of things and we forget that it's about energy, then we're not actually being served. I can't tell you how many times a client says to me: "I've had ten readings/I've studied my chart for 20 years, but what you just told me in an hour about my chart helps me make sense to myself." And that's because I'm doing this energetic approach. It's all about energy. We are changing and our astrology needs to change with us.

Chiron is a huge part of that because it teaches us the value in learning about ourselves as energetic beings. As you'll hear in the course, each person is an antenna for energy relative to what the Chiron placement is, so house, sign, and aspect. Each person is an antenna for energy.

Mostly, how we understand energy is through or as emotion, and so Chiron stuff has a lot to do with emotional stuff, but the core of it is about being sensitive to energy. Because there are a wide variety of kinds of energy out there that we experience, some of it feels bad, some of it feels good; we apply labels and meaning to the energies we experience, to the emotions that we experience. And then, of course, we seek to repeat or seek to find those that make us feel good and we tend to reject and avoid and shun those that make us feel bad.

The Chiron evolution at this time involves while learning to manage one's energy, while learning to manage the creation of the world around oneself in terms of the energy he or she is holding, we detach from the meaning that we have assigned to emotions. We learn the real process of healing, and Chiron teaches us the value in healing.

Not to get too ahead of myself, but one of the major teachings of Chiron is to look at the point, to understand the point of pain and suffering. As each person is an antenna for Chiron energy, all kinds of great energy is experienced, all kinds of horrible energy is experienced, but the meaning that gets associated with them – "I'm going to pursue pleasure, I'm going to seek joy, and I'm going to avoid pain, and I'm going to avoid suffering"—that's a natural human response. We don't *want* to feel pain. Well, at this stage in our evolution, we have to understand what the point of pain and suffering is. What I've been shown by these Masters and my Guides is that the point of pain and suffering is to teach us the value of choosing compassion.

So, if you are looking for one keyword for the process of using the "key," which is understanding energetic sensitivity surrounding Chiron, that word would be *compassion*.

Each of us has a choice on how to respond to the energy in the world around us. Not many of us respond to joy with negativity. Joy can be infectious. We feel good when other people feel joy. We're happy when people are happy. When we sense pain and suffering in the world around us, we don't like to experience that. Some of us take it on as a mission to help heal people and to support people, and to caretake, but many of us don't.

So, in this transition right now, what we're supposed to look at is the value in choosing compassion in the face of pain and suffering. When we experience difficulty within or without, the pain and suffering, and we shut down, we close our hearts, we don't want to feel that. We choose not to feel that emotion, that energy. We cut off a part of ourselves. It is not head-in-the-clouds, pie-in-the-sky, fluffy New Age nonsense to say that love is the answer to everything. Maybe that's become a cliché in some ways of thinking in some circles, but this choice to have compassion in the face of pain and suffering is the choice to love.

Chiron empowerment, Chiron growth, Chiron evolution centers on the choice to be loving no matter what you experience. Again, this is in some ways outside the normal scope of astrology. But astrology is just a language telling us about the human experience, and the human experience – being this journey of understanding ourselves as energy, having physical experience, and therefore astrology should always be supporting our evolution as energetic beings, which is to say spiritual beings. In some ways this course is going to depart from tradition.

In some ways everything I do – or most things I do – departs from tradition because I'm looking at this from the energetic, spiritual standpoint, with us as energetic beings and love being energy.

When we talk about fear versus love, we talk about there being two motivations. There are two kinds of ways of doing things and one is with love, which can also be called faith, and the other one is with fear, which is essentially an absence or withholding of love – it is acting without love. When we look at things through those eyes, in that light, there is only one ultimate choice, and it is to be loving.

What we tend to think of, what we talk about as love, and what we represent in our culture as love is not what I'm talking about. I'm talking about when we encounter anything, we respond with openness, openness to share our energy. I'm not talking about crossing streams of energy or mixing energy; I'm talking about showing the truth of who you are, which is love, which is loving. When people are suffering, they will tend to see it in terms of material manifestations. It's not always true that people understand the energy about what they're experiencing and so it has to come out in the physical plane. It has to come out in the material world.

So, something about the body is broken and that creates suffering, something about the material world: "I don't have food. I don't have a house. I don't have relationships. I don't have love. I don't have acceptance. I don't have a family. I don't have connectedness. I don't have connection." All of those things are outgrowths in the physical world of the energy someone is carrying. Because it looks like a lot of things that are difficult for us to deal with, almost. A person on the street asks you for money – that's one of these manifestations. What we really need is love, what we really need is compassion; we really need the energetic connectedness, the energetic connection. These other things, these material world or manifest situations, arise from our capacity, from our feeling of energy.

When you're confronted with pain and suffering, no matter what it looks like – somebody who is sick, somebody who is dying, somebody who is destitute, somebody who is abused – all of these situations have real-world remedies, of course. All of these situations have these practical routes through them, and yet what the person at the spiritual level needs is compassion.

We have a lot of models of what this might look like, people who devote their lives to helping the poor, the downtrodden, etc. But in our daily lives we can do a tremendous amount – and these people are extreme examples – like Mother Theresa, etc., these people who walk into the middle of the storm of destitution or something like this and do commit their lives to doing this kind of work. And that is one kind of example.

What we're being asked to do now is to respond to any and all pain and suffering with compassion, which requires us to have an open heart. We'll get into this more deeply in the Myth and Archetype section – but a lot of us look at the prospect of opening our hearts as a very dangerous idea. If we do that, we'll be totally emotional, we won't be able to control ourselves, we might start weeping if we're holding pain or grief from the past, and there are strategies we're going to work on in the Chironic journey in the Myth and Archetype section. But in our daily lives to respond to any and all pain and suffering with compassion is extremely important. That provides a spiritual evolution. It's not obvious, but when we do this, we spread love in the world. And again, this is not pie-in-the-sky, head-in-the-clouds, New Age fluffy nonsense.

This is how we solve our spiritual issues, how we solve our spiritual problems, which have a lot to do with this Chironic energetic sensitivity. Because you're walking around being an antenna for other people's energy, which includes their suffering. How do you respond to it? Do you shut down? Do you open your heart? Do you think that because they're suffering, you should suffer too? Do you understand in what ways their suffering is their story, is their journey, their experience? That involves learning energy management.

Astrology buffs or aficionados will know that the old axiom, "As above, so below," in talking about the relationship of our lives to the planets, and I update that. I go one step further and say, "As inside, so outside," because, as we create the world around us, the world becomes a reflection of our own energy fields.

When you encounter suffering and you don't look at it and you don't respond with compassion, we can know for sure that within you there are parts of you that need compassion and you don't respond to them. So the big part of the Chiron journey, which we'll get into later, has to do with learning how to treat ourselves compassionately. When we do that, then we can understand how to treat others compassionately.

Getting back to where we are now, relative to 2012 and all these opportunities to shift and experience ourselves as energetic beings, what we're looking at now is a divergence in levels of consciousness. Those of us who go down the path, who respond to the invitations to learn about our history and how we created the world around us, how we have created our own worlds around us – that's going to be one level of consciousness, where we open and adapt to this view of seeing ourselves as spiritual creators, creating all of this. The other level of consciousness, for those people who do not choose to change in the way that you do, the way that the others do – things will seem to stay the same, but get more intense – the same themes, the same patterns, the same issues, but more intense perhaps, probably faster. The ways that problems can manifest in the material plane will become faster because, the same way that the ways that we can solve and heal and release these, and understand this new perspective – this higher view, this bird's-eye perspective on ourselves as spiritual beings – also increases in speed.

So, divergent levels of consciousness. Those of you who go through this process of change will find yourselves speaking a different language. You'll find yourself using language--not just a different vocabulary, but using language in a very intentional way, in a very different way, that actually brings through the energy of yourself as a divine, creative being.

Some of you will begin, if you have not already, to channel and to live lives essentially connected to your higher self, or your Guides, or the Masters that you're aligned with. And that will naturally change your relationships, because a lot of other people will not do this. They won't understand what you're talking about, and you will have some sense of being able to understand what they're talking about, but you won't be able to relate to it and they won't be able to relate to you.

What I want to close this section with is: Understand that as you go down the Chironic journey, which is an initiation into spiritual maturity – not just what traditions have said spirituality is, but what the Ascended Masters who hang around to help us, what *they* tell us that spiritual change and evolution is – as you go down that path you are going to be living in a different world. You'll be more connected to your intuition – specifically with Chiron, living a life where you are willing to sense what is going on in the world around you, comes with, has built into it, living in harmony with the flow around you. This is about creating a world around you that matches your vibration, so you'll naturally be guided to live in a certain place. You'll be guided to go here and go there. You'll feel that inner wisdom nudging you to do things. That's part of the Chironic journey.

As we experience divergent levels of consciousness, again, no judgment. No judgment on how fast you may or may not be doing your path, no judgment on how fast or how much or how anyone else is doing his or her path. Learning how to love ourselves as divine creators. Learning how to respond to the world around us with compassion. Learning how to, by responding with compassion, how we can end suffering and pain in ourselves and the world around us.

Going forward in the rest of this course, you're going to learn not just Chiron through the signs and houses and aspects and transit progressions, etc. –how to look at, how to understand the technical side of Chiron in a chart – but you're also going to be learning about how to manage energy, how to come out of the Chiron victimhood into understanding the spiritual purpose of this energetic antenna that each person is carrying.

So I'm very excited. This is the end of the introduction. And I hope you're excited too. So keep listening, and roll up your sleeves and get ready to learn all this stuff that I've been channeling for a couple of years that people find really, really useful in helping them to change their lives.

Myth and Archetype

When we talk about myth, it's important to understand that myth is always a tool of social instruction. A myth is a story that gets handed down through generations in order to teach people how to be good members of the group, society, or family of which they are part.

So, myth is always about teaching people how to behave and how not to behave. We always have to be, well ... I guess my word is *suspicious*. I'm very Uranian – I have Uranus in the 1st house, conjunct the Ascendant. I feel we always have to be a little suspicious of what we're being taught or at least be cognizant of the real messages that we're being taught through our mythologies. They tend to be cautionary tales: "Do this. Don't do that. Be this kind of son or daughter. Be this kind of spouse. Be this kind of employee." It carries over, not just from the moldy oldies that we inherited from our Greek and Roman forebears. For example, sports figures attain a mythological status. People who hold the office of the president or the prime minister of any country have a certain mythology attached to them. They become, in essence, role models for how we should and shouldn't behave.

You can think about those presidents, for example – presidents of the USA that are revered for certain attributes – they are mythological figures. It makes sense, myth being a tool for social instruction. You need to know what are appropriate behaviors in the family system you live in, the school you go to, the community you live in, the country of which you are a part. You need to know this stuff. It just happens that after a while, we can find that we're not really living these stories as we receive them, and that's where I begin looking at the difference between myth and archetype.

So myth is social instruction; archetype is actually how we live it. Archetype is the portion of our psyches that lives the story, that runs the story in question. Check out the *Living Myth* book if you want a full exploration of this that goes beyond Chiron.

The Myth of Chiron

I want to tell you the story as we received it. It will be, in many ways, very familiar to you if you're into astrology enough to get a billion-hour audio course on Chiron. But this myth as we received it is that Chiron is a centaur – Chiron is a half-horse, half-human being. He is immortal and he is a healer and a musician and a teacher. He does a lot of different kinds of things. We sometimes hear mention of him as a teacher of heroes before they go on their great quests, and we sometimes hear of him in mention of the other centaurs and his relationship with them or something like that.

What we usually hear about – and this is how we have really taken on this story in astrological circles the last 30-plus years, since it entered our vocabulary – is that Chiron is the wounded healer. He is wounded by a poisoned arrow. The accounts vary as to how exactly this happened (some say it is his own invention, some say not), but it's an accidental wounding by a poison and because he's immortal, he can't die, so he's in suffering. He's in this mode of suffering.

He does everything he can to try to heal himself, but none of it works. Eventually he works out this deal whereby he can trade places with another immortal. This is with Prometheus, who is having his liver eaten out every day by a giant liver-eating vulture, and Chiron can give up his immortality and free Prometheus in the process. He works out this deal because there is nothing he can do to help his suffering. He's immortal and he's been poisoned by this really potent stuff.

So as this comes to us culturally, there are certain kinds of pain that never go away, that we cannot get rid of, that we cannot heal, and that are only solved by death. I happen to think that's a very limited way of looking at anything, this kind of black-and-white thing that can actually generate some pessimism, but this is the story that we received. As we've worked with it in astrology over the last few decades, we get the idea of Chiron as wounded and wounded healer. We talk a lot about what it means to be wounded and the idea that we cannot actually help ourselves with our own wounding, but that we can help other people with their wounding if it is similar.

This idea and the myth as we have received it through astrological circles is that we feel a pain that we cannot address, but we can help other people with that pain. Now if we just continue with our pain, then we're wounded. If we choose to help other people with that same kind of issue, then we are wounded healers.

At one of his astrology apprenticeship programs, I heard Steven Forrest mention something on Chiron. I don't think at that point he was using it a lot; he wasn't talking about it. He was still feeling out how he felt about it, and what he wanted to say about it, and how it came through to him. But one of the things he said is that it has become a convenient excuse for whining because this idea we're taught is that we have this portion of pain, which makes us suffer, that we can't do anything about.

Chiron came into our vocabulary in 1977 – that's when it was discovered – and this was in the middle of the Pluto-in-Leo generation's explorations of generating and following and consuming the self-help movement. One of the things about the Pluto in Leo generation as an aside is that all of these individuals at the soul level are focused on self-expression. They're focused on what it means to express the self and have the personal voice heard. A lot of what was happening in the '70s with the self-help movement as it began, what really seriously blossomed, was kind of an attitude of "poor me" that formed part of that foundation. Not all of them were living unhealthy Chiron stories – and not all writers and teachers and people who were following the stuff were – but culturally, as a collective, a lot of the understanding of Chiron energy was informed by that level of awareness that particular kind of vibration in the collective consciousness when Chiron was discovered.

Now, whenever a body is discovered and named, and it therefore enters the collective consciousness, it's time for us to learn to deal with that energy. We need to learn to understand that archetype within ourselves and learn how to deal with the energy it represents.

So Chiron actually comes in, in full swing of the self-help movement in the '70s and, given my perspective on Chiron, I think it just took us a few decades to begin to understand that focusing on this pain that we can't get rid of is not productive, because then we just end up whining about how we're suffering. And again, a lot of people do take it a step further and become what is known as this wounded healer, but it's still defined by wounding and healing.

One of my intentions for doing this audio course is to help us get beyond wounded and get beyond wounded healer so that we can understand the point of pain and suffering, and we can understand ourselves more as energetic beings. But as we have been for this last (as of this recording) 33 years, working with these ideas of Chiron as wounded and wounded healer, that has actually opened up a tremendous vista into ourselves and to how we're wired, so I don't discount any of the work that's been done. But we're ready to evolve our consciousness surrounding Chiron, because we are evolving.

There is a lot of great work on the psychology of Chiron and how it manifests. As I've explored how other writers and astrologers have looked at Chiron, there are several who have gotten deep levels of understanding who have really impressed me. But again, a lot of that (most of that, frankly) stops with the psychological approach. And we will never solve this deep need for human meaning through psychology alone. We'll never heal the kind of pain that is represented by our Chiron placements through psychology alone.

As we have received the myth, it's easy to focus on the pain and the suffering and not really ever understand what to do in response to it. As we received this myth and as we've been working with it, especially in astrology, and we come up with these ideas of wounded and wounded healer, it's easy to be stuck in one of those roles. It's easy to create the world around us in terms of being wounded or being somebody who helps other people with a similar wound.

Like I said, there's a lot of great work about the psychology of Chiron, but that's not enough; it's just not enough as we are changing. So what I do is I retell the story in order to get at the real heart of how we live the archetype. I do that across the board, and that's one of the things that *Living Myth* is really useful for, as it retells these stories to reflect how we actually live the archetypes.

With the Chiron archetype the first thing to notice is the fact that there are two wounds. The one that we focus on in the myth is the second wound, when Chiron is inadvertently poisoned by this arrow. The first wound happens at birth. The actual story varies between sources but, in essence, his mother, who is a nymph named Philyria is out frolicking with her nymph gal pals like usual, and Kronos (whom we know better as Saturn) sees her and says, "Wow, I've gotta have her. She's hot!" She does not want to be had by him, so she takes the form of a horse and she runs away. He takes the form of a horse and overtakes her and essentially rapes her. She goes back to her humanoid form, and when the little baby is born – and she's looking forward to this, however the baby was conceived because this is her baby – when he's born he's half-horse, half-human. He's a centaur. And she essentially reacts with:"Get this monster away from me!"

So he is taken away from her because she rejects him at birth, for just being who he is. He is taken away and he is raised by some other gods and he is taught healing arts and martial arts and all of these wonderful things. He lives a very interesting kind of life, where he is very resourceful and whatever it is that he wants to know, he learns it, and then he turns around and teaches it to other people.

As we talk about the wounding of Chiron and we focus on the pain we can't get rid of, we think it's about this inadvertent wounding of the arrow. That's actually a red herring that's a misunderstanding, a misdirection from what the real pain about Chiron is.

I've been working with people for a few years about getting into this deeply in themselves, about what this real Chiron wounding is, this wounding at infancy, this rejection by the mother. It could also be a rejection by another parent figure, a primary caregiver, but it is very often Mom, and sometimes Dad if there is a lot of direct imprinting and reliance on Dad as a primary caregiver. If Dad's not around that much, or if Mom's with baby 24/7 and Dad's there sometimes, it's probably not going to be Dad, unless there is a karmic connection that needs to be explored through the Chiron wounding with Dad.

What happens is that there is some kind of inadvertent rejection by the parent. Baby does something that feels natural and the parent either corrects the action (i.e., "We don't do this!") and prevents the baby from reaching something or from finding something, or from moving in a certain way or from doing something, expressing some energy. And it's a molehill. Through everybody else's eyes, it's not a big deal. Baby's just doing this. But what happens is, because Mom or parent is everything, because the caregiver is the source of everything, the caregiver is God and Goddess and Creator and love incarnate, the source of love, and food is love and all of this. From that Baby's perspective, everything comes from the parent, including love, and love is everything. So when this behavior is rejected or censured or sanctioned or the baby is given a look which conveys rejection or punishment, the baby gets imprinted with, "I shouldn't be this part of myself."

As we explored earlier, Chiron is an energetic sensitizer. What happens is that we are so sensitive to the reactions of other people in this given part of life (represented by our Chiron sign, house, and aspects) that we internalize the reaction of the other and make a mountain out of a molehill. The original molehill that seemed mountainous was this rejection from the parent.

What's happening is that people are running around – fully functional adults are running around with this wounded infant, feeling sensitive because Mom or Dad or Caregiver rejected him or her in the past. When I do this work with clients, I will intuitively dial back to the age it happened at first or where it first made a real impact. It varies from a few hours, a few days, up to about 18 months, to have the real, impactful imprinting take place. The infant will have sensitivity to this issue running 24/7, but the events that make the greatest impact will happen before the age of 18 months. Then, for the rest of infancy, the rest of childhood and the rest of life, the wounding gets repeated because we are so sensitive to the reactions of other people that we take any kind of hint of negative reaction – as a personal rejection of this natural part of ourselves.

So, saying it's a mountain made out of a molehill is not to belittle the part of us that experiences this pain of rejection. What I want to get at is that, through anybody else's eyes, it's a molehill, because the people who trigger a Chironic sensitivity and the wound that might have been attached – for the vast majority of us was attached and not processed over time –they don't see it as a mountain, and they cannot understand why we are so sensitive to this part of life, why we are so sensitive about expressing this part of ourselves. When people who are very Chironic or people who have a deep Chiron wound who go to express this part of themselves, and other people can see the fear that goes with the risk of expressing it, it doesn't make any sense. And this is categorical.

For example, say that you're dealing with a 40 year-old man with a prominent Chiron. Let's say Chiron is conjunct his Sun. He's 40, you figure he's fully developed, he's fully functioning, he has a job, he has a family, he takes care of himself, he's dependable, he's reliable, he's mature. But then he gets into creativity, which is a Sun issue. When he gets into creativity, part of him will expect some form of rejection. So you might say, "Wow, you write poetry, and you should go read it." And he would never do it, or he would do it, he would risk, but the intense cache of emotion and fear that goes with it will not make sense to anybody else. Maybe we'll try to explain it away by saying that he has stage fright, or he's shy, but it's so much deeper. It's like the threat of rejection; it's the threat of losing love. "If I express this part of myself, I will not be loved." And this is the imprint from when this person was an infant. We can assign baby behavior to all of the energies of the zodiac. So, with the Sun we're talking about shining, and we're talking about being bold and being the center of attention.

In this random, imaginary 40 year-old guy's situation, he might have, suddenly, at eight months old, burst out in a display of what we might call creative energy, but to others it looked like he was demanding to be the center of attention all the time. So he got imprinted with the fear of rejection if he did that, because "it's obnoxious" and people don't always let kids get away with stuff like that. But from his perspective, this is a mountain, this is central to who he is – Chiron on Sun – and he needs to expressive himself creatively, but he can't do it because he was so hurt when he did it as an infant.

One of the ways I work with people is to dial back to that age and to understand what that baby needed at that moment, and then we figure out how, today, how here and now, this 40 year-old guy who is otherwise fully functional, how he can give that part of himself – that infant that's been imprinted with this fear of rejection and fear of the loss of love – how to give himself what he needed then.

Essentially, a lot of Chiron healing involves a process of learning to parent inner infants that needed but never got certain kinds of love and acceptance.

That's the end goal: love and acceptance, compassionate love, compassionate acceptance.

There are different responses to carrying a Chiron wound from infancy. One response is to shut it down – to shut this part of ourselves down. In the case of this 40 year-old's Chiron-Sun, to avoid all arenas of life where he might have to creatively express himself. He might seem in many ways like a drone. He might seem half-robotic because he's trying to avoid being solar, like expressing the energy of Leo or the 5th house. He's trying to avoid being the center of attention, for example. All creative urges he has, which there will be many, he will tend to edit.

That's one kind of way that we do that. We tend to try to shut the part down, so that we can ensure that we will not be rejected for doing it. We all need love and acceptance, especially the part of our lives that is being run by an inner infant, who has this Chironic pain.

The other kind of response is to identify as wounded and to pursue this part of ourselves, but in one way, feed off the rejection. In the example of the first person, the response is "Wow, I don't want to experience a loss of love. I don't deserve that." In the second example, when somebody expresses the Chiron and gets the rejection, it can be internalized as meaningful. The rejection itself can be some kind of stand-in for love. Now obviously, it's not a parallel, it's not analogous, but if you are giving me attention by rejecting me, at least you're giving me attention.

So there are some of us who feed off that rejection, even though it hurts a tremendous amount and is never fun. We've all met people who develop an identity around the reasons for which they are rejected. That's one of the ways that we live Chiron journeys. That's one of the ways we experience this archetype.

Regardless of where Chiron is in our birth charts – regardless of sign, house, and aspect, regardless of whether it's involved in the karmic story, regardless of any details about Chiron – there is something true about Chiron that applies to each of us. That is that when we express our Chirons, we are obviously unique. When we can get over this wounding from infancy which involves parenting the inner kids – the ways that they needed but didn't get this compassionate love and total and utter acceptance, unconditional love and acceptance – then we are free to appreciate the ways that we are unique.

This kind of sounds like a truism, but Chiron offers the opportunity to learn this from the inside out, to appreciate uniqueness, to appreciate difference.

Whatever you do, whatever your Chiron is about, when you act on it, you will be obviously unique.

So, what does difference mean? What does it mean to stand out from a crowd? All of our reactions to this, all of our default reactions to this and answers to those questions have to do with our conditioning. Remember that we carry this infant until we process it. Each of us will carry this infant, afraid of rejection, until we figure it out. As that infant is trying to get us not to be rejected, there is a lot of conformist, fear-based behavior that we engage in, to make sure that our wound is not triggered.

The truth is that each person is unique. But when we are guarded, energetically and emotionally, because we've experienced the pain of rejection for being unique, for standing out, for sticking out like a sore thumb, or for being the only person in the room who's different, that conditioning will naturally lead us to one of those two responses that I mentioned earlier: blocking that part of ourselves or indulging in self-pity because we're rejected and developing an identity around it.

We're talking about the influence of a part of us that is very, very young. This part of us does not have the faculties of reason and verbal communication. In our infant brains, in babies up to 18 months old, they are not reasonable. You can't reason with them; they deal with everything via feeling.

I work with clients now both in one-time readings and in ongoing sessions who are working on deep Chiron issues, who have sought traditional therapy, psychotherapy and counseling from traditionally trained people and they can spend years and years going at these issues and never really making the kind of progress that feels meaningful to them. This is because the part that is hurt, the part that needs attention, can only be dealt with energetically, which is to say emotionally.

A while back, I had a client with Chiron on her Sun in Aries, and she didn't have consciousness that the issues she wanted to work on had to do with Chiron-Sun – feeling different, having her own sense of creativity – being bold – because that Chiron on the Aries Sun will limit some of the boldness and instinctive action due to the fear of rejection. But she had spent nine months *talking* about it. Which is essentially talking about the ramifications of it. Talking about the results of this wounding.

In an hour I told her this Chiron story and made it applicable to her based on her particular Chiron configuration. Her response was that it was more useful than nine months of therapy. And this is true of many of our deepest issues that we seem unable to crack. We seem unable to get at it, no matter what we do about it. We can go to other people to get energetic/energy work, we can talk about it, we can seek astrology, we can do all kinds of therapeutic things, but until we consciously shift our experience of that part of ourselves and welcome it and love that part of ourselves, that is the only way to heal that original Chiron wounding. Once we do that, then we are able to experience Chiron as a gift, to get beyond wounded, then get beyond wounded healer, and to experience all of life through our energetic faculties.

This is a giant thing to talk about here – a very critical, very important thing – about how we relate to our emotions and how we relate to what we understand as our heart. A lot of times I talk about this in terms of our 4th chakra, our heart center, which is in the center of our chest, the emotional center of the body. We all know this from – if nothing else, when the little cartoon skunk falls in love with the cartoon cat, and the cartoon hearts emanate from his little skunk cartoon heart. (That's one of my favorites.) We know that's where love comes from, we know that's the source of it, and that's where pain comes from or that's where it's centered in the body. That's where we feel it.

Regarding Chiron, the big teaching about this is that the heart either opens or closes. Chiron opens for something that feeds us and supports us and inspires us and makes us feel loving, and it closes for things that don't, for things that are destructive and hateful and angry and chaotic.

As we live these Chiron stories, being walking antennas of energy and picking up all kinds of things in the world around us, when we carry this core Chironic wound of rejection from our childhoods, from our infancy, what happens is that we're closed off to many kinds of experiences that life has to offer because we're afraid of having that button of pain pushed.

We're pretty amazing in that we learn over time, and we always want to seek the repeat of what brings us pleasure and joy and happiness and avoid what brings us pain (unless of course we're getting off on identifying with pain).

Continuing with the example of Chiron-Sun, there would be an echo with Chiron in Leo or Chiron in the 5th and also Chiron aspecting the Sun in various ways. Continuing with that example, the fear of rejection will actually keep that person from enjoying being around Leo people or being inspired to create and express that creativity and to speak up about one's personal opinions, because the Sun is not just about singing, dancing, painting, and music. The Sun is really about expressing ourselves and having our voice, shining, having ourselves seen, really being seen for the complex beings that we are.

A lot of times when we live these Chiron stories, we learn how to shut part of us down. That part is our heart. A lot of people brought up in Western cultures were taught that the mind is the solution for everything, the mind or the body, but they're not taught that the heart is the solution for everything – unless they're going to be mothers or nurses, or something like this. There's a very specific, kind of limited bandwidth in our culture across which healing compassionate energies are allowed to go, or expected to go or encouraged to travel.

What happens is that we don't know what to do with what is in our hearts, so we're carrying this wound of rejection. We're carrying experiences, the memories, the pain, and the suffering of having been rejected and we're trying not to trigger it.

When you come to somebody like me and I say, "Alright, it's time to open your heart," a lot of people will have a reaction like: "Oh I can't do that, because if I do that, I'll lose control, I'll feel pain, I won't know how to function anymore." Because, as we live in this Saturnian culture that says, "Order, structure, and discipline are paramount," what can't be controlled is demonized, and that extends to the level of using our hearts, understanding our emotional natures. From the Saturnian perspective, the heart/emotion is out of control and the roller coaster that it can take you on is unacceptable. It is not supported by structure-based discipline, that kind of mindset.

So, when we're challenged to get into our hearts, we find ourselves challenged to overcome a lot of conditioning about what it would mean to do so. As with anything, the fear of it is worse than actually doing it. It's not true that opening up the heart means that you spill all over the floor. It might mean that you need to cry about something, it might mean that you need to grieve something, you need to feel something difficult, that you need to process the loss of a loved one, whether through death or separation. It might mean that you need to process your frustration and feelings of anger and despair about some part of life that, between you and me, is probably karmic and lasting over many lives and deeply imprinted in you.

It is true that we have to process what is called emotional baggage when we do open our hearts, but this is one of the Chiron teachings: To be the energy of antenna that we are, we have to be able to open our hearts.

The 4th chakra in a human is the primary sensor of energy. All of our chakras sense energy, but the 4th is the one that connects the series of the lower four and the upper four, so it is in common, it is in each group of the seven chakras and ties together all the practical, material-based things in our lower chakras and all the higher, thought-based and spiritual things in the upper chakras. The heart ties it all together.

I work with it also as a truth meter. Where truth is what comes through on the vibration of love and when we can feel our hearts, we can use our hearts to be as sensitive as we naturally are wired to be. We can navigate the world, understanding what's true and what isn't, registering immediately what is of "higher" or "lower" vibration. We can navigate the world through that.

This does require that we deal with what we might be carrying in our emotional history. This Chiron work, this learning to shift our perspective on ourselves as energetic beings having these physical experiences, does require emotional archaeology. It does require that we go through all of these difficult things. In the work that I do we change our minds about what they mean, the meaning assigned to it.

When it comes to Chiron, assigning meaning looks like this: "If I do this thing, I will be rejected, so therefore this part of myself leads to rejection. If I feed this, if I let myself be whole, if I express this part of myself, I will be rejected." Now, what it *really* means is that we're sensitive to energy. We're sensitive to the reactions of other people. We're sensitive to the energy that moves through other people when we're highly Chironic, and every one of us has the capacity to be highly Chironic. It's not just that the chart placement matters. Everybody who is doing anything about Chiron, which is the vast majority of us, is living some part of the story. We're sensitive to the energy in other people, and we're also unique. This Chiron part says: "What I'm doing when I express this part of myself is different from the status quo I live in." That's what it means.

Now, if we can unwind the meaning of the reactions of others and withhold assigning meaning to our experiences of this energetic sensitivity, then we unravel this mountain and it is revealed as a molehill, and then we get the bonus of being able to appreciate difference. The end goal of the Chironic process is, in part, being able to experience difference. Being able to experience our own uniqueness without judging it, without editing it, without shaming it, without being afraid that others can't handle it or will not love us if we express this part of ourselves.

When we start living our Chirons out loud, what happens is some people say, "Wow, you're kind of freakish, and I love you for that." Some people say, "I don't understand that, but I wanna try." Other people say, "You're weird. Get away from me." However it is, when you are naturally yourself, your relationships will edit themselves into more authenticity, and the ones that are built on you being inauthentic will naturally go away.

Part of the end goal of Chiron is to accept our individuality and difference, as well as the individuality and difference of other people. When we express Chiron express difference. This idea that each person is unique is rooted in the fact that because everybody is unique, everybody has a different perspective on things. As we grow up in Saturnian cultures, where normalization and conformity are the rules, when we express our Chirons we're always a little different.

The more that we can let go of the meaning that we have attached to being different, the better. In terms of the process of healing Chiron issues, the first step is identifying the inner kid imprinted with the Chironic fear of rejection. You can look at your own, you can look at the people around you, your students and clients and understand this: What was this kid trying to express? How did that fear of rejection stop it?

That 's the first thing – identifying what the issue is. So you know if Chiron natally is in the 2nd house, we're talking about self-esteem and self-worth. If it's in the 3rd house, it's about communication, expression, exploration, and curiosity. If it's in the 10th house, it's about reputation, ambition, and receiving respect. So you can go around the wheel and look at what this issue is. You have to identify the part of the person, which will be an inner kid, that's imprinted by Chiron.

The second step is healing that by becoming the loving, nurturing parent you or they didn't have. That's actually one of the longest parts of the process: loving ourselves in the ways that other people didn't love us or seemed not to love us. Even though they loved us and we knew that, there was a certain thing we didn't get. To be spiritually mature beings, at the Mayan Calendar and this evolution of consciousness, etc., we have to get to the place where we love ourselves in the ways that someone else seems not to have. Very critical.

The third step is decoupling sensitivity from meaning, which involves being willing to experience all of what life has to offer. When you heal the inner kids, this kind of follows naturally, because you're less willing to assign meaning, because you're not in fear that you need to protect yourself from rejection or from a loss of love.

The fourth step is understanding what the gift of sensitivity is – that is, this enriching, human experience of feeling all you can feel, and that involves learning about energy management.

Number five is accepting the value of compassion, which is the deepest teaching that Chiron offers. Compassion will transmute all suffering, will end all suffering.

Number six is using compassion, while learning to move beyond the identity as wounded or wounded healer, or even moving beyond the identity of healer.

When you get deeply into Chiron processes, what you find is that you stop identifying as what hurts you or hurt you in the past and you stop identifying as what you do for other people, how you help support or heal other people. When you get beyond that identity, then you are what I would consider fully human.[4]

I don't have a lot of judgments on the speed of the process because, for example, I have the capacity to channel this material for you, to teach this stuff and to help people learn this stuff, and yet, admittedly, I do live my own Chironic process. It's a long-term thing where I'm healing my own Chiron wound of fear and rejection. But I'm not identifying as my wound. Even as I process the layers of it, I'm not identifying with it, and also I'm not identifying being a healer; I'm simply bringing through some information for you that might help you, that might help you shift perspective on your own situation.

There's a real value in not identifying as either of those things. It's not that there is a finish line and you're great if you get there, but it's that this process is a deepening into your own sense of humanity and uncovering what I think is the truth about being human – with following this archetypical journey, this archetypical process all the way through, and teaching you about this value of compassion.

When you generate love, when love is your first response, you change the world around you. And I don't mean that you fix problems or that you make life better for other people. You change the world around you because of the energetic commands that you're issuing. You're *being* love. You are loving and that changes the world around you. That opens up the door to enjoying being here.

Because of this particular kind of relationship that humans have developed with pain and suffering and talking about it being Chiron – the archetype being a convenient excuse for whining, that victim mentality coupled with the mindset that "things happen to me" – when you start creating the world around you as love, you can actually enjoy being here.

Most of us don't like to be here. Most of us don't like to be here because we have experienced a lot of difficulty, a lot of pain and a lot of suffering. Regardless of what we think it means about us, it is difficult to exist in a state where we feel that pain and suffering a lot, or all of the time. Also, because of our karmic journey calling us to learn all aspects of this thematic material that our souls choose to learn about, we always experience all the good and all the bad in a given area of education. But some of our lives seem stacked up with the negative versions of the lessons about the energy. So there are a lot of people who don't

---

[4] This is the Masters' vision of how humans can develop, maturing in this stage of our evolution and leading to the next.

want to be here, who don't want to be in their bodies. A lot of people who don't want to feel what they can feel.

You might be one of those people who's toying with the idea, who's flirting with stepping through a door into opening your heart and finding out what's in there. Every single person has the capacity, has the potential to do this, and every single human has the choice of whether or not to do this. The fact that you're drawn to my work (or that you're drawn to these particular channelings) – and you're drawn to this particular course, which is centered on channeling about what love is and how to love ourselves better and how to love ourselves in all the ways that other people have not loved us – says that you're prepared to make that choice. You're prepared to make an informed decision about whether or not you're going to be in your body and be in your heart and continue evolving as a human and heal all this stuff from the past that's waiting for you to look at and feel.

Going through this Chironic process brings you into your heart, opens your heart, and supports you feeling what you can feel. That's very important, but I think what's more important is that people understand that this is a choice and that this is something that is waiting for them if they want to go down that road. In many ways this has a lot to do with diverging levels of consciousness where some people will be living in one world as of 2012 (if you're not already) and then everybody else will be living in another kind of world.

Regarding myth and archetype, the last thing to get deeply into is that nobody said life would easy. When we look at the myth, Chiron has this pain and suffering from his inadvertent poisoning, and he does everything to heal himself but it won't work, so death is preferable. We need to take this as a reflection that the culture as a whole – the one that is transmitting this story and teaching this story, where it's easy to hear that death is better than some kinds of suffering – these cultures are shaped by people who have not had access to this teaching. This new telling of the story can help us understand how to value the energetic sensitivity in each of us, the energetic antenna, and how it adds to our experience of being human.

Our ancestors have not had that available to them on a collective level. All these shifts that we're living through, where we can learn about ourselves as energetic beings and spiritual beings having these physical experiences, this is unprecedented. This has not happened before in the entire history of humanity or this planet.

When I started thinking about generating a big work on Chiron a few years ago, the phrase that kept coming through to me was, "What are we really teaching?" with this thing about the wounded healer, the wound or the wounded healer and suffering and how we have to end suffering at all costs – what are we really teaching?

And I was looking at this myth as a vehicle to teach this message and I frankly was pretty upset by it, when I understood (when I saw that message and understood the implications of it) that *death* is the answer, that finding a way for ourselves to not have to experience the suffering anymore is preferable to figuring out a way to change our minds about what is happening.

So … "What are we really teaching?" I felt that we were teaching ourselves that in some arena of life, in some way, it was okay to whine and stay there. And that just really got the hair on the back of my neck to stand up – it gave me the willies that any kind of myth might be – admittedly probably inadvertently – used to teach that death was better than suffering. That just *really* got me going.

This idea that death is preferable to suffering takes us into this place where we have to look at what we think life is, what we think life is for. This Chironic process leads us to be able to experience all the energy that we can, which in many ways comes out as emotion, or comes *through* as emotion.

From my channeling about the soul's journey and what each of us is actually doing here having these human experiences – which is to learn what it's like to be spirit in a place like this, forgetting that we're spirit and, ideally, ultimately remembering – I look at this and what we think life is for. Those of us who have suffered a lot might think life is all about suffering and might look for ways – not necessarily to end our lives, though some of us do – but we might look for ways to make sure we don't feel all we can. We watch TV, we eat foods that make us numb, we drink, we take drugs, we gamble, we get lost in entertainment of all kinds: movies, TV, porn, whatever it is. We can get lost so that we don't have to feel the things that we don't want to feel.

As I spent a lot of time meditating about this Chiron teaching the last few years, it really altered how I was thinking about what life was for, so I hope that there's a by-product of all of this teaching in you and in the people that you touch and affect as far as changing their minds a little about what is the point of pain and suffering. I think the end of the archetypal process with Chiron is really accepting that there *is* suffering, but we have a choice about how to respond to it.

What is Healing? What is a Healer?

Given what you've heard so far, now we have to start talking about what healing is. What healing is – and who the healer is. When we get into this process of maturing our Chirons, our Chironic sensitivity, and going through the archetypal process of healing ourselves, this changes how we look at wounded and healing. When we go through this, the old ideas that other people are suffering and need help kind of go out the window.

At present we have this idea of being wounded in a way that we cannot help ourselves – that very prevalent idea about Chiron. As we work with that and live with that, what happens is that we think that we need someone else to help us. The spiritually mature Chiron helps itself, though. This happens after all of the essentially whiny, inner kids are nurtured and brought back into the fold and are not causing a lot of chaos because of their fears of rejection and abandonment because they are different. With a mature Chiron, the perspective that other people are needed for a healing process dissolves.

To the parts of a person that have been holding onto this pain and suffering, this is a terrible prospect. The whole point of this Chiron need is that somebody else does something for us. But this is the terrain of spiritual maturity. Everybody who is teaching spiritual topics will tell you that this is where we're headed – understanding how to take care of the self, understanding how to meet your needs, because then you're not waiting for someone else to do it.

As we talk about these inner children – these inner infants being imprinted with this sense of loss, this sense of rejection and perhaps abandonment – those little kids are waiting for someone to do something. As we grow up with this wound from infancy, this sense of rejection for just being who we are – if we (and most of us do) allow that fear of rejection to shape our lives and we wait for someone else to do something for us, then we're just waiting for someone else to do something for us.

This is one of the ways consciousness goes into two streams, where we have this divergence of levels of consciousness: those people who are willing to take care of their own needs, and those people who are still waiting for someone else to meet their needs. When you look deeply into this, you'll find parts of yourself that may sardonically or sarcastically respond with, "Well, if I really did that, then why would other people be necessary?" If that happens, understand that those parts of you are keeping you from self-sufficiency in order to ensure that other people do things for you, to keep that pattern in place. If the only use that a person finds for other people is to support this woundedness in whatever way it takes shape, that's where the most Chiron healing is needed.

So, what is healing? What does it mean to heal something? Chiron is a teacher for us in this and right now, with the way the energies are shifting in consciousness, the notion of healing itself can shift. Chiron is actually a significant teacher here: *What is healing? What does it mean to heal something?*

In the old way of looking at it, Chironic healing is not really possible. It's a very depressing view, this idea that the pain that you feel can never be healed and if it could in any way be mitigated, someone else would have to do it for you. It is so disempowering. And it is an utterly disempowering view of what it means to be a human and to feel emotion.

So, let's take that back. Let's understand in what ways feeling emotion is actually a gift. We have to look at the different kinds of healing, because there are medical applications of which healing is a very obvious process. But here we're talking about – something's broken, something gets fixed. It's not the same way with energy. It's not the same way with our emotions, which are energy. How we can heal emotional issues is by owning them, by owning these parts of ourselves, by giving attention to the parts of ourselves that have felt they haven't had the right kinds or the right amounts of attention in the past.

Healing comes from being whole. We hear a lot in metaphysical circles about the links in etymology of these words. "Heal" means "whole" or "wholeness." Healing is actually a process of accepting what it is and who it is that we are, accepting the energies that we're running, accepting what we are feeling. When we accept them, then we stop judging them, and we stop creating shadows of parts of ourselves. We stop labeling things as too much to look at, too painful to experience. Compassion is the key to this Chironic healing. Once you have awareness of it and you accept it, you hold it with compassion. You view all these parts of yourself with compassion. Compassion is love. So compassion for self, which is self-love, is the key to healing all Chironic issues.

In the old way of looking at it, yeah, maybe we don't know how to do that, so we seek help from other people, and this idea that you cannot help yourself with issues that you can help other people with – that's a very limited view. It's a misunderstanding of the Chiron story, in that it's actually a literal adherence to the myth, which misunderstands the archetype as people actually live it.

With healing comes awareness, self-awareness, self-acceptance, and self-love. When it comes to energetic emotional issues, including Chiron pain and suffering, then the only healer is the self, the person we're talking about. The person who has the wounds is the only person who can really heal him or herself.

There are a lot of people who are called healers who will take exception to being called healers, because as they've undergone this process themselves, they understand that the best thing one person can do for another is to offer tools – to support someone in gaining insight and information, and being a sounding board or giving feedback or simply "holding space" for a person to go through this process on his or her own. These are the healers who understand that true healing has to do with awareness, acceptance, and compassion. Therefore they understand that what they can do for you is offer the reflective awareness, the reflective acceptance, and the reflective sense of compassion.

Another layer of the Chiron myth that we haven't really understood is that when Chiron is whisked off to be raised by Apollo, after his mother rejects him at birth, he's taught all these arts. He's taught all these healing arts and martial arts and all of these things. And he doesn't whine; he doesn't sit around and bemoan his circumstance. He is alone, and we have to know assume that the rejection from his mother is painful. He's also not a centaur like the other centaurs; the rest are wild and uncontrollable. They're famous in the mythologies for ruining people's wedding parties, for example, and mistakenly killing each other in drunken brawls, and just kind of ruining everything. And he's not. Being half-man and half-centaur, he stands apart, he's not accepted by the community – any community – and so he lives on the outside. He accepts his difference. His response, even in the mythology, is to develop resourcefulness, which we know leads to self-confidence, and he ultimately becomes a teacher for all these people who are doing these very important quests, projects, and tasks: Hercules, Jason, et al.

The Chironic process is about going within and accepting the difference and relying on ourselves. That's what's waiting for anybody who goes through a significant Chiron healing process. You go from wounded to wounded healer to something beyond that, where you don't identify with the wound or being a healer – you identify with yourself as a unique being. When we read Chiron's myth like this, we can understand an endpoint to this archetypal process of gaining self-sufficiency and the way to get there is to shift our minds, to shift our ideas of what healing is and who heals us.

A lot of us, especially people who are going to be drawn to this kind of inquiry, will have experienced incredible results with healers, probably having gone to a practitioner of some kind and saying "Wow, this person did a great job." The best of them are simply holding space to provide you with information or reflection that you are ready to receive. You're the person who drives your healing process. You're the person who makes it happen. Nobody can do something for you that you're not willing to have done and nobody can tell you something that you're not ready to hear.

This works in my practice. Even if I understand from a person's chart the kind of energy dynamics happening in that person's life and energy field, I don't know how it plays out specifically, because they're just symbols in a chart – they just tell you about the relationships of energies. For instance, that square from Saturn to somebody's Moon. I don't know if that comes out at work, I don't know if it comes out as a parental relationship, I don't know if it comes out as a teaching thing, if the person's in the military and has authority problems … I don't know all of those details. I don't know any of those details. What I do is I ask the person. The person responds. I say, "Tell me about this issue with authority," and what that person tells me not only answers the content so that I know what to work with, but also tells me what that person is ready to hear in response.

And as I work with Spirit Guides, they tune in to how the person responds and then tell me things based on what that person is ready to hear, what that person's level of consciousness is ready to receive about the situation. Putting this on the client – putting this on the individual *all* the time – is ultimately to empower that person to understand what role he or she has in the healing process. Some people do think that I did something. Some people do think that I'm the person who "did" the healing. When people comment about that and thank me for what I do, if they need to hear that they're the ones that made it happen, then I do. I always make those comments when they're appropriate.

So, who's the healer? The individual is the only possible healer. What does it mean to heal? You gain awareness, you choose acceptance, and you respond with compassion to all the parts of yourself that feel out of whack. Transitioning from that old way of thinking, the infantile expectation that other people "should" be helping us into becoming the person who is aware of being responsible for the healing, instead of just kind of wandering around, waiting for someone to do something for us – *that's* an incredibly potent Chiron learning.

Chiron in the Houses

The houses represent different parts of life, different arenas of life. A house is where the action takes place. When we have a body in a house, we have an emphasis of action in that house. That body works through, primarily, the parts of life represented by that house.

The house in which Chiron is is where that person shows up as different. Automatically, it also represents the history of the wounding. In all houses, in all signs, we can assign or translate the symbolism into what a baby might do, and we can always trace it back. The original wound is always about stuff that has to do with this house, parts of life in this house.

If we're in a wounded phase, then this is the house we'll try to edit. This is the house, the parts of life that fit with it, that we will try to edit out of our lives to avoid experiencing that pain of rejection. Everything that has to do with this house will contain a lot of buttons in our emotional life that get triggered, so we'll avoid it as much as we can and we'll be hypersensitive to it.

As we edit this part of life out – or we *try* to – we may even not let others in our life become aware of our sensitivity to these things, so there'll be something that we avoid. In attempting to edit it out, we avoid things that have to do with this part of life, and we hope that nobody notices. Eventually people notice, but if they don't have the kind of vocabulary of astrology or some other kind of interpretive art that helps understand or explain how people are wired, they won't get it.

The feeling or sense of being wounded in the house relative to Chiron is that "I've done this before and I've been hurt. Why should I do it again?" If in the wounded healer phase, we will have an identity surrounding our role in parts of life represented by the house where our Chiron is, we'll have an identity surrounding what we do for other people who are hurt in this part of life or who need help and support. The wounded healer phase has a lot to do with identity as a healer. It is an extension of identifying with the wound but with a different take on it.

The third phase is when we're beyond the wound and beyond the identity of a wounded healer. These are the parts of life where we provide an example of uniqueness and can teach others by example to have compassion for anybody and everybody because of the way that they're unique.

To contrast these three phases: For somebody who is in the wounded phase of any house, if you start talking about something that fits within that house, the person probably will not respond and may probably cringe. They might try to hide it just not wanting to be conscious of this conversation, or would change the subject or leave. If in the wounded healer phase, that person could assert the identity of what it is they do for people who have problems in that kind of situation. If beyond that, they can hear what you're saying and not assign a bunch of meaning and potentially participate in a conversation like anybody else would.

One thing to say about this identity as a wounded healer is that it involves forcing some issues. The identity of being somebody who helps others with problems is a way of clinging to the wound. You think you can't deal with the wound on your own, but you have this perception that you can help other people with the thing that hurts you. No matter how you approach it, it's still clinging to the personal pain. There's a kind of whacked-out motivation. It derails a lot of other things in the personality and in the person's life. So, always I want people to go from wounded into beyond identifying as the wound or the wounded healer. That's really important.

Being beyond identifying with the wound or as somebody who helps people with that wound, being in this third phase -- there's no meaning that gets attached to any of this. What it leads to is being able to participate in the world in a way that will undoubtedly, unavoidably reveal and celebrate your own uniqueness. You can see this in people around you who have been through something but don't stick to it and don't cling to the identifying of having gone through it.

Moving on to the houses specifically, beginning with the 1st house.

1st House

The 1st house is about our bodies. It's about decision-making, leadership, revealing and showing ourselves. It's about instinctive action.

The 1st house is where we burst onto the scene, no matter what we're talking about, no matter where we are, no matter what we're doing. The 1st house is where we begin things and where we jump in and show ourselves to be who we are, as a first impression.

The wound here is about how one uses the body and, ultimately, how one makes decisions and how one makes instinctive choices. Whatever's in the 1st house, we tend to wear that energy without being conscious of it. Here's that instinctive side of Mars/Aries. It's about action and doing and being. It's not about a lot of analysis and being conscious of what we're doing.

So things that are in the 1ˢᵗ house we tend to wear on our personas, and we tend to learn about ourselves with that energy through the reactions of other people. When Chiron is in the 1st house, there is this sense of being different, and if the wound is very, very strong, there is a sense of not having the right to *be*. This is part of Chiron working in Aries in the 1ˢᵗ house, because you burst onto the scene and announce existence in the 1ˢᵗ house. If Chiron is there the wound will say, "Maybe I don't have the right to be here."

The Chiron wound in the 1ˢᵗ house will affect a sense of being bold. It will affect a sense of beginning things, as far as using the body in decisive ways, making decisions, and leadership. This is a wound to the will, essentially, being related to Mars. Until the wound is processed, the experience of all 1ˢᵗ-house things, including sexuality and desire and attraction, etc. The experience of that will be colored by the woundedness, will be colored by the expectation of being rejected just for being who one is.

First impressions will be a gigantic issue because of this perception of something being wrong with the self, wrong with the body. Every time I see Chiron in the 1ˢᵗ house, there is something about the person's physical body that is perceived to be very different, so different that the person is not going to be accepted because the person stands out. It could be ears that stick out, it could be a scar on the face, or it could be a nose that maybe is perceived to be too big. It could be proportioning of the body, it could be a feature of the body that is perceived by the person to be worthy of rejection, or to be a reason that somebody would reject him or her. It's simply that this perception that the body, as it naturally is, is not acceptable.

When people with a 1ˢᵗ-house Chiron can change their relationship with this perception, they can understand that every single person is unique, that each body is unique, but as long as they identity with the wounded part, there is going to be a perception of sticking out, having some part of the body being unacceptable or being an eyesore a trigger for rejection.

What ends up being true is that other people might notice the unique thing, but they don't care. When you're in junior high, people might notice it and pick on you about it, but in general, people don't care. Carrying the wounded infant around, however, it becomes very, very important. Other people might notice what it is that's so unique but they won't attach the same meaning to it that the person who has a Chiron in the 1ˢᵗ does. In all ways of life that relate to the 1ˢᵗ house, the wound is in the sense of being different.

In the wounded healer phase, the person will have made some peace with the ways that he or she is different but will also wear a badge on the sleeve about being different for it. So there's that identity from that person maybe helping other people with self-esteem issues or body issues, but still there's the identity that persists about being the wounded self.

Beyond the wound, beyond identifying with it, somebody who accepts him- or herself unconditionally might say, "Yeah, my ears stick out," or "Yeah, one leg might be shorter than the other." By fully and totally accepting him- or herself, that person can be an example of total and utter self-love, self-compassion, and self-acceptance for other people. When the person wearing the energy of Chiron on the outside without being conscious of it processes the wound, then what's worn on the outside is this compassionate approach to everybody. It's a very kind of healing balm.

If you ask somebody who is beyond that identification with the wound about it, maybe they could tell you a story from history, but it won't mean anything. That person won't have a lot of meaning associated with it. The sense of being different is no longer forming the identity. It's just accepted as a natural feature of life that everyone is unique.

Ultimately in any of these houses, the real gift to give with Chiron is accepting the ways in which one is different. That's going to be the bottom line for the gift that we give to others throughout all the houses and all the signs.

2nd House

The 2nd house represents skills, resources, value systems, self-worth, and self-esteem. A lot of times we hear about the 2nd house being about money and skills and resources, but there's this chain of ideas that are linked together through the 2nd house, where you get from self-esteem to money. Whatever you find important is your value system. That's going to dictate what skills you choose to gather and develop and perfect, and those are going to dictate where you put them to use, and that's going to dictate what kinds of resources that you get in response. One of the resources we talk about is money.

There's this chain that goes from value system to self-esteem to money, but it also has to do, ultimately, at the very bottom line, with survival. So we look at all the things that are necessary to survival. Skills are necessary, so that you can earn money so that you can have food so that you can continue surviving. So this is a whole chain that goes with the 2nd house.

The wound when Chiron is in the 2nd house is to the capacity to develop self-esteem. It is to the capacity to love the self and utterly accept the way that one is wired. In the 1st house, it's just the body and how the body shows up and is very "present-tense" being. In the 2nd house it's more about this conception of self that the unmediated action of the 1st house can't process, can't relate to.

The wound here says, "What I think is important doesn't matter, what I think is worth gathering as a skill, the things I consider worthy of learning, are not that important. How I use the skills that I have isn't important; they will be rejected." All of these things – my interests, my value system, my skills, the ways that I want to earn money, the ways that I prove myself to myself, the ways that I establish self-esteem – are pointless because others will always reject me.

When a person has identified with the wound, this part of life will bring pain and the person will try to avoid it. How that looks is somebody following someone else's game plan, even though it's very obvious that it's not important to the person and even that the person doesn't want to do it. It could be, for example, that a person with Chiron in the 2nd really feels strongly about a certain career choice. What's randomly coming to mind is park ranger. For whatever reason, for whatever else we can see in the chart, that's very important to her. But maybe the parents, maybe the person comes from a family of attorneys, or even there's a family business – a construction business that everyone in the family is expected to work in, and to this point everyone has. So whether it's a kind of career that's a tradition or an actual business that the parents want the kids to go into, this kid, this 18 year-old kid who's going into college, really wants to be a park ranger, and that would break these patterns.

As important as this is to this young person, the other people's value systems are going to seem that much stronger because the person's self-esteem is kind of in the toilet, with Chiron in the 2nd and being in the wounded phase. If the person us intrepid, he or she might stand up and say, "This is what I really want to do," asserting that self-esteem, asserting that sense of self, that 2nd-house strength. But because of the deep sensitivity of the wound, anybody else saying, "Well actually, no, this is more important and this is what you're going to do," that can make that young person feel overpowered.

So when you have Chiron in the 2nd and there is perpetuation of the wound, a lot of times I see people who do things that are important to other people. They've allowed other people's value systems to take over because of their self-esteem. If a person is a wounded healer here, again there is identification with helping people who have self-esteem issues, and that's perceived to be a way of helping oneself. It doesn't *really* though because, again, it is still identification with the wound.

Beyond the wound you find people who do things differently for their own reasons, which are obviously different, and they accept it. So what happens is, whatever somebody with Chiron in the 2nd is going to do about his or her own value system, how it is he or she wants to make money or what skills are considered important and how those skills are put to use, the person will show up as different. Being beyond the wound and beyond the wounded healer, this third phase is simply accepting that each person's value system is unique and that each person must go through the process of developing his or her own self-esteem and that just because it's hard to do that, doesn't mean that other people's ideas of what should be done, should be done.

The gift to give other people is that of embodying the example of accepting this difference. People here who heal this will have some skills and talents and interests that nobody else in their lives can figure out. For example, someone with Chiron in the 2nd might want to adopt a language different than their native language, being interested in other cultures, might think it would be a better one and somebody else might reason, "Well there's all this stuff going on in South America or in Europe or even China having become a major world player," so there's kind of interest there, but this person might pick some obscure little country in Africa to read about and to perhaps visit. And there's no judgment on the fact that nobody else can get at why it is important. Even if other people are judging it, you just accept that this is what's going on, and "I'm interested in these kinds of things and that's how it is."

What ends up happening is that Chiron always actually develops unique resourcefulness. So with Chiron in the 2nd house there is this capacity to understand the use of skills that nobody else can see. It is not just being weird or having unique sensibilities, it is that the person can understand how to apply certain skills in ways that nobody else can understand.

There is a very important point in the story of Chiron where, instead of going off and being sad and letting the sadness take over (which is not in the mythology, but how we seem to think we should live the archetype), Chiron develops all of these skills and perfects them and puts them all to use. And in those times, somebody who is proficient in music and the martial arts, the healing arts, and this and that, well that's a Jack of all Trades, and that's not common.

What it turns out is that Chiron was uniquely positioned to train the heroes before their quests, where they needed all of this information, but nobody before that could have recognized the value in having all these disparate skills, especially as he wasn't really accepted by the other centaurs or the communities surrounding him. He lived kind of out in the pale, out beyond the settlements.

There is a resourcefulness, and when it comes out in the 2nd house as a plus it is the ability to see around square thinking about how resources should be come by and used. The person with Chiron here can see them in new ways and see that, and that is also one of the gifts. It is not just being clever, but it's about applying things in new ways and, in doing that, the person can be a natural example – living *by* example – for others of that compassionate self-acceptance in uniqueness when it comes to skills, values, and resources.

3rd House

The 3rd house has to do with perception, communication, the local environment, and exploration and curiosity – all parts of life that relate to this. When Chiron is in the 3rd, there is a wound about information in and out: the process of learning, communicating, speaking, and also of thinking and perceiving. The wound can come out as, "I shouldn't say what I want to say. I can't think what I really want to think." That might sound crazy to some people, because you can think whatever you want, but if that thinking leads you to do things that get you rejected, that's going to be a protective strategy, which is an attempt to edit the natural way the mind works.

If the person is deeply in the wounded phase, which is going to be a default for some part of the life, there's a lot of pain surrounding communication, either from what other people say or what the person has said that has gotten him or her a lot of rejection. It's also about curiosity, so therefore exploration. Some people with Chiron in the 3rd have been wounded by asking really brilliant questions of the wrong people and at the wrong times; however, the energy can be manifested as this wound about exploration and curiosity.

These people might have intense inner worlds in their minds and not communicate that to other people. They might have issues in school because school is one of the ways, one of the conditioning processes, that really gets into our 3rd house. The 3rd house is about information coming in and out, being constantly fed information and then being expected to pump out (usually the same) information in response. It's being tested on how well we learned. Chiron in the 3rd is going to naturally affect all of these processes. It could be hesitancy to speak, it could be that the mind works differently, it could be that the way somebody has to study in order to really learn something is very different than other the way other people study. And maybe some teachers don't get that.

So you can have really bright kids or really bright adults, for example, but maybe the grades don't reflect that and so nobody might see how they actually be smart. If the wound is perpetuated, that kid (or adult) will be unable to participate in the education process like everybody else is, because it will be such a charged area for him or her. If the person is in the wounded healer phase, then of course, there's an identity surrounding helping other people communicate differently or helping others figure out how to ask better questions, etc.

When the person is beyond the wound in the identity of the healer, they can be an example of uniqueness regarding communication and mind and speech for others just by having total self-acceptance of whatever Chironic reality has resulted from this placement. For example, somebody who is curious about all kinds of things that nobody else has any interest in, somebody who asks a lot of questions about topics that people don't find important, or somebody who wants to learn a lot of information or information in ways that are different from other people.

This also will come out rather literally in many, many people as the way that they speak. Some people with Chiron in the 3rd may have a speech impediment or may have a nervousness about communication that leads to something that looks like a speech impediment. Because the energy of information in and out is different, it can also come out as hearing issues, it can come out as sight issues, or perhaps just the way the mind works and the way the person experiences the world around him or her is different.

Because this is the house of exploration and Chiron is going to make it different, it could be any of these things. It can also be just that the person is not interested in learning "the program" because Chiron will naturally provide a uniqueness. The reasons for any physical manifestations will also have a lot to do with karma as well, and conditioning, and what the soul has signed up for.

So you don't look at Chiron in the 3rd and automatically assume somebody's deaf or blind, but there *is* a uniqueness in how the mind works and how the information comes in and out. Learning, reading, hearing, and seeing are not the only ways that information comes in, so this also can show up as sensitivity to tactile sensations, to taste, etc. All of our physical senses take place in the 3rd house.

The core of the energy is that the information in and out works differently. A person might be extremely sensitive to light or to sound or to smells, for example. The whole sensing faculty of the person is hypersensitive. When someone can accept this about him- or herself there is a possibility to be an example of somebody who just accepts that everybody thinks differently, everybody's communication is unique, everybody sees the world in different ways. *What if the blue that I'm seeing is not the same blue that you're seeing?* These are the kinds of questions someone with this placement might ask.

The person with Chiron in the 3rd who processes this uniqueness and this sense of difference will come out on the other side with an utter self-acceptance and therefore an acceptance of other people. They will understand with compassion that everybody's mind, communication style, communication means, are all unique, and that there is nothing wrong with being unique.

4th House

When I look at the 4th house, I always see in someone's chart an energetic inheritance from the people that he or she comes from – ancestry, heritage, but also the literal family. At its root, the 4th house is about who we are when no one else is around. It is about our inner selves. Sometimes I talk about it as our psychic basement. It's who we are when we're alone. And for the vast majority of us, this gets imprinted on us very early. You are who you come from, you are the places you grew up, you are the people, you are the ethnic heritage, you are the religion.

So there's this idea of energetic inheritance that I work with when I look in the 4th. When I see Chiron in this house, I know that it's not just *this* person who has Chiron in the house of emotion, family, connectedness and home, but there is some wound to the emotions running through the entire family system. There will be a wide variety of responses with this placement because some people's families accept Chiron sensitivity when it comes to emotions and some of them don't. When we look at the 4th house, we are looking at the wider arena of home, family, belonging, connectedness, having roots, having a connection to our own history and our family's history.

One way of working with the Chironic wound in this house is focusing on emotional sensitivity, because we're talking about Chiron being an energetic antenna, an energetic sensitizer, and emotions are energy. So this house placement has a unique layer to it because how we learn about ourselves through and from our families has a really intense emotional component.

When wounded, somebody might think that he or she doesn't have the right to feel what he or she feels. To everyone else that sounds ridiculous, but to the person with Chiron in the 4th, there has been rejection for being emotionally wired the way one naturally is emotionally wired. There's been a rejection for feeling what the person feels. That wound, that molehill, that incident that becomes made into a mountain, can lead someone to feeling that he or she doesn't have the right to feel what he naturally feels.

This placement also affects the sense of connectedness to other people. With Chiron here, there's a rejection happening from the family – it's within the family, it's running throughout the family system energetically, but the person with Chiron in the 4th will experience being cut off from family in some way whether literal or energetically or emotionally. That can look like being adopted, or it can look like going from living with parents to grandparents. While the person may not be completely, literally disconnected, he or she might disconnected in some way from his or her parents. There is a sense of separation. It can also be that the parents and family are always around, but that the person can't relate to them on an emotional level, or relating to them in such a way is not acceptable, so there's a sense of disconnection. In essence, this sense of belonging and connectedness are disrupted when Chiron is in the 4th house.

If we're in the wounded healer phase we can help other people with these feelings of disconnectedness, but we have an identity surrounding our relationship with emotions. When people with Chiron in the 4th are beyond the wound and beyond the identity of healer, there is this capacity to share emotionally and to listen to other people's emotional stories without attaching meaning to them. They can be an example of this energetic sensitivity, the person who is sensitive to energy who is not caught up by any of it. This is Chiron in the house of the Moon. There is a lot of potential for very deep, unedited compassion, because of this Chiron healing in the house of parts of life relating to emotion.

The person who is beyond the wound will understand that everybody has unique emotions, that everybody is, because of his or her emotional nature and expression, unique. And so this person can show by example how to honor one's internal self and to heal the sense of disconnection by remaining connected to the self. When we do that, then it is possible to connect with other people in the right kinds of ways, but first one has to accept in oneself this uniqueness of emotional expression.

5th House

The 5th house is about spontaneity, creative expression, and play, but essentially it's really about being in the moment and shining. It's a house related to the Sun and Leo. It's about expressing the experience of being you. It's not just knowing that you're you, it's not just *being* you, it's *performing the experience of being you.*

When something is in the 5th house we need to have our personal touch on that expression.

When Chiron is here there is a wound to personal expression, to self-expression. There is a wound to creativity and to the playful, childlike part of the self. A lot of times this will come out as specific, obvious wounding scenarios in childhood, but really what we need to take with us as we mature and age is that the part of us that is childlike needs to undergo some personal healing. When someone is in the wounded phase with Chiron in the 5th, there is this fear of performing. There is a fear of expressing the self, a fear of showing what's going on creatively. This will dampen the person's ability to be spontaneous in any way. Friends can say "Hey, let's go do this!" and that person might think, "You know, I shouldn't even have friends like this, because this is too dangerous." Or maybe, "If I show you who I am, I'm going to be rejected." Or, "If I really express my creativity, my sense of boldness, if I really try to shine, I will be rejected." There's a fear of all that kind of personal expression and spontaneity and playfulness.

If in the wounded healer phase, there's an identity surrounding helping other people creatively express themselves. Getting beyond the wound and identifying as a wounded healer, the person will have accepted that each person is unique, each person's creativity is unique, and each person's sense of self is unique, and so therefore the expression and communication of that is unique. So, the healing is in accepting that everybody is unique. Going through this compassionate self-acceptance phase, when it leads to giving this Chironic gift of being able to share the creative self, the personal self, and not judge the reactions of others.

When somebody with Chiron in the 5th does express creatively, it will be different, because everywhere the Chiron is it comes out as uniqueness. The person who processes this fear of rejection and this rejection of self that gets imprinted early can give the gift of spontaneity without judging it and can actually affect other people and inspire them to honor their own creative selves. Even with people who don't have Chiron in the 5th, there are those of us who feel that our creativity might not be welcome where we are. Somebody with Chiron in the 5th in revealing a deep sense of vulnerability in creative endeavors will inspire a lot of people to honor their own difference when it comes to their creative expression.

6th House

The 6th house is about duty, responsibility, and about being detail-oriented – all the arenas of life that fit in with this. It's also the house of unequal relationships. Traditionally we might talk about the 6th house as the house of illness or health.

How I understand this is that there is an awareness in the 6th house of minute processes, including of the body, an ability to track changes in patterns, an analytical ability to make connections about why things are happening the way they are. I always look at a heavy 6th house as somebody who needs to develop, if they have not already, a sensitivity to how the body responds to different stimuli. And with Chiron in the 6th house there is going to be a wound to the analytical side, the duty-oriented side, that part that feels that responsibility is important.

A lot of times when I see Chiron here I see people who manifest a lot of health issues. There are two avenues into health issues when we have Chiron in the 6th. One is that your energy antenna is working at the level of the minute processes of the body. Developing Chiron sensitivity is very easy physically when we're in the body, but there is a necessity to shift the perspective of "This is going wrong" or "I am sensitive to this," or "I am allergic to this" to "I'm manifesting these health issues." There is a need to shift that perspective to understanding how to honor our reactions, our body's reactions, to these minute processes.

For example, when someone with Chiron in the 6th comes into see me there is very often a discussion that ensues about why the person eats what they eat, because the body responds to food immediately. You have a sense when it hits your mouth of whether or not this is good for you. When the person with Chiron in the 6th can honor that, then there is a way through that sensitivity to understand in what ways that this is actually a gift. This energetic antenna of Chiron is a gift.

The other avenue into the health thing is if somebody is having a woundedness about taking responsibility for something, physical illness is a very convenient way to manifest an inability to follow through on commitments and to take responsibility for things. So these are two angles on health in the 6th house when I see Chiron here.

As far as duty and responsibility, there is a lot going on with being rejected for being someone who is committed or who has taken responsibility. If you have taken on a project and you're abused for it, or you're shunned for having done it, you're going to avoid taking responsibility for things. This is the house of unequal relationships, where we learn things from other people and, once we become very knowledgeable, we teach people who are less knowledgeable than we are. This is a great way that Chiron in this house can evolve: by being conscious of what one doesn't know and then accepting it, and accepting that there are things that other people know. So everybody needs to learn if they want to get better at something one of the bottom lines of the 6th house being improving things.

If the person is in the wounded phase, relationships with people who are more skilled and more educated will be difficult, because the person has difficulty accepting that what he or she doesn't know is not reflective of his or her worth. There can be a lot pain and hypersensitivity that stem from relationships with mentors and teachers as well for similar reasons.

If in the wounded healer phase, the person will have shifted some of the identity, but they will still have an identity associated with duty and responsibility and perhaps a feeling of being "less than." So the real nugget that has to get processed and shifted in the person's awareness and consciousness level, in order to get to beyond identifying as the wounded healer, is that every single process can be improved.

We have to develop a certain humility when faced with learning new skills and new tasks and in proving that we can do things. Especially for someone with Chiron in the 6th, it's important to be accepting humility in the face of learning something new and learning from other people who are more knowledgeable than they are. Accepting that humility can take us into understanding that, on a very deep level, everybody doesn't know something that they wish they knew. Everybody wishes that he or she were better at something than they presently are.

What happens in the 6th house a lot of times is that while there's a certain kind of evolutionary or soul level intention to learn humility, sometimes we are humiliated. Look at the vast difference of emotional quality between choosing humility or being humble and then being humiliated. When Chiron is here, a lot of times we've been humiliated for something that we don't know or can't do well. This might come out as: "I've given up too much, and when I do give it up, I'm rejected, so why should I do that in the first place?" The person who evolves beyond the wound and identifying as the wounded healer will accept that there is something that everybody doesn't know and that there is a real skill and a real test of quality of character in choosing to be humble in order to improve what you find worth improving.

And that leads to the gift that Chiron can offer in the 6th house. What people with Chiron here can offer, which is accepting what they can do well and what they can't do well, applying what they can do well in useful ways in the spirit of service, and improving something so that it can be useful to others. The important thing is not to get caught up in feeling "less than" if we don't do something well, and learning how to apply humility and a strong work ethic in order to make something better, so that it can be offered as useful for other people.

Lastly, teamwork is also associated with the 6th house. Teamwork is where we humble ourselves enough to join with other people to accomplish some goal. The

11th house is understood to be the house of friends and groups, but the 6th is where we go through the process of being humbled enough to, essentially, submit to a group. So submission is a big part of the 6th house. With Chiron in this house there is an issue of what it means to submit and what it means to accept that one is in some way "less than." This is a house of adaptation to unequal relationships. It is about giving something up for a group effort.

In order to achieve some long-term goal, we do have to sacrifice things. In order to be of service we have to give up some of our needs and desires. People with Chiron in the 6th will have a history of (or will have a certain kind of relationship to) being asked to sacrifice something for a greater good. This includes working on teams and being part of any group effort. When somebody crosses the line or rounds the corner to the place of having healed these Chiron issues, the person accepts that, in various scenarios, everybody's got to give something in order to improve something, to make something better. Taking responsibility for things and other people requires being willing to sacrifice a few things about one's own agenda.

In the 6th house is where we learn that as choosing humility or where we find ourselves forced into humbled by some situation or circumstance. But the Chiron here in the 6th will be fear, one of the default modes will be fear that "I've given up too much, and when I do give up, I'm rejected, so why should I do that in the first place?"

7th House

The 7th house is the house where we meet the other. It's traditionally thought of as the house of other people – friends, spouses, lovers, business associates, business partnerships, etc. This is where we learn about ourselves through our interactions with others. Every relationship that fits in this house teaches about fairness, harmony, equality, balance, justice.

When in the 7th house, we take reflections about ourselves from other people. When Chiron is in the 7th house and a person is in the wounded phase this person will expect rejection from other people. The truth of this is that the level of sensitivity to other people and what's going on with them is dramatically increased. It's not that people will reject someone with Chiron in the 7th house more than anybody else, but the person's radar for what's happening with other people is heightened.

The wounding in infancy had to do with what's fair, so the person is expecting to be rejected and will not risk being hurt by another person. In the 7th house, in order to really be worried about fairness, harmony, and equality – what it takes to create fair relationships – we have to take responsibility for being heard as well as listening to other people. A lot of times, when the wound is very active, when the wounded phase is highlighted, the person won't risk being heard by other people, because there is an expectation that there's an automatic rejection waiting for them.

Some people who are living in the wounded phase will be loners. Some of them will be around people all the time, just not fully representing who they are, not really revealing who they are. There's this idea that "If I tell you who I am (the 7th house idea), I'm going to be rejected by you. It's not okay for me to really reveal, just to tell you who I am."

As we learn about what's fair, we learn about what desires and what boundaries in relationship are healthy. Someone with Chiron in the 7th house may want something from another person, not get it, and then assign a lot of meaning to that. It could come out eventually as assuming that there's a pattern, or creating a pattern, of "I can't ask for what I want in a relationship." Here's that 7th house learning about what's equal. "I can't ask for what I want, because the answer's automatically no." Or "If I reveal what I want then I'll be rejected." So there's a kind of perpetuated imbalance in relationships when Chiron is here if a person is in the wounded phase, in order to avoid risking rejection. In the phase of the wounded healer, there is an identification that develops around helping other people who have this heightened sensitivity or who experience rejection.

Just as with all the other houses we've talked about so far, in this phase, when there's healing that's taken place, there's a kind of proprietary self-definition around the wound itself and it looks like progress, but it isn't actually progress. Beyond the wound and beyond identifying as this wounded healer, Chiron in the 7th house has the capacity to accept that each person is sensitive to the reflections of others. These people can accept that everybody is receiving data in reflection from other people.

Just because this person is so highly sensitive, when the disidentification from the wound and being the healer happens, the person can accept that everybody experiences this to some degree; that everybody is vulnerable within relationship and that everybody risks revealing who they are and saying, "This is what I want, this is a good boundary for me, this is what I need when I'm in relationship." These people can allow the understanding that everybody has this going on, to generate compassion, and to be a trigger for compassion.

This process will involve not taking things personally. One of the lessons here, to get from wounded to beyond identifying with the wound is to understand that because everybody is vulnerable and everybody has a sensitivity to the reflections and the reactions of other people, that the way that people react to you has to do with *their* situation.

The person with Chiron in the 7th will, by default, take the reactions of other people as indicative of the person's worth of having relationships, or the person's worthiness of being in relationship and being treated fairly. Once they process this wound and stop taking things personally, the reality they eventually see is that how people treat you has everything to do with them and nothing to do with you. Everybody is just working on surviving, surviving within their relationships, and maintaining their own self-esteem and their own way of living and their own beliefs, and maintaining some kind of direction down their life path.

These people with Chiron in the 7th are highly sensitive to this fact, but it doesn't have to carry so much meaning for them. Once the corner is turned and the person is no longer identifying with that wound and taking everything personally, the gift of compassionate understanding is given to anybody and everybody in relationship.

Meeting people who reveal their insecurities is another thing that someone with Chiron in the 7th is going to be very sensitive to. That person who has come out of identifying with the wound can hold a space for compassionate understanding for other people and essentially give the gift of putting them at ease about how their process of forming relationships, how they feel vulnerable, and how they are sensitive to the reactions of other people is unique.

8th House

The 8th house is where we engage in relationships that require trust. In the 7th house, we're building trust, but in the 8th house we cross a line, we cross a threshold, we open to another – we reveal something intensely personal about ourselves. By comparison, the 7th house is more chatty: "Who are you, and this is who I am" – where we're learning how to find a common footing.

In the 8th house, it gets a little intense. It involves all arenas of life – it's not just the one-on-one relationships of the 7th, but it's deepened, intensified. It's how we reveal ourselves to each other and what it takes to create trust. This house is traditionally said to be the house of sex, death, and other people's money. Really, this has to do with sharing resources, where we learn how to rely on other people and how to be someone on whom other people can rely. When you're talking about sex, death, and sharing money and other resources, there is a certain brute honesty that always wants to come into play. At some points we have to reveal ourselves in order to get whatever job done we're talking about.

In the 8th house everything hinges on the capacity to trust. Because this is related to Scorpio and Pluto, there is a certain element of learning about power in this house – learning about who gets to have power when. When we reveal ourselves and become vulnerable – when we're injured, when we're hurt, when we're betrayed – we're that much more sensitive to what's going on, to that pain.

With Chiron here, the wound is about trust. The wound that will be perpetually created – until the person crosses the threshold of not identifying with the sensitivity – will be about trust. People here will have manifested or created many reasons not to trust people, many situations, many intense interactions with other people, whether it's about sex, whether it's about money, whether it's about life and death, but always coming down to who can be trusted when.

The Chiron sensitivity in the 8th house has a lot to do with being able to feel into the deep, secret motivations of other people. As Chiron is an energetic antenna, what it's picking up on when it is natally in the 8th house is that, with these other people that we meet and are potentially going to exchange intimate energy with on some level, we can sense what's going on in their motivations.

Every single person has shadow components, or parts they might not act on but they can sense; that they can sense, that they – when honest – would own. Or perhaps when they're betrayed would strike out in vengeance, or they would seek to hurt another when they're hurting, in order to seek some kind of justice. Someone with Chiron in the 8th gets close to somebody else and can feel those inner motivations. Even if those other people don't act and don't identify with those motivations the person will be afraid of those parts becoming active.

Again, Chiron in the 8th in one sense is all about trust, but on a deeper level, it's really about learning who can be trusted when. If a person is identifying with the wound, everything about trust and intimacy is going to stir these issues and cause a lot of hypersensitivity to the motivations of others. When other people carry any kind of thing that might seem overpowering or not trustworthy, the wound gets triggered. If in the wounded healer phase, again it looks like progress, but it's not really, and will appear as somebody who is a champion for issues of abuse, or trust, or betrayal, but the wounded healer, this wounded healer is still identifying with the wound.

Beyond identifying as wounded healer is this acceptance of sensing the deep, dark secret motivations of other people and at the same time not let it mean anything. The real empowerment journey with Chiron in the 8th is about trusting one's own radar and then understanding where to categorize the results that come in. What's needed is an acceptance of the fact that everybody has portions of themselves that they might not own, that might seem to threaten safety and security, that might seem to cause betrayal, and might seem to be worth not trusting. But the reality these people will eventually accept is that everybody, inadvertently, at some point betrays somebody else. This is part of learning about relationships.

The Chiron in the 8th beyond the wound, beyond the wounded healer, accepts the energy that comes in and doesn't attach meaning to lying and betrayal by others. The wound is not being triggered because the point of the energetic sensitivity is understood.

How this can come out as a gift is in utter compassionate acceptance of all of the kinds of motivations that people have. This person can become a natural counselor, because everything that you could think of to tell this person, every dark thing, everything you don't want to talk about, this person accepts it, this person understands the energy and can resonate with the energy without judging it. And not judging is what I mean by not attaching meaning to it, allowing it to be what it is, and teaching other people by example to let it go. This will, of course, help other people heal issues of betrayal and having been lied to, and feeling that nobody is trustworthy.

Every time we look at other as not trustworthy, we're having a doubt that we're going to be able to trust ourselves. The person with Chiron in the 8th can ultimately teach people that the person to be concerned with trusting is oneself.

9th House

The 9th house is about all of the areas of life where we seek some kind truth, where we seek something that we don't have, and where we seek something that we can imagine and we might believe in but have not yet experienced. So when we live in the 9th house, we can be on a perpetual search for truth, for justice, for some kind of something, an ideal. This has to do with the guiding principle by which a person lives his or her life – philosophy, religion, imagination, and intuition. This is Jupiter's house and it is related to the right brain and how we know certain things that we can't prove. So there's this house where belief comes into play. When Chiron is in the 9th house the wound is about expansion, risk, or believing in something involving education, imagination, religion. In a lot of people I've seen in my practice, it comes out as religion. Actually, it *looks* like it's about religion, but it's really about belief and an experience of being wounded in the area of belief.

A lot of times people who are living a 9th house Chiron story would seek the truth of something behind something, but they get stopped by organized religion or a philosophy or a moral edict, somehow. Usually, it shows up as people in the person's life who subscribe wholeheartedly to some version of truth that doesn't feel real or accurate to the person with this Chiron placement.

The wound is a wound to the capacity to believe in something, to have an overarching life philosophy or an overarching idea according to which one lives. As stated above, a lot of times it comes out as religion, but not always. It can also come out in the imagination. In the imagination, we create, we fashion these essentially fictional worlds, which we can then create in the manifest world. But the wound with Chiron in the 9th will be, "That's not possible. That's not true. My imagination is not going to create something. I can't hold a belief in something because it hurts too much."

Because of the nature of Chiron lending itself to making everything different, what a person with Chiron in the 9th does believe, or would believe if he or she let himself believe it, would be different from what is surrounding that person. So if the person really does give in to imagination and gives in to belief and taps into that intuitive side that knows things that the rational side cannot prove and cannot explain, it will set this person apart.

When in the wounded healer phase, there is an identity surrounding being different when it comes to belief and imagination and the capacity to have faith, risk, and trust. Again, it looks like progress because the person is able to talk about it, but because of the identifying with the wound, it is not progress.

Beyond the identity as a wounded healer and identification with the wound, this is where the person can accept that, when it comes down to it, each person's beliefs are unique. Each person's imaginative side leads to uniqueness. The person with Chiron in the 9th will be hypersensitive to the reactions of others when it comes to imagination and belief. That's the Chiron sensitizer here. But when the person crosses the line and can cease identifying with the reactions of others, no longer judge being different and have the self-confidence to understand that being different is actually a gift, then there no more wound to be triggered.

The person with Chiron in the 9th getting to this phase will be able to believe in the self enough to be able to believe in the visionary self and the capacity to imagine. They will have faith in the part that can develop this overarching principle by which to live and can have enough confidence in that. They will be at a place when other people say, "Wow, that's weird," they won't take it personally or let any of the reactions of other people mean anything. By giving in to this part, by really feeding it and living through this part of the self, the person will be revealed as different.

As the person evolves to believe in something and hold a vision within, then other people's reactions stop mattering. As the person persists in holding this vision, other people can be inspired. The person can teach others to come out of "group belief" and to understand more about the uniqueness of each person's vision and capacity to believe in things.

So, the person with Chiron in the 9th can provide an example of a unique way of developing a personal belief system. In many ways this can actually reinvigorate, for example, religion. If individuals were in touch with what they truly believed instead of what they were told to believe (or thought they should believe), religion would actually change. This, of course, would threaten the status quo, but again that's the Chironic gift: to support individuality by embodying an acceptance of one's own uniqueness.

10th House

This is the house where we explore having a public life. It's where we explore developing a persona or a public self, and creating for ourselves a place in the outside world. In contrast to the 4th house, the 4th house is everything inner and private and at home; the 10th house is everything outer, public, and not at home.

The 10th house doesn't have to be work per se, but in the way that we live in Western cultures, it is about work because we become identified with what we do for a living. It can a place in the community. The 10th house relates to how we wish to be seen in the world, the kind of place we would want to have in the world even if we perceive we don't really have one.

Ambition, hard work, being respected for doing something well – that's what we want from our 10th house placement and situation.

With Chiron in the 10th house, there is a wound to the feeling of being respected in the public sphere. The deep, energetic sensitivity with Chiron as an antenna for energy when it is in the 10th house is about the ability to get respect, the capacity to have respect – to not only do things well and present them publicly, but to be respected and lauded for what one does well.

There's a feeling in some of these people that either they don't anything well, or that they do something well but nobody's going to recognize it. This kind of wounding that gets perpetuated is about rejection of the public self. When this comes out at work, where there's a normal amount of criticism of the person's job performance, the energetic sensitivity to these issues will actually intensify the criticism and draw more of it.

Somebody with this position who has difficulty at work might not be seen by employers as a good employee, worth investing in, or even as somebody who should hang around for a long time. Some people with the placement will be job hoppers. Other people will lack respect for themselves and might stay in some job that is kind of crummy or crappy, where they are not treated well. They might garner a lot of abuse at this job, because of this energetic thing they're carrying. They might stay there because any other job would be worse. This sense of rejection of the public self is what's at the core of this.

The wounded healer identity is not progress, but it would be standing up for the rights of people who are not treated well in public and similar kinds of actions. Beyond identity with the wound or being a healer, it's where he person can accept and not take personally that everybody has some vulnerability when it comes to expressing ambition or creating a long-term public face, and that everybody is fallible and nobody is perfect. The heightened sensitivity here is to all of the issues surrounding this vulnerability. While this person feels this strongly, a lack of identification with what it might mean enables that person by example to help other people gain confidence.

When you're a little kid and people ask, "What do you want to be when you grow up?" and you say, "I want to be a fireman" – that's a very 10th-house situation. There is this ideal of this public persona. A lot of times people have become identified with their jobs and these jobs are institutions which people then fit within.

With someone with Chiron in the 10th, the little kid will be asked, "What do you want to be when you grow up?" and the kid might say something like, "Well, I want to be a fireman, but I also want to help starving children." This answer might seem incongruous to the part of us that is very clear and categorical with what has to do with that 10th house persona.

If every single person were encouraged to develop that public persona with as much uniqueness and imagination as possible, the world would be a radically different place. You'd have people who would want to do certain jobs, but then have certain avocations where they really make a difference in the world. Or they have some job that's kind of boring but then do some exciting thing in the world that allows to contribute their own person uniqueness. That's what we're talking about. A person with Chiron in the 10th needs to develop, needs to trust in and then offer his or her own unique contribution in the public sphere.

When the person has crossed the line from identifying with the wound then they are in a position to believe in their unique contribution enough to develop something they can actually offer in the public sphere. So naturally, the job or career for a person who has this placement needs to reflect a certain level of individuality. Chiron is a maverick and needs to be different.

11th House

The 11th house is where we work with other people, where we find other people who believe the same things we do. We want the future to look a certain way, but we know we can't achieve it by ourselves, so we find other people to ally with and work with who feel the same way we do, who want the same kind of world that we want. As a result, this is the house of friends and groups, of people that we associate with. It's networking, it's politics, it's associations.

The 11th is the house where we learn what group effort can achieve. With Chiron here, the default wounding is to the groups and people with whom one is associated. It has to do with choosing friends as well as choosing groups to be a part of. The wounding is about being rejected for the kind of vision of the future one has. How it plays out a lot of times for people with Chiron in the 11th is that they'll associate with groups who cannot recognize their individuality; who cannot recognize their unique contribution, and so the natives are very sensitive to the reactions of groups. That's where the energetic sensitizer comes in.

When the person is wounded, the person will either not associate with groups to avoid being triggered or will associate with groups but try to hide his or her own uniqueness. This is very damaging over the long term, but in order to protect the sensitive part of the self and not trigger the wounding that's what these people do very often.

They won't actually be able to completely hide their sense of being different because wherever Chiron is, we're going to show up as different. What truly shows through as unique is the kind of vision or goal a person has or the kind of groups that the person chooses. It could be that the person chooses groups that end up contributing to the wounding more than necessary. It might seem to others that if a person with Chiron in the 11th would only learn to pick the right groups, then everything would be okay. But what happens is, you get people caught in this cycle of rejection that leads them to picking the wrong groups in order to continue the cycle. That's just what we do with Chiron: We perpetuate cycles until we figure it out, unfortunately.

The wounded healer phase would be somebody who fights for individual's rights within groups. Again, this is identifying from the wound and it can look like it's coming from compassion but many times can come from anger about having been rejected oneself.

Beyond the wound, beyond the identity as wounded healer, Chiron in the 11th will be very sensitive to how individuals fit within group dynamics. They will be sensitive to how an individual's vision, how an individual's desire to create the future and unique contributions to group efforts, can play out – and also how the group dynamics might not be able to absorb that.

You have two kinds of drastically different kinds of possibilities here. One is within a group of people. One person stands up and says, "Hey, I have this great vision. Let's talk about this." It can either be inspiring to the group, or it can be hated by the group because it's different from the consensus reality that's been developed over time. It doesn't matter if the Chiron person (in this latter example) has been in the group for 50 years or two days. It doesn't matter. But there's this cohesion that results from the group mind, which belongs in the 11th house. At its worst, it's a mob mentality. At best, it's a collective of people working toward a common goal.

The difference between people being inspired by the Chiron person's vision or hating it and wanting to step on him or her is the Chiron person's attachment to the reaction. What happens is that if the person stands up and says, "Hey, I have this cool idea!" and the group says, "We don't want to hear it," the Chiron person can say, "Great, thanks for letting me know," and go on to find another group of people where this particular unique contribution is honored.

For the Chiron person, when they make this transition, when they "wake up" to not identifying with the reactions of groups of people who are established and goal-oriented, the person will be free to find the right kinds of groups.

When someone with Chiron in the 11th is belonging to completely the wrong group but hasn't spoken up enough with self-loving confidence in order to find that out, he or she has to explore his or her own individuality within the group context and be willing to change groups. They need to "wake up," to find another group that has a different goal and a different dynamic and a different sense of what it takes to move into the future.

A lot of groups seem to have common goals, but those goals aren't necessarily future-oriented; those goals are to stay exactly as they are. There's nothing wrong with that, but someone with Chiron in the 11th who has the capacity to envision interesting things for groups and really understands a lot about group dynamics won't fit in with that kind of group and needs to learn to move on if necessary.

12th House

The 12th house involves parts of life where we identify as more than just our ego. The 12th house is where we learn about the greater fabric of reality that surrounds us. Things that belong in the 12th house take us out of our normal experience of space-time. This is the house of escapist behaviors, addictions, mysticism, meditation, and getting lost in creativity, ecstatic dance, music, and art. It's where we identify as more than just what we think we are – what our egoic self thinks it is, which often involves in getting lost in some flow, some current of life that surrounds us. When Chiron is in the 12th, the relationship with these parts of life is what has been wounded.

A lot of clients who have Chiron in the 12th, this childhood triggering, this childhood wounding comes out as having relationships with disembodied beings, be they spirit guides or nature spirits or angels. But then the beings go away, so there's this sense of disconnection and rejection by spirit, or rejection by this greater fabric of reality that's beyond our egoic sense. In some people this is felt to be a connection to the universe itself, a feeling of being at home in the universe – feeling as though one has the right to exist as a spiritual being. It can appear as a wound to the person's relationship to God or Goddess or the creator principle. Some have felt that the universe isn't looking out for them. Whatever the details, there's a sense of disconnection from the spiritual side of life or from the unseen parts of life.

As I work with spirit and spirituality, I look at this as related to the fact that we are energetic beings having human experiences. Some don't work with a concept of a deity, don't talk about having a specific kind of deity, but rather this relationship with the energy of the reality around them, the things that you can't see and touch. Whatever you call it, it's all the same in the 12th house. It's about relating to the energy of the universe and the world around us, especially the unseen.

When Chiron is here, very often there is a wounding to this sense of connectedness to this kind of reality. Some people are very conscious of the split and feel abandoned by God or the Universe. Other people have not explored the idea of spirituality or connecting energy or feeling the world as an energetic being. Those are two extremes, but either way the wounding is about connectedness to other realities and to feeling the self as a part of a greater reality.

There can also be a response of taking things very literally in order to avoid triggering the wounding that comes from feeling that disconnection from that part of life. Somebody here might be surrounded by people who seem connected to spirit or connected to art in an inspired way or something similar, and the person just won't get it.

The 12th house represents all of these idealized, wonderful, spiritual things, but also escapism and addiction. Chiron anywhere in the chart can lead to addiction or escapist behaviors that lead to addiction because the pain of disconnection and rejection can be so great that we retreat into something that helps us numb out. In the 12th house, it's kind of a classic symbolism here. Chiron in the 12th might be very directly inspired to numb out in order to not feel the pain of disconnection. When you see Chiron in the 12th, do not assume that there is addiction or escapist behavior, but that's one way that it can come out.

When the person identifies with the wounded healer, then of course he or she is helping other people and identifying with his or her capacity and history of standing up for other people, helping them to process this disconnection. But again, because it is associated with the wound, it is identified in terms of the wound and so just perpetuates it.

Beyond the wounded healer and beyond identifying with the wound is a sensitivity to energy, where one feels the universe, one feels the flow of the energy of the world around him- or herself. One understands one's place within that fabric and is not attached to any of it. When you have this antenna for energy in the 12th house, it is extremely sensitive to energy of all kinds everywhere, perhaps not even locally. One might even pick up on the feelings of a faraway friend, not having spoken with them in years.

When the person with Chiron in the 12th manages to *not* associate with any of the feelings that come through this antenna, then there is a capacity to be an example for other people of how to handle such incoming energies. Ultimately, it will bring peace for these people to live in relationship to the energies in the world around them, as it will allow them to express their unique individuality. In a way, this essentially brings the normally "invisible" 12th house into manifest form. When there are planets in the 12th house – whether they're dwarf planets or asteroids or centaurs or planets in the 12th house – we're challenged to bring a part of that world through our consciousness into the real world, into the physical manifest world, in order to concretize something.

When we talk about Chiron in the 12th, we're talking about bringing through the energy of compassion – being able to sense all the different energies flowing around one and accepting this fact, accepting these flows of energy and compassionately responding.

Having a sensitivity to the spiritual concerns and spiritual needs of other people is also part of the gift of this placement. In the 11th we're talking about having an understanding of group dynamics and how individuals fit within them. In the 12th house, it's having an understanding of how people relate to spirit, how people can relate to these unseen parts of life. Whether or not the Chiron person identifies as spiritual, whether or not he or she meditates or chants mantras, etc., there is a sensitivity to the realities of individuals attempting to connect to something outside themselves.

When people with Chiron in the 12th stop identifying with the energies that pass through them, then they have the capacity to show others how to accept one's place in the greater scheme of things and how to experience the energy around oneself and the energies of the cosmos directly.

Chiron in the Signs

A sign is a lens through energy works and is therefore a kind of a motivation. It's a method and a motivation for the planetary body or acting energy. The acting energy here, of course, is Chiron. The sign that Chiron is in determines the behavior of the planetary body.

Chiron's orbit is highly elliptical, which means that it's more like an oval stretched out – not circular. As a result, there is an uneven distribution of Chiron in the signs among the population. The longest time it spends in its 50-year orbit is approximately seven years each in Aries and Pisces. The least amount of time it spends in any sign is Virgo and Libra, which is at the other end of the scale at about a year and a half each. Consequently, when you're looking at charts you'll see tons of people with Aries and Pisces Chirons and not so many with Virgo and Libra.

Aries

Aries is the energy of unmediated instinctive action. It rules things that begin quickly and doesn't edit itself and look around at what other people are doing, and figuring out how to be them. The key phrase for Aries is "I am" and it is this bursting on the scene, this moment of beginning and this sense of announcing, "Here I am!"

When Chiron is in Aries, the wound is to the sense of freedom to announce one's existence in the world. The wound is to behaving in an unmediated, unedited way. Aries energy is a part of each of us and, for people with Chiron in Aries, it will be edited as long as they are in some way identifying with the wound or afraid of being wounded again. When we do Aries energy well, we allow ourselves to flow in the moment. We don't think about things, we don't analyze, we don't ask the opinions of others, we just go and do something. We allow ourselves to flow with this energy of announcing existence and beginning things.

Given whatever house we're talking about, the person with Chiron in Aries may have a doubt that he or she has the right to exist in that area of life. This editing of the natural flow of energy will also make them self-conscious about a lot of different kinds of things. The energy of Aries has to do with physicality and using the body, responding instinctively with the body in various ways. Think about all the different ways that could come out: sexuality, athletics, or in any kind of way that a person uses physical energy to respond to something in any given moment.

To avoid triggering the wound, people who are still identifying with the wound will try to edit out their instinctive responses to any given stimulus. The wound is sourced in some kind of rejection about responding instinctively to something, responding without thinking. The response, in order to avoid the wound, may be pausing to think every time Aries energy threatens to come out. But the energy can't be edited, so what's created is this loop of self-doubt and the person tries to hold back the immediate, instinctive response energy. This can lead to a backup of energy, a buildup of Aries/Mars/1st-house energy, which can be destructive if the person does not find an appropriate outlet for the energy.

When people with Chiron in Aries cease to identify with the wound and also get beyond identifying as a wounded healer, what is waiting is an incredible sense of presentness – being present on an incredibly deep level – an absolutely pure presence, awareness, consciousness of the moment and a willingness to respond in any given moment to any given stimulus. As they do this without taking it personally, not identifying with what the original stimulus might mean.

So there's a healthy detachment waiting for them. As the Chiron in Aries at this phase will be expressed uniquely, the response in the moment will be unique. This is the ground for Chiron, and so the person with Chiron in Aries will respond to things with an incredible sensitivity to energy and a conscious choice to hold compassion and love.

Taurus

Taurus energy seeks to slow things down. It seeks to ensure survival as its bottom line. In order to ensure survival, one has to make sure that all the elements in play at any given time are focused on in turn and are stable, ordered the right way and can be put to good use, etc. There's this whole chain of control-oriented behaviors with Taurus energy because the bottom line is stability and slowness in order to ensure survival. Where Aries announces itself, Taurus starts to get practical about how to continue surviving. All energies working through the lens of Taurus want and need to work at their own speed, their own pace, as well as for their own reasons.

When Chiron is in Taurus, this way of expressing energy is going to be attempted to be edited. The original wounding with Chiron in Taurus is the that way the person needs to do something and the speed at which he or she needs to do it is not acceptable. There's a rejection of that person's method of attempting to slow down and working on one's own terms at one's own speed in order to achieve something.

When we're talking about baby behavior, this involves being rushed through something. Baby takes too long to do something and the parent needs to keep the schedule going, so he or she kind of moves through it. The baby is wired to be hypersensitive to being edited in this way. That's where the wound comes in.

Living according to one's own value system, choosing the speed at which one accomplishes something, as well as the reasons behind doing it – this is the source of the wound and that's what will be attempted to be edited. This relates to the 2nd house in the sense that it does have to do with self-worth and self-esteem.

With Chiron in Taurus, doing Taurus healthily leads us to self-esteem. Doing Taurus healthily leads us to be able to understand why we're doing what we're doing and to be able to achieve things at our own speed, at our own pace, and for our own reasons. That all contributes to self-esteem.

Taurus is a natural part of our energy fields. It's one of the 12 energies of the zodiac, one of the 12 lenses through which we experience life. When a person attempts to edit this in order to avoid triggering the wound again, there will be a great deal of inner conflict. "This is what everybody's doing, X and I really need to do Y or need to do X in a different way," and hence the Chiron difference, that sense of uniqueness. There's going to be tension because, "If I do that, if I differentiate myself for why I do things or if I go too slow, then I'm going to be rejected." There's that fear of re-opening and re-triggering the wound. In other words, they will need to slow down. They will *want* to slow down, take their own time, take their own roads, do their things for their own reasons. Yet that fear of rejection can cause them to have a lot of inner conflict about fear of triggering that wound again.

When the person is beyond the wound and beyond identifying as wounded healer, what's waiting with Chiron in Taurus is an absolute flow with their own rhythm. When they do flow with that rhythm it will set them apart from the people around them. That's just a natural sense of Chiron difference and uniqueness. When they honor that, then they can actually affect other people, being an example of someone who can slow down and do things at their own pace, at their own speed, and for their own reasons. When they can help other people connect to that route of developing self-esteem, then they help other people connect to their own rhythms.

There is also a tendency to experience things through the senses because that's one of the ways that we understand ourselves as unique. "I'm getting information from this thing as I touch it." So there's a sensual, Venusian aspect to this placement. It is also about what we find important enough to learn, and so there's a tie-in with skills and resources related to with the 2nd house and Venus, here with Chiron in Taurus. Whatever they find interesting is what will set them apart. Their challenge is to stop identifying with other people's reactions to their sense of being different.

Gemini

Gemini is about exploration, specifically of the world around us, the world that is immediately around us, curiosity, gathering data, including through all of our senses – touch, sound, sight, smell, etc. It is the sign where we open our minds.

With Chiron in Gemini, the wounding is about the mind being open. The wounding is to either the reactions from asking questions, expressing curiosity, and exploring things with reactions from other people being that it's not okay to ask those kinds of questions. Or maybe the person has a reaction to the answers that are received: "I wish I hadn't asked that question." Each of those two can be equally wounding, equally damaging.

It will come out in different people in different ways. For some people it will be asking questions, opening up to new ways of doing things, being exposed to other people's reasons for doing things. Those that could trigger the wound, as long as somebody is still identifying with the wound and terrified of repeating that rejection scenario.

It can also carry over into these people trusting or not trusting what their senses tell them. For many of us, that might sound a little ridiculous. But it's not intuition; it's the logical left brain connections that we make about things – deductive logic instead of inductive. If the data in front of you get you in trouble, part of you may try to edit out being conscious of those data or trusting that they should be paid attention to.

For example, you see body language, you see cues in somebody. That's not intuitive, that's looking at the result of life on someone's body and you're observing it with your eyes. But you know that asking questions and making observations about things can trigger other people's pain into being hard on you for asking questions. So this is one way that Chiron in Gemini can play itself out.

71

You observe data, but you know if you use them you'll get yourself into trouble – at least as long as the person identifies with that wound.

In other scenarios, asking questions will trigger people's deep pain, their own Chironic woundedness, for some reason. The energy of Gemini can be very casual about the use of information and one of the evolutionary reasons for Chiron in Gemini is to sensitize us to the use of data, to the use of observations and the data that come from our senses and our left brain.

It's very easy to hurt other people when we observe things about them or ask questions about things that they might not feel comfortable talking about. When somebody with Chiron in Gemini does allow that sense of curiosity and learning about the world and gathering data to flow unimpeded, that person will show up as different. It could be the kinds of questions, that the questions asked are emotionally penetrating, which is very different than regular Gemini questions. Gemini is about data, the surface. Chiron in Gemini will sensitize that person in this arena.

When a person with Chiron in Gemini gets beyond identifying with the wound or the wounded healer, what's waiting for him or her is essentially a talent of having all of these data-gathering tools and a sense of curiosity and exploration that can actually uncover and honor difference in self and others. If the person expresses curiosity in a natural way, it will set that person apart. So there is the task of not identifying with the reactions of other people. The person with Chiron in Gemini can really get behind the appearance that the left brain and sensory data present and deepen the experience of energy behind any apparent situation.

Cancer

Cancer is the emotional experience, the emotional lens. When we do things through Cancer we seek to feel how they operate, how they are affected by the world and how they affect the world around us. When Chiron is in Cancer, the wound is to the emotions, to the sense of safety and security and can feel like, "When I express my emotions, I am not going to be safe." This is the rejection scenario surrounding the feeling.

What happens is that when Baby gets imprinted with this wounding, it has to do very often with the parent looking in the eyes of this baby and seeing this incredible emotional sensitivity and recognizing it in him- or herself. Many clients I've worked with who have this placement are working on healing family issues. Chiron tends to be a source of these issues. The baby is radiating this invitation to connect on a deep, intense emotional level – this incredibly vulnerable, sensitive level – and maybe the parent doesn't quite know to deal with it, what exactly to do with it or how to deal with it.

The wounding is to having the right to feel what you feel. "If I really feel this, then I'm going to be rejected. If I really run this energy, if I really open to feel as much as I can, then I'm going to garner or earn rejection for being that way." The emotional nature, the feeling sense, the way of responding to the world in a feeling way that will attempt to be edited. Yet this is a natural mode of expression, so there will be a lot of tension that builds up. "This is what I need to feel and I'm not sure how to honor that, because if I do I might lose the love and support of people in my life who are most important to me." That's how the thinking can go with Chiron in Cancer.

While people with Chiron in Cancer identify with the wound, we recognize emotions as a major part of our humanity. Even while we live in this very Saturnian culture that doesn't honor and exactly know how to deal with our emotions in healthy ways, we still recognize that our emotions are a major part of who we are. The person with Chiron in Cancer can feel that his or her own humanity is not acceptable, is not okay or, if expressed, will get him or her unloved. So you have this essentially supercharged emotional sensitivity with the wounding, that "I can't experience it." Not only just that the person can't do anything with it, but "It's not healthy for me to experience it, because then I'll be cut off from everybody." "It's too much" can be part of the wounding with this placement.

This part that is trying to protect the rest of the self will say, "Well, your emotions are just too much for other people, and when you express them, it overwhelms other people." So there's that part of that wounding: "If I'm really flowing with who I am, when I really permit myself to be who I am and live from that place, then I won't have the support of other people. Other people won't know what to do with me." That's the sense of rejection when we're dealing with Chiron in Cancer.

What's waiting for these people when they stop identifying with the energy that flows through them, when they stop identifying with the wound and stop having any idea of being a wounded healer, is a heightened capacity to the flow of emotional energy. This person might encounter another who has a lot of pent-up emotions for one reason or another, and offer that person a single look in the eye, and a real open-hearted 4th chakra compassionate response to that person's suffering. It doesn't take sitting down with that person for three hours and talking about the feelings in order for that person to feel better.

There is a receptivity to the energy of that pent-up emotion, when that person feels acknowledged in a very deep and very sincere, open compassionate, open-hearted way. The person with Chiron in Cancer person can learn to be not attached to the meaning of that energy. So that person can feel your frustration, your anger, your desperation, your destitution, these desperate feelings for four seconds and make a real connection with you energetically through just a glance or a touch on the shoulder and then let it go. These people can model for the rest of us how to feel intense emotion and not be attached to it – how to feel *any* emotions, *all* emotions, and not be attached to them.

Leo

Leo is about personal expression. It is about performing and expressing one's own perspective. The planets working through this sign can be seen as the part of the self that is trying to perform the experience of being the self. It's not just that "I want to tell you" or I want to show you the thing I made – rather it's that I want you to understand what it's like to be me.

So Leo energy doesn't have to be about creativity because it is about whatever the person chooses. However this person chooses to express, there is a personal side to it, a creative aspect to it, because it's performative.

With Chiron in Leo, the wounding is that, "If I do this, if I shine, if I tell you who I really am in a personal way, then I will be rejected." In one sense Leo is about responding to the world, responding to situations, environments and other people with a personal stamp, a personal signature: "This is what I think. This is how I respond."

There are a lot of people who are creative and we all love a creative person. But until they stop identifying with the wound, those people with Chiron in Leo will have a lot of emotional charge about the reactions of other people to the expression of self. They will be highly sensitive to the reactions of other people. What happens is that what you express creatively might challenge somebody else's confidence in his or her own creativity or in expressing personal opinions and having a personal mark on the world around them.

Let's say the person with Chiron in Leo stands up and performs something. There's a room of 25 people and three of them feel challenged to confront their own unwillingness to be creative. The person with Chiron in Leo will pick up on that, will be sensitive enough to that insecurity, and will internalize that as a sense of rejection. And you can say, "Well 22 people *loved* what you did," and that person may have an intellectual problem reconciling that because three people in the room represented rejection, the wounding for the expression of the self. So they're hypersensitive to the reactions of other people when expressing their own creativity.

When they stop identifying with the wounding and are not playing wounded healer, what's waiting for them is being able to run a natural sense of creative energy that will set them apart. Expressing their opinions, expressing their experience, conveying through some creative or conversational or literary way the experience of being them. When this challenges others' insecurities, the person with Chiron in Leo, when not identifying with the wound, will accept this and will be compassionate and sensitive, and essentially hold space as an example of somebody who honors the creative self and doesn't get wrapped up in the reactions of others.

Virgo

Virgo is where we seek to improve something. Where we seek to analyze, discriminate, make choices about what we're going to work on, be specific and be intentional about making something better. In the process of doing that we learn about being humble and we learn about duty, responsibility, and the benefits and costs of having a strong work ethic. When Chiron is in Virgo, this is what's wounded: the part that can analyze, discriminate, make choices and make something better.

With Chiron in Virgo, what the person has been rejected for is discriminating, making choices, and analyzing. After that initial wounding, the person's natural inner critic and inner judge will step in and supply harsh criticism about future choices made. So the rejection is, "I made this choice and that got me a lack of love. I chose *this.*" Now imagine here a baby reaching for something and not getting to have it, not getting to make a choice. That method of choosing, that lens of self-expression that is this choice, is called into question as a means of getting rejection. So they're all suspect: being really analytical, being really clear that connecting the dots – A to B, B to C, C to D – all of that will get you in trouble. So there's a wounding to the analysis and discrimination part of the person.

How it comes out in daily life is in making choices. "How can I be sure that my thought process in leading to choice A is correct?" The reality is that we make choices and then we find out they might not have been the greatest ones and we learn from them. The person with Chiron in Virgo will have a really heavy voice of criticism, though: the inner judge and critic will be very, very strong. You can

75

see how this is a twisted form of that analysis and discrimination because it is informed by the emotional wounding, a projection of the fear of the loss of love.

When they stop identifying with the wound and the wounded healer, what's waiting for people with Chiron in Virgo is a sensitivity to how this analysis, these thought patterns, and how people go about choosing things can inspire insecurity due to a fear of making wrong choices. People with Chiron in Virgo can have compassion for people in this process, can inspire trust in others that the choices they make in any given moment will lead them to the right place and teach them how to detach from the meaning of making a "wrong" choice.

When someone with Chiron in Virgo employs that analytical method in order to discriminate – the process of analysis and discrimination will set them apart. If they're not identifying with the wound, they will no longer take to heart the reactions of other people, which might sound like, "Your thought processes are a little off." They will be able to accept with compassion that those people are simply being confronted with looking at their own thought processes and seeing that the Chiron in Virgo person is working differently.

Where otherwise there might be criticism, the person with this placement can hold a lot of compassion for how people choose things, what people chose to do, and how people choose to live. They can be examples of people whose decisions and choices come about via thought processes that are completely authentic, unique, and original.

Libra

Libra has to do with creating fairness and what we do to create balance, harmony, equality and justice. Libra is the sign of the other, a sign of relationships, and it emphasizes the process of *learning* moderation, balance, equality, and justice. The process of learning these things requires interacting with other people – and we naturally have to interact with other people in order to learn. It might be easy to look at Chiron in Libra and look at it being about relationship, but it's really about this process of finding equality, justice, balance, and harmony.

When Chiron is here the source of rejection is the threat of the loss of love. "If I attempt to balance this, if I attempt to make peace, if I attempt to be moderate, I will be rejected." It will come out in someone's daily life as a belief that fairness isn't possible, or "The ways that I need to live in harmony, the ways that I need to seek balance with other people and within myself and with life aren't okay." And again, Libra is a natural part of our energetic expression palette. There's going to be a lot of inner tension because we all seek balance, peace, and harmony in some way and to some degree. The Chiron in Libra wounding is that it is not going to happen, because if it does, then "I can't afford to have it happen because I'll be rejected if I speak up."

This also comes out in cooperation, and that's probably where a lot of the wounding as a baby happens where the baby opens energetically to some kind of balanced and fair interaction, but what happens is the baby isn't energetically heard because part of the Libra process we go through to learn fairness and harmony is being heard by and hearing other people – and not. Even highly evolved, sensitive, post-modern 2010 parents aren't always focusing energetically on what's happening with the baby. There are times when that baby's input – which at that point is energetic, emotional – is not taken into account, and the baby is going to be extremely sensitive and reactive to the energetic responses of other people.

How this can play out for someone who is now a fully functioning adult but still has this Chiron wounding active, is this assumption that they are not going to be heard by others and that their needs are not going to be taken into account by others. So there can be a real dampening of the spirit to seek equality with other people when trying to form healthy relationships. The need will always be there, but the actual methods and willingness can be dampened significantly in order to avoid triggering the wound that says, "I won't be heard. I'm not going to be taken into account. My needs are not going to be honored and treated as I would honor somebody else's needs."

What's waiting for people with Chiron in Libra when they no longer identify with the wound or being a wounded healer is they can be incredibly open and vulnerable when it comes to the reactions of other people and not taking those reactions personally. They can understand that everybody's insecurities come out when we come together in relationship. They can understand to some degree that everybody is afraid of not being heard and having unfair relationships. They can become wonderful models of compassionate listening to people with whom they're in a relationship and to anybody else. They can become remarkable models of compassionate listening because they're not attached to what the other person is saying as a personal reflection or indictment or a potential source of rejection.

Scorpio

Scorpio as a lens of expression is about penetration, digging below the surface, and understanding what's found below the surface once you get there. The method of Scorpio is to dig below anything that is apparent, with an understanding that everything that is apparent and on the surface reflects, hides, tries to hide, and/or tries to reflect an inner motivation. Scorpio is all about finding out what that inner motivation is.

With Chiron in Scorpio, the wounding is to sensing into things below the surface. The wounding is also about trust, but it is related to digging below the surface. The person with Chiron in Scorpio is outfitted energetically with an antenna for the inner motivations of others. Intimacy is one of the routes to the true experiential, energetic, emotional understanding that Scorpio needs. And while intimacy can lead us to think of sexuality, it's really about honesty – plain, deep, frank honesty – about who we really are inside. As a person with Chiron in Scorpio approaches intimacy with another person, if what the other person says and does and what that person is feeling on the inside differ, the person with Chiron in Scorpio will be able to sense that difference and will not trust.

So the wounding is in taking personally that other people are not honest with you. The fact is that each person has a sense of wanting or needing to protect the self when it comes to developing intimacy with another person, building that deep bond where we expose ourselves in whatever way is happening in the moment. A lot of times people are not fully honest up front when confronted with that kind of interaction with another person.

The person with Chiron in Scorpio takes the energetic discrepancy between behavior and true motivation personally, as a betrayal, as a rejection. When the person is no longer identifying with the wound and is no longer playing at being a wounded healer, what is waiting for them is a sensitive, accepting, loving, compassionate response to when other people aren't honest. It's that simple.

Among my clients who have Chiron in Scorpio, there is a tremendous amount of really intense, dramatic life experience, life stories and relationship issues that accompany this. Everything I've said here is the kernel – it is the core of it. It's about being sensitive to other people's dishonesty and taking it personally. So when they don't experience that, when they don't choose to be attached to other people's energetic issue with perhaps not being as honest as possible, then they are a model for accepting other people when their motivations even aren't loving.

When somebody is not completely honest, the motivation might seem to be loving since it has to do with protecting the self, but it is fear-based. The person with Chiron in Scorpio will always be sensitive to that, especially the discrepancy between, "This is the appearance I want to show you and the reality I'm experiencing." There is also a level of this that the person with Chiron in Scorpio, when they're in the wounded phase, will not understand. It takes getting beyond the wounding, not taking things personally in order to comprehend that there are times when somebody represents him- or herself in a certain way and does not know the truth of what's happening inside, but the Chiron in Scorpio person will be able to sense it. When wounded, there is a sense of betrayal felt: "I can't trust you."

When not wounded, when beyond the wound, the sense is, "Aha, I understand that you might not see this about yourself and I can have compassion for you that you're not capable right now – or you're not in the stage of your evolution yet – where you can really connect with that deep, true motivation."

The person with Chiron in Scorpio, as a model of compassionate love and compassionate self-loving, can be compassionate with these other people and help them see how to connect their inner motivations with their outer descriptions of themselves. That's the gift they can give.

Sagittarius

Sagittarius as a lens of expression is about expansion. It is also about belief in the sense that we can aim for something, to call it into existence by focusing on it in our imagination. It relates to this element of belief of holding an ideal, holding an idea in our right brain, in our intuitive knowing, holding that in there and then going for it.

When Chiron is in Sagittarius, we're talking about a wound to the risk of expansiveness, of the capacity to hold a belief and to eventually move toward it. There is a wound to capacity to hold a belief, being able to believe in something, and to move through life in an expansive way. The wounding is to having taken a risk of some kind, most likely in infancy. You can look at the house in question and that will tell you some more vocabulary words to plug in but, essentially, there is a risk and an expansiveness that seems to get in response some form of rejection and the threat of a loss of love.

Whatever Sagittarian behaviors are employed, whatever is happening with this person, it will set them apart, because Chiron is a natural differentiator. As the wound is to the willingness to take risks, Chiron here can dampen all the different ways that people have the opportunity to expand or imagine a better world for themselves – or to live in bigger ways or live into a bigger version of themselves, a more confident version of themselves, a more robust, jovial, vivacious sense of themselves.

As the person with Chiron in Sagittarius identifies with this wound, they will attempt to edit the joyful, boisterous part of themselves out. In our culture – or at least as we have received astrology for a few thousand years – Jupiter energy is considered the best. Jupiter is the ruler of Sagittarius and Jupiter is fabulous, Jupiter is great. So, this sense of natural optimism and buoyancy and resiliency that most people identify as a very strong, positive trait, is damaged.

When they stop identifying with the wound and they're not trying to be a wounded healer, what is waiting for the person with Chiron in Sagittarius is an acceptance that the reactions of other people when it comes to them being "big" have nothing to do with them – for example, if you risk making a big, personal expression or risk telling people what you believe.

Being beyond the wound just takes all of this away. Beyond the wound, a person with Chiron in Sagittarius can accept all the ways in which expressing belief makes him or her different without being attached to other people's reactions to it. They know that everybody believes something that makes them a little unique.

Capricorn

Capricorn is the mode of working toward things in the long term. It's the mode of concretizing ideas, making things manifest. When we do Capricorn well, we have a long-term goal and we work toward it incrementally and slowly and we value the experience of going through something over time. We develop a skill and are recognized for what we do well by other people, by our community. We gain respect for doing something well when we do Capricorn in a very healthy way.

When Chiron is there, this part is wounded. The wound is to working at something over the long term, concretizing some idea, and bringing it into manifest form. It is also a sign of developing maturity by choosing to sacrifice things that might be nonessential in order to focus on what is essential.

The wounding in infancy can be about competency, about corrected after doing something. We translate all of these signs and houses into baby behavior. The vocabulary and the possibilities get narrow, but if the baby is doing something – perhaps playing in a certain way and is corrected – that can be a source of Chironic Capricorn wounding.

There is a sense of autonomy that goes with Capricorn, a sense of doing things for oneself and being an authority on something. For people with Chiron in Capricorn as they age, the wounding is to their capacity to develop a sense of self-respect by being respected by others. The wound is about working toward things in the long term, taking care of themselves on their own, standing up on their own two feet, being in the world, or becoming a person who is worthy of other's respect.

The Chiron wounding will be activated whenever it is time to get serious about something, to get serious about a project, and roll up one's sleeves and develop a long-term strategy. The wounding will say, "If I do this I will be rejected. I don't have the capacity to stand up on my own two feet in this way and to develop into somebody who is respected for what I do well." When the wound is triggered it has to do with respect, it has to do with competency, doing something well and being recognized for doing something well.

Many times, the inner voice of Capricorn criticism will sound like: "You're not doing it well enough. You're not doing it right." There's a kind of resonance with Chiron in Virgo where the original wounding happens, but Capricorn's inner judge and critic is fully capable of taking it on and berating the self from the inside out instead of needing someone else to do it. That wounding can derail the person from developing any kind of long term plan and perpetuate thoughts like: "I don't know how to do this. I'm not capable of taking care of myself. I'm not capable of being an adult."

When these people are beyond identifying with the wound and beyond attempting to be a wounded healer, what's waiting for them is to be able to have compassion with the self for having doubts about standing up on one's own and achieving something of lasting value in the long term. They can also become a model of compassionate acceptance for other people, recognizing that everybody has at least some that doubt about their capacity to develop something over the long term, to become respected for being good at something. So these people can be a compassionate leader in the sense of being energetically sensitive to these vulnerabilities that every adult has to some degree.

Aquarius

As a lens of expression, Aquarius seeks to be different. You might think Chiron is very at home here, but there is definitely a Chiron wounding waiting to be explored, and it's about creating freedom. It's the part of us that seeks to be unfettered by convention and by circumstance – a "don't fence me in" kind of energy. Aquarius naturally is an inventive, original energy within us and – aside from Chiron – it is already unique. And when Chiron is here, that sense of creating freedom for the self is really what is hampered – the sense of originality, the sense of independence in creating freedom.

So the person will be very sensitive to the reactions of other people when it comes to setting oneself apart, to being different, to doing things in a different way. Aquarius is a natural part of the zodiac and therefore a natural mode of expression for all humans. When Chiron is in Aquarius, the wounding is: "If I set myself apart, I will be rejected." There isn't room for innovation here. The original wound in infancy had to do with doing something differently, specifically differently from the norm, from the way the parents or the family do it. It could be in any manner of things, and the house where Chiron in Aquarius is will answer a lot, fill in some vocabulary word gaps for you. The sense of being different, being innovative, setting oneself apart, and being free of convention is what is not supported or will seem to garner rejection.

For as long as the person with Chiron in Aquarius identifies with the wound, there will be some measure of fear about setting oneself apart. Even when one does set oneself apart it's going to be different from how other people do it. That's part of the key with Chiron in Aquarius. You have this marker of uniqueness, this maverick energy.

So these people need to learn how not to take personally the fear that other people have about mavericks, about people who stand out from the crowd. Other people have fears and they're not sure how to deal with those of us who are different. So this Chiron journey through Aquarius is in honoring the self in order to be as unique as one needs to be without taking the reactions of other people personally.

When the wound is no longer identified with and there is no identity of wounded healer, then what's waiting for people with Chiron in Aquarius is being a model of compassionate self-acceptance. No matter how weird you might be, no matter how strange you seem, no matter how different you are, there is always the capacity to love and accept yourself. The gift that people with Chiron in Aquarius can offer other people is to accept the ways in which they are different and accept it in other people. They can accept that everybody has some fear about being different, and they can look you in the eyes and be an example of accepting difference. That's the gift they offer once they get beyond that wound.

Pisces

Pisces as a means of expression is about surrender and going with the flow. It's about relinquishing control, whether voluntarily or not – where we flow with something outside of ourselves or with what is bigger than us, or where we're forced to go with the flow. This is a natural mode of human expression, just as each of the 11 other signs is. When Chiron is here, this sense of surrender is what's wounded. "If I surrender, I'm going to be hurt. If I open up to the world around me, I'm going to be rejected."

Another way of talking about surrender when it comes to this Chiron wound in Pisces is vulnerability. When we do surrender to whatever is happening around us, we open ourselves up to experiencing the energy around us. With Chiron in Pisces, what most of these people are sensitive to is all the energies around them. So when they open up, when they surrender to anything, they're opening up to be energetic sponges for the world around them. What they take personally is any of the negative stuff that they pick up. Chiron anywhere in the chart is a call to learn strong, healthy energetic boundaries, but Chiron in Pisces can look like it has an uphill battle when it comes to managing one's own energetic field, because this porousness is necessary – being one of the twelve modes – and yet it also brings pain.

The sense of rejection for the person can come from the Universe itself. "If I open up, you're going to throw all this negativity at me." With Chiron in Pisces, one of the things that happens is we don't notice the good as much as we do the bad – meaning when you open up and you're vulnerable to the energy around you, you don't notice the good because it doesn't hurt you, doesn't traumatize you. It doesn't force you to lose your footing and have to try to start over with something. This wounding is to the sense that the Universe is a kind place, that "I get to flow with reality around me." That's the wounding here.

When they stop identifying with the wound, what they're doing is ceasing to identify with the energetic sensations that they feel. They are ceasing to identify the sensations with emotion that they either want more of or want less of, that they want to approach or avoid. When they process the wound and are no longer identifying with it, they are able to open to life and all of the energies and not cling to any of them, not make meaning out of them, or stick to or allow any of them to stick to the self. In doing so, they can become an incredible model of compassionate loving acceptance for everybody and anybody and everything – all modes of being, all ways of being. When you don't take any of these energies personally, you can accept that they're natural.

So these people can walk around the rest of the world, just being loving acceptance that the totality of everything is actually good and is filled with variety and diversity. This will also lead them to not judge what other people are feeling and experiencing because they are clear that they don't have to take it on. The energy doesn't have to follow them around, it doesn't have to linger within their systems or affect them or hurt them.

That is healing for the sense of being connected to the rest of the Universe – not just the capacity to surrender, but to that feeling of connection to the rest of life in the Universe.

Chiron Retrograde

Retrogrades in a birth chart work differently than when a planet appears to be moving forward (in direct motion). The energy is focused inward, so however it might work for everybody else in the world, for someone who has a retrograde it works in a different way. With Chiron retrograde, this compassionate response, this sensing energy and the meaning that gets attached to the energy that's felt is just a little bit different. The major reason someone has a retrograde is to retool how and why that energy is used.

If we're talking about Mercury retrograde, the mind and the thought processes can work differently. The point is to not think other people's ideas, not communicate other people's ideas, but to develop one's own. With Jupiter, it's about belief. Perhaps the person has in other lives developed or started to express other people's beliefs and not really figured out what he or she believes. These are just two examples.

When we're talking about Chiron retrograde, the reasons for having compassion, the reasons for sensing and responding to energy in the world around a person need to be reworked. It's a kind of retooling or a rewiring of the energetic antenna. The person with Chiron retrograde may sense just as much energy in the world around him or her – may sense the pain and suffering, the emotions, and the energy of other people – just as much as somebody with Chiron direct but the response is going to be different and it needs to be different.

So some of these people will respond with an open heart and essentially jump in with this energy of compassion, this helper energy, this nurturing energy, the healing energy. But there are situations for people with Chiron retrograde where they need not to. There's a lesson with Chiron retrograde about when to be compassionate, when to help, when to heal, when to support other people's pain and suffering and when not to.

Very often that kind of education, that kind of learning invitation, will manifest as being surrounded by perpetual Chironic suffering, or at least having certain people in one's environment who are chronically Chironically suffering. They have to learn how to withhold not the compassion, but withhold giving energy to these people, to find the right reasons to do it, to develop healthy ways and motivations for responding to them.

When someone has Chiron retrograde, the default is going to be one of two things: Either to give openly or give without question, or to withhold this energy because it doesn't feel right to give or help. One way of looking at it could be dragging the self down in other people's suffering. The evolutionary intention behind Chiron retrograde is to develop one's own means and motivations for doing it.

So there needs to be a time in someone's life who has Chiron retrograde where compassion is essentially withheld. Or compassion can be had, but the response of doing something about the feelings, the pain, and the suffering of other people is withheld.

Every person has an emotional center and, underneath levels of pain and suffering and responses to abuse and betrayal, everybody wants to respond to others with compassion. We want to help each other, we feel we're connected, we feel that we're the same. Beyond pain and suffering, beyond our own wounds, we want that connection with people. But when somebody has Chiron retrograde it's imperative that there be a period when the person does not help other people. During this time, that can be very, very difficult. The person can say "Well, I can feel that person needs something, but for some reason I simply cannot give it. I simply cannot do it."

During that period – which could be a year, several months, or 30 or 40 or 50 years – the person needs to spend time with why it is important to be compassionate. When he or she does that, the beliefs about why it is important to be Chironic and what is important about being Chironic, about helping other people with their suffering and why that's valuable will be revisited.

This, of course, can result in a lot of loneliness when you can feel the suffering of others and you are choosing not to do anything about it. This can really weigh on you and it can lead to a lack of connection, which then leads to loneliness. If someone is defined by what he or she does as a Chironic helper or healer for other people, especially, then this period is difficult but necessary for a course correction to retool Chiron's function.

After a period of time, ideally the person will arrive at a healthy understanding of when it's important to give and when it's important not to give. For a lot of people with Chiron retrograde, what is often the case is that there were people in the environment – likely in early childhood – where somebody is perpetually suffering, and perhaps they want to help alleviate that person's suffering but they understand they can never really help them until the others help themselves.

With Chiron retrograde, this is one of the big lessons. When is it important to give? When is it important to withhold the giving? Or when is it important to withhold an energetic response to someone else's emotional suffering? There are times when responding to someone else's suffering perpetuates that suffering. As a result, sometimes this process involves a sort of tough love where, "I can see you're hurting and I recognize that it's for your own good that I not do something about it, because you have to learn how to pull yourself out of this emotional muck."

Not everybody learns how to do this, however, so the person with Chiron retrograde going through this process needs to understand that other people's suffering is not their responsibility. Anybody in touch with his or her Chiron will have at least one part of themselves that asks, "What kind of person are you if you can see the suffering in others and do nothing about it?" This situation is also very Piscean/Neptunian, where we're very much tapped into the energy surrounding us. But with the Chiron retrograde, this question needs to be answered, and prejudices about people who don't help other people need to be addressed.

What it all boils down to is better energy management, taking better care of oneself. People with Chiron retrograde need to learn how to do just this. The potential for the people who choose to go through this process, or who allow themselves to be dragged kicking and screaming through it and stick around, is that they understand more about the true nature of healing and suffering. They understand that the true invitation of pain and suffering is to teach us to choose compassion and that as we have compassion for ourselves, as we are able to see the difference between giving to others and giving to ourselves and able to take better care of ourselves, we can actually help other people exponentially more because we are healthy in this respect.

This process will come up at some point in everyone's life who has Chiron retrograde. Going through this process allows a person to really develop a way of taking care of the self, so that when he or she does give of the self, when responding to energy being sensed in the environment, then it's not a compromise to his or her own health.

When I see Chiron retrograde in charts, I see people with family members who suffer, people with family members who don't know how to process their own grief or their own pain and suffering. This often happens in families because families are incubators for our karma. Sometimes they are crucibles, yes, but they begin as incubators for all of our karmic issues, which are sometimes about learning through having horrible boundaries and giving away too much. This is why a soul would choose to have Chiron retrograde – to be surrounded by people who are suffering and feel that you have to give because you love them but you can't and then eventually there has to be a point where things get cut off. This is one way we learn lessons when it comes to living with the energy of Chiron in healthy ways.

Of course the people who are closing the door, as well as the suffering people who feel the door closed on them, don't understand it. That's just part of the process for this energy of compassion – to stop leaking compassion externally because it needs to be directed inward in order to learn the life lesson associated with it.

Once the person with Chiron retrograde has gone through this process they are able to understand the right uses of healing energy, and able to understand the right use of compassion as a balm. This is when compassion actually looks like tough love, when compassion requires not helping somebody, which is actually very difficult for any of us who haven't gone through this process.

Another situation that arises with Chiron retrograde is simply not knowing what to do with the influence of Chiron energy. Again, this fits the mission of needing for this energy to be turned inward so one figures out for oneself what it is, what it is for, and how to respond. You'll find people with Chiron retrograde who don't know how to deal with the pain and suffering of other people. This is simply a reflection that they don't know how to deal with their own pain and suffering. We can know and we should accept with compassion and detachment that they don't know how to respond. They are learning this and it is a major life lesson.

Let's say someone's heart is pouring out onto the concrete in front of the person. They might feel like a deer caught in the headlights. They might feel disconnected, like, "I don't know what to do with this so I'm not going to care about it." There is going to be a level of detachment. When we see this, we think there's maliciousness or cruelty or indifference involved. It's important to respond compassionately to this person's inability to respond with compassion. If you're seeing this, it's part of your own Chironic journey to learn to accept where somebody else is in his or her development or process without judging it.

To sum up, people with Chiron retrograde have to find their own way. Some will not be connected to their sensitivity. Some will not know what to do with what they feel because they have to retool how to do it and why. Some will overgive and then stop giving for a period in order to figure out how to live in a more healthy way. The bottom line is that the soul is intending to learn better energetic boundaries – to learn how to take care of oneself better, how to manage one's energy better, to give the self what one needs in order to give other people what one can afford.

This is not about being miserly. It's not a stance of "I don't have enough" or that there's a scarcity of love or a scarcity of support and compassion. It's not about that at all. Rather, it's about ensuring that you care for yourself in a way that supports you in achieving your other goals – in achieving any goal that you have – and in performing your soul's mission.

Relative to the first part of this book, we're talking about where we are now in this invitation to understand ourselves more as energetic beings having physical experiences, and by doing so, understand our true spiritual nature and more of who we really are – not just who we *think* we are or who we've been told for thousands of years that we are. Learning how to take better care of ourselves energetically is part and parcel of that evolution.

Natal Aspects to Chiron

Aspects in natal charts tell us about the relationships between energies within the person's psyche and energy field. It's very easy to understand aspects within a person's chart by looking at the outward manifestations. Yet as we're talking about Chiron, one of my goals is to help you learn how to think astrologically, which is thinking in terms of energy and how bodies in the chart and their relationships have everything to do with energy. I want to put your attention on the inner experience of these aspects, because when you understand that, then you can change any outer experiences of aspects that do manifest already.

You can think of aspects as conversations between energies within a person. Two functions of the person in aspect have a conversation that then plays out in the person's outer life. As previously, we have to look at where a person is in relation to the wound or identifying as wounded healer in order to understand how the aspects manifest. I've talked many times about if the person is identifying with the wound, this is something that can happen, and if the person is beyond identifying with the wound, this is another kind of thing that can happen. But we can't know from looking at a chart how a person lives the aspects in his or her life – it's all energy and we all have free will.

Because we're talking about relationships between different parts in someone's psyche and energy field, whenever one party in a relationship changes, the other one can't help but change. This is something I see as an energy practitioner in the work that I do. As people shift consciousness, the people around them can't help but shift in some way as well. It also works on the level of when we're having an argument with each other. If I go back on my own before I even speak to you again and I change my mind about what's happening, it shifts the energy between us and you can't help but – in some way, in one direction or another – shift as well. That is the same for aspects in a natal chart.

Looking at Chiron in aspect to natal planets, there can be a certain tension about how the person feels about the experience of being highly energetically sensitive relative to whatever part we're talking about. As soon as you or the person learns more about Chiron and learns how to make different choices, then the dynamic within the energy field and psyche of the person that is reflected in his or her natal chart will shift because consciousness is changed about an aspect involving Chiron.

The aspects I'm going to cover here are conjunctions, sextiles, squares, trines, inconjuncts, and oppositions. I'd like to say a couple of things about these six aspects before I begin talking about them in relation to bodies in the natal chart.

The first thing to say is that no aspect is good or bad, no aspect is easy, no aspect is hard. These experiences are determined by conditioning, choices, and beliefs – which are all wrapped up in one another. Looking at a natal chart as a representation of energy, we begin to lose the idea that this aspect is good, that aspect is bad, this is easy, and that's hard. They all have the potential to be difficult or easy depending on how we're wired and how we use our wiring, how we choose to live and how we function as a conscious being. I'll give you some examples of that as we run through all these energies.

Conjunctions indicate a fusing, a merging of two energies. It's like two energies that are joined at the hip. You can't talk to one without the other. Visualize it this way. Within the psyche of a person there is a meeting happening with all these different parts – Mercury, Moon, Chiron – all these different functions are together in one room having a meeting. There are different roles that different bodies have in the boardroom, but the conjunction represents the two people who are sitting over there and never have separate opinions, who always agree and always support each other. They're kind of like the same voice, the same person. With conjunctions you can't talk about one energy without talking about the other; they are automatically merged.

With a sextile it's about stimulation and triggering, so the two energies in question feed off of each other. That can be a good-natured thing, encouraging nice tickle and poke in the ribs. It can also be a negative thing where we push each other to action to get a reaction out of the other one, which poking and rib-tickling fit as well. It depends on how we receive that energy, but it is stimulation and triggering us into action.

Squares indicate friction and pressure to change. Two energies in a natal chart square to each other have different ways of doing things, different opinions about how and why things should get done. They expect each other to change, to do things differently. The pressure they apply on each other is about causing the other one to do things differently. Squares always ask us to change. When we're talking about natal squares, the two parts of us seem unable to get along. Squares are thought to be "bad" and that is because we don't want to be pressured to change. When we open up to what we can learn from changing, however, squares can actually be the most beneficial in our overall growth. When we There is a way to resolve the tension of the square, and I'll talk about that as I talk about Chiron in aspect in each body.

Sextiles and trines are often said to be good and easy, and it's not always true. Sextiles can trigger you into making stupid decisions. Trines are considered easy because there's a supportive or boosting energy, but we can also be supported in laziness and complacency. We can get boosted into complacency with a trine. So there's a support between the two bodies. They speak the same language, they want the same goals – at least they can respect each other's goals – and they're not asking each other to change.

The inconjunct is an interesting one. The inconjunct is about 150 degrees, and it is as though the two energies in question cannot be in the same room together. They don't simply have different ways of doing things and ways of seeing the world – they have fundamentally conflicting ideas about every single thing you can imagine. While the disagreement is fundamental, it appears as though they can't be in the same room together. They simply have to open up to each allowing the other one to have their say. I'll get into that when I talk about Chiron inconjunct different bodies.

The opposition, which is about 180 degrees, represents confrontation and (like the name implies) opposition. With an opposition, two bodies are on the other side of the wheel, so each has opposite ways of doing things and different opinions about why things should be done, as well as how they should be done. This can look like a standoff with gunslingers about to have a high-noon contest out in the street, or it can be two energies that understand that they can see each other in ways that each cannot see the self, and so they can learn from each other.

Regarding orbs, conjunctions I use up to eight degrees unless it's aspecting the nodes. With sextiles I use six and use the same for the nodes. With squares I again use eight unless it has to do with the nodes, then I'd use 10. For trines I use eight. Inconjuncts I tend to use very small ones, up to three degrees. With oppositions I use eight unless we're talking about the nodes, in which case I use 10.

Sun

Within a person the Sun is ideally the one that makes all of the decisions. Using a boardroom analogy, the Sun is the CEO, the person inside you who is running the meeting in your psyche. In order for our Sun to be healthy, we have to maintain a sense of rationality, we have to express ourselves, we have to consider and then make our opinions count, and we have to shine. That's one of the functions of Sun: not only organizing all of the rest of the parts of us into one voice – or as much as one voice is possible given all these different agendas within us – but also to shine, to take responsibility for expressing ourselves creatively.

Being human is about being creative. It is not about things we traditionally think of as creativity, or at least it doesn't have to be. Your Sun, no matter what sign it's in, no matter what house it's in, is about you expressing who you know you are. When the energetic sensitizer Chiron comes to the Sun as an aspect to Sun, this person within you making the decisions is affected by a deep sensitivity to energy. How this is experienced and how it is expressed will depend entirely on how the person perceives this energetic sensitivity, what the person thinks is happening, and what he or she believes is happening about this.

Some people respond by being a very compassionate person. Some people respond with a real sensitivity that is a vulnerability and a woundedness. As I've mentioned, everything with the aspects here depends upon the person's relationship with the wound. In this case, with the Sun involved, the person who is making the decisions, the final arbiter within the psyche is sensing energy in one way or another. Most of us are taught that the Sun is this rational, grounded, sane, "with-it" energy. Ideally it can be, but when you add Chiron you're talking about that person having a wound, having a sensitivity to energy that results in a wound. The experience and the expression of this, what it means to have Chiron in aspect to the Sun, will depend entirely on how that person relates to the energy, the sensitivity and whatever wound has been developed because of that.

Sun Conjunct Chiron

The conjunction of Chiron and the Sun merges the inner CEO, inner decision maker, with the antenna of energetic sensitivity. Depending on how the person relates to this sensitivity, this could be a very compassionate leader who takes into account the fact that others have feelings, for example, but it can also be somebody who is hesitant to shine because of the wound. Basically when that person is solar, when that person is bold and lives out loud, he or she will be receptive, very open to receiving the reactions of other people to that. Now the person is just shining in some way, but because of he or she being so sensitive to the reactions of other people then everything gets blown out of proportion.

These people can turn a corner, if they need to come out of woundedness, by understanding that everyone's solar expression sets them apart as unique. They just happen to be tremendously sensitive to the reactions of other people, which are probably projections or meaningless. So what they receive is just information about people's energetic reactions – it's not meaningful about them or their creativity.

92

Lots of people with Chiron conjunct the Sun will have difficulty expressing their own creativity because they perceive that other people don't value their voice. The feeling is that other people will not love them if they express their creativity, shine, take up a lot of space in the room, want to be the center of attention. These people feel like if they bring something very shiny and shining to the world around them, then they will be rejected for it.

Sun Sextile Chiron

With the sextile to the Sun, the triggering comes in. The person inside who's making all the decisions, the CEO, who is holding together all of the different voices in the room, is being stimulated and triggered by energy. The energetic antenna is poking him or her in the ribs.

The experience of this depends on what the person thinks the energy is about and "What does it mean that I can pick up this energy on other people? And what does it mean that I can sense things in the environment? Here I am, the Sun. I'm supposed to be calm, cool, rational, collected, but I'm really picking up on a lot of things I can see and I can't justify, can't explain or prove." The person's relationship with energy, his or her willingness to be energetically sensitive and the wound that results from that will determine a lot of the experience. Basically, the person is saying, "I'm going to go do this, I'm going to go be my Sun," and is being stimulated, triggered, poked, and pricked by energetic information, which includes the suffering of other people. Because of the triggering effect– when Chiron triggers the Sun – this can be the energy derived from energetic sensitivity in the form of other people's emotions. The other way this can be expressed is that the person's solar expression, including creativity, can drive, can push, stimulate, and push along the person's sensitivity to energy.

The best strategy for the sextile between Sun and Chiron is to allow energetic sensitivity to be real. Allow the information from the emotions of others to be real and yet develop good boundaries so that you can be stimulated in positive ways, but not triggered into action in silly, superfluous, or wasteful ways where you leak energy.

Sun Square Chiron

The square is trying to get change happening. Each body in square says to the other one, "You're doing it wrong. Here is how you need to do whatever it is you're trying to do." This is the inner CEO, the part inside who is making all the decisions, being squared by energetic information, energetic sensitivity, and the suffering of other people.

The square can make us feel that we're being pushed off course because it's a 90-degrees angle – if you're staring straight ahead, this energy is coming at you from the side and that can knock you off balance. There can be this feeling that, "If I allow this information in, I'm going to be knocked off course. I'm sensitive, I'm aware of your suffering, but if I pay attention to it then my conscious mission (as inner CEO) will be thrown off course." In other words, there can be this sense of "I can't get done what I'm trying to get done if I pay attention to the feelings of everybody around me, or the energetic information in the world around me."

Because this is a square, the healthy way to go about this is to allow energetic sensitivity to change you. Of course, the Sun might insist on having control and so that might be a difficult process. But that is the highest ideal: to take in the energetic information, but not let it mean: "You're not doing it right. You're not doing your Sun right. You're not making decisions appropriately. You're not expressing yourself in the right ways." It's just that this information, when it is let in, will change the perspective of the person inside who is making the decisions.

Sun Trine Chiron
The trine from Chiron to Sun natally will boost and support energetic information of a kind that more or less is spoken in the same language as the Sun. It is the same language because the trine is a boosting, supportive aspect. A really positive potential is that the person takes in energetic sensitivity, the information derived from that, including the suffering of other people, the emotional realities of other people, but doesn't feel that it has to knock him or her off course. It doesn't change the mission, but it can enhance and add to it.

As with the conjunction and the sextile, the trine can benefit, but with the trine it's more obvious to people that it's not a threat. A manifestation of it we don't want to encourage is to be conscious of this information, but not let it change you, because it's not trying to force you to change. The Sun-Chiron trine wants to encourage a proactive relationship with what this energetic sensitivity brings, what this information can bring, how the perspective can change. It's not pressuring. The lazy/complacent way of experiencing this is: "Oh yeah, I can see that you're suffering. Yeah, I recognize that, yeah." And it's not that you have to do something about it when you're aware of someone's suffering, but that's a natural human response – that we can get kind of "lazied" out when experiencing this trine in a certain way.

Sun Inconjunct Chiron

Inconjuncts are very difficult because the energies in question have fundamentally different approaches to everything. In this case Chiron inconjuncts the Sun and the information that comes from energetic sensitivity will knock the person off course. In fact, it might feel like getting pushed off a *horse*.

I was recently talking with a student about this, and I said, "It's not that an inconjunct between two bodies pushed you off your horse – it's that you got knocked off your horse, the horse ran away, you twisted your ankle, you're not even sure how to get back up again, and your footing is not going to be the same when you get up." This inconjunct is like that. Most people who have a Chiron-Sun inconjunct will have zero idea what to do with energetic sensitivity. Meaning, when they encounter somebody's suffering, they absolutely can't keep their crap straight. The person inside making the decision, the inner CEO, just can't get it together if he or she allows this information to come in.

So this is one of the aspects where it's really easy to have a default stance of cutting off the energy from other people as a survival strategy because the inner decision maker, the part of the person that is trying to maintain a healthy sense of self and ego, gets totally discombobulated by the reality of what is felt when that information comes in.

The strategy with an inconjunct is to allow each energy its voice and in this case, to stay grounded and sane – positive solar traits – and to be sensitive to others. The person needs to understand a tremendous amount about energetic boundaries and how to be grounded, how to be stable in oneself and then occasionally or periodically open up to the energy of Chiron as the sensitivity comes in from other people.

Sun Opposing Chiron

With the opposition from Sun to Chiron we have a standoff. Gunslingers are in the street and one is ready to take the other one out. Conversely, here are two people who can respect each other even though they have different views and can see each other in a way that the other can't. With Chiron-Sun you're talking about the way you make decisions, the way you shine, the way you feed your creativity, the way that you express your individuality. This is in direct opposition to the sensitivity function, this energetic antenna. How this can play out is when the person says, "I'm going to be solar, I'm going to express my creativity and I'm going to shine." Suddenly there are all these other people around whose whining or pathetic woundedness gets in the way and steals all the attention.

These people need to learn how to recognize the woundedness of other people as reflecting something in themselves, but it doesn't have to stop or get in the way of the solar expression. For example, if what I express is difficult for some people to experience because it triggers their wounding, I'm going to be really aware of other people's pained reactions to my creativity, my creative product pushing their buttons.

The person has a choice as to how to respond to this. "Is this going to limit my solar expression, or am I going to learn more about my creativity through the reactions of other people?" Opening up to letting the creativity be enriched, letting the solar self-expression be enriched by what is found in this energetic sensitivity, this energetic antenna, can be rewarding. Though at first glance it may seem to threaten the Sun's urge to take center stage, and that's where we get this gunslinger idea. We can either assume that we're threats to each other or we can learn how to learn from each other even if we don't get along and don't really like each other. There's kind of a mutual respect that can be developed.

Moon

This is the part of a person that is responsible for creating happiness. This is also the part that is conscious of feeling, aware of emotion, concerned with nurturing and nesting, and creating stability, safety, and security. So this is interesting to have Chiron as an energetic antenna in inner conversation with Moon, the marker of emotion and feeling. Chiron will sensitize whatever it is involved with, so when it's involved with the Moon it is not necessarily an intensity of feeling, but it can be. Depending on the aspect, whether it is a boost, trigger, friction, or pressure, it can make the Moon or feeling function much more subtle. It can add the energetic sensitivity to the emotions which can intensify and deepen, but it can also simply bring subtlety.

The relationship with the Chiron wound determines a lot of how this happens. If we are judging emotions and we are judging pain and suffering, then our emotional reaction will be intensified. Once we work through a wound, we can then get into the realm where Chiron can benefit the Moon by the energetic input enriching the emotional sensitivity.

Moon Conjunct Chiron

When Chiron is conjunct the Moon, the Moon nature is wrapped up entirely with the energetic sensitivity. This is one of the places where a person needs to really learn some good energetic boundaries – how to give back energy that doesn't belong to one, including emotional energy, and how to take back what does belong to one and to really learn not to be overly porous when it comes to emotional needs and emotional expression. This is a real gift, to sensitize one's emotions and heart to energetic sensitivity and the emotional inner realities of other people, including their pain and suffering, while not absorbing that suffering. The Moon is a place where we open our hearts, the part of us that is heart-open, and Chiron can represent other people's suffering. We can take stuff on from other people by default, especially in the ways that we've been living for many thousands of years. We have not learned how to give back the energy (which is emotion) that does not belong to us and to maintain our own boundaries. When we do it looks like we're being cruel or cold or callous. And it's really time for us to learn how to take that back.

This conjunction may open the floodgates of "energy and suffering in, and energy and suffering out." People who have this conjunction really need to learn what emotion is theirs and what emotion is not theirs, to learn how to consistently sort through what they're feeling and to have some boundaries. When I say boundaries, it's not protection, it's not walls, and it's not armor. I see boundaries as "This is what I'm available to experience. This is the kind of energetic experience I'm going to have." Moon conjunct Chiron can represent an extreme of this misunderstanding that we have about energy and what belongs to us and what doesn't.

Moon Sextile Chiron

The sextile from Moon to Chiron triggers the emotions. The energetic sensitivity from others will affect this person. It is not the same porousness that the conjunction can have, so it doesn't have to be that the heart is constantly open and the person feels subject to all the pain and whims of the suffering and wounded and whining. It's not that, but it's that this information comes in and presses a button, pushes the emotions to respond. If the person is not grounded, if the person is not clear what does or doesn't belong to him or her, then this can really be a distraction. Ways to handle this well include recognizing what is one's own, energetically and emotionally, and what is not and then to be really clear and intentional about how one is going to respond to what is one's own and what is not.

Moon Square Chiron

The friction with this aspect is the pressure to change. Chiron says to the Moon: "Well, I know that you're feeling a certain way, and this is what you would like to do to make yourself happy, but here's this ever-present source of energetic information (including other people's suffering) that is going to push you off your course if you let it in." That's the default fear. The higher, more mature way of experiencing this is to allow the energetic information you receive to change you. It would be beneficial for someone with this square to observe the pain and suffering of other people and not assume that being conscious of it and responding to it would destroy their mission – their happiness mission, their Moon mission. There's a real skill here in overcoming the fear of what it would mean if the person really opened up to the information coming through over the energetic antenna. The bottom line is that the emotional reality – what makes a person happy and how that person nurtures him or herself – must in one way or another take in the information from the person's Chiron function. It must take in this energetic sensitivity. But the native has the choice on whether to be pushed and pressured or to open to change, and that is the fundamental invitation of every square.

Moon Trine Chiron

With the trine between Chiron and Moon, there is some kind of supportive internal dialogue happening between the emotional function and this energetic sensitivity, the feeling-happiness function of the Moon and this energetic antenna that is Chiron. There can be recognition of the suffering in the world around one and of the energetic inner realities of individuals in one's life and no perceived need to do anything about it. But there can be a more conscious way of experiencing this trine.

The information from Chiron, the awareness of other people's emotions and the energy in their fields, including the pain and suffering, can actually support whatever one's Moon is trying to do to create happiness. So energetic boundaries are important: "I want to help you, but I also have to take care of myself." The trine can really teach somebody how to open to this energy and not let it drain you and then closing to it when you need to go take care of yourself. That can enrich the person's lunar experience, the *creating happiness* experience, if the person is willing to go back and forth and not just assume that the channel needs to always be open.

Moon Inconjunct Chiron

With the inconjunct, Chiron says, "Here is energetic information, here is information in other people's suffering, here is an energetic awareness of other people's pain," and you can't figure out what to do with it at first. By default, this inconjunct says, "If I let that in, I'm thrown off course, I'm ruined." In the case of Moon, "My happiness would be destroyed. Happiness for me, safety and security, apparently would be impossible to create and maintain if I allow all this other energetic information in."

That can look like feeling really knocked off course by other people's feelings and needs. Some people, with this aspect will not exactly know how to maintain their own sense of self, because their emotional function is always being knocked off course by other people's suffering and pain. As a result, they might not know how to take care of themselves.

A good strategy with the inconjunct is to learn to go back and forth, to say, "Right – there is that information, I can see that you're suffering, but I'm also extremely clear about what my needs are, and what I need to do in order to maintain energetic health, to be happy, to nurture myself, because I can't always let you (wounded people) in. I can't always do that."

It's a survival strategy to avoid the input of the Chiron information, but it is really important for the person with this aspect to overcome that and to choose consciously to maintain health and occasionally or periodically let in that other side, too.

Moon Opposing Chiron

Here is the standoff between what one needs to make one happy and the emotional realities and suffering in people in the surrounding world. This standoff can seem to say by default, "This is what I need to do to make myself happy, period. If I let you affect me, then you're going to ruin it." This opposition with the energetic sensitivity, the awareness of what's happening within other people, the subtext, the subtle energies within other people, mostly comes out of pain and suffering: "If I let that be real and if I let that in my consciousness, then it will prevent me from being happy." That's the apparent situation with the opposition from the Moon's perspective.

If we can shift that to: "I see you in a way that you cannot see yourself, and I recognize that you see me in a way that I cannot see myself," then there can be valuable information from the awareness of other people's suffering and that person can shift to: "Aha, yes, I can see what's going on with you," but then come back and have that information help the person adjust his or her own needs and emotional nurturing capabilities and situation. The awareness of human reality, gained from observing the suffering of other people, can support one in taking better care of oneself emotionally and therefore creating happiness, security, and safety.

Mercury

Mercury represents a person's communication function and perception. It's how a person thinks, how a person hears and speaks, and what a person is interested in. It's also the curiosity function – what gets somebody interested in something, what they want to learn, what they want to know about. It is literally communication, so it will have to do with how the person uses his or her voice. The senses of the body are affected when Mercury is involved: touch, taste, smell, sound, and hearing. All those things have to do with Mercury. The bottom line with Mercury is that's it's information in and out – that function. When it comes into contact with Chiron, what is energetically sensitized is information in and out. It is not just how somebody hears something, but also how somebody interprets it. The computer of the mind, which can be thought of as Mercury, is affected by this energetic sensitivity.

The way the mind works, what is considered interesting, how things are communicated and how things are learned are affected by the awareness of energy. People who don't have Mercury-Chiron aspects could learn this or not learn that. Let's say there are 20 kids in a 3rd-grade class. The ones who have no Chiron-Mercury aspects are just there learning– unless there's retrograde or karma involved with education – but generally speaking, these kids will learn as they are expected to learn. The Chiron-Mercury kids will be aware of the energy of the teacher – unconscious of it, but feeling the energy of the teacher, of the other kids, residual energy from maybe, "Mom got mad at me this morning," and this residual feeling of energy that can last. So Mercury-Chiron people are sensitive to the energy of things and it affects the information in and out, and their mental processor and their communication faculties.

Mercury Conjunct Chiron

The conjunction of Mercury and Chiron is going to merge the information-in-and-out function with energetic sensitivity. By default, the person can be very confused because there is an energetic undertone that is actually more real to the person than what is presented verbally. I can tell you "I'm fine" if you're a Mercury-Chiron conjunction, but you'll be able to sense if I'm not.

There's a real need here over the course of these people's lives to learn how to integrate the subtext of energy with the literal thing that's being seen on the surface, and to learn how to honor the subtext and not think that just because it's subtext and nobody's naming it directly, that it shouldn't be.

Because Chiron leads us to difference when we honor this part of ourselves, in the Chiron-Mercury person how the person's mind works is naturally different. Obviously with the angle we're looking at in terms of being sensitive to energy and how that mind is joined with that energetic antenna – that is different. But even when that person moves through that sensitivity to the point that sensitivity is no longer a problem, how that person communicates, what that person is interested in, and how that person learns will all be unique and set that person apart.

Some people with this aspect might see auras or colors in people's fields or see discarnate beings. The way that the mind works and all the senses work are sensitized to the experience of energy. There is going to be a need to communicate openly and directly in these people, probably with all Mercury-Chiron aspects, but in particular with the conjunction, because the person cannot use his or her mind without experiencing Chiron. These are some who can communicate about energy, can translate some of these seemingly ineffable, seemingly ungraspable, foggy concepts about energy and really bring them into form and say, "Oh this is my actual experience," and they, in turn, can teach other people through their own experience of feeling energy.

Mercury Sextile Chiron

The sextile between Chiron and Mercury triggers the energetic sensitivity, the awareness of energy, as it concerns the person's mind and speech. Sometimes this will come out as somebody who talks nervously. What the person is actually triggered by is energetic subtext he or she perhaps can't understand, is not conscious of and wouldn't know what to do with, because the subtext is always what we don't want to talk about and that is a lot of what Chiron brings in. It's this idea that, "Even if I tell you I'm fine, you might be able to sense that I'm not." But my sensitivity or my suffering might trigger your mind into action, so you might think it a lot, but you also might overtalk in order to avoid that discomfort, not knowing what to do with the energy you're feeling.

When the aspect goes the other way and Mercury triggers Chiron, using the mind and the communicative faculties triggers a sensitivity to other people and triggers a sensitivity to energy. There can be a back-and-forth dialogue: "What I sense in you energetically, what I feel is going on, that you might not even be aware of, that I might not even know how to communicate clearly about stirs me talking to you, and my talking to you gets me more insight into your energy field and that triggers me."

Mercury Square Chiron

This is friction, pressure from energetic information to communication, thought, perception – all things Mercurial. The square says, "Whatever it is you want to think about – whatever it is you want to focus on, experience, and think about and communicate – if you open up to energetic sensitivity in other people, then it's going to derail things." It's going to push the person off course in a way that prevents getting that goal done. This can be something like, "I have something really important to tell you about something that I'm experiencing." So you and another person agree to have tea tomorrow and you sit down together, but that other person's cat is really sick and he or she thinks the cat is going to die in the next couple of days. But that person knows you want to tell him or her something really important about you, so they're going to wait, they're going to give you the space to communicate. If I have a Chiron-Mercury square, I'm going to sit down and say, "I really need to tell you this," but I'm going to feel that you really can't hear me because of your own pain and suffering. So I have the choice of whether or not to feel unserved and unappreciated and unacknowledged because your need seems greater than my idea, or I can allow what you're saying to get in and that would actually change how I think about the world.

There's a real need for those with Chiron square Mercury to open up to this information and let their minds, interests, and their expression be altered by what they feel and experience. Underlying all of these aspects, you need to learn better energetic boundaries. You need to open up to the subtle information about energy in other people's fields but also learn exactly what to do with it that is healthy, so that you don't feel derailed, squeezed out and drained from being conscious of other people's pain and suffering.

Mercury Trine Chiron

The trine from Mercury to Chiron says that there is a flow between the information-in-and-out faculties of a person and the energetic sensitivity of that person. What the experience and how they go about things is in some ways aligned, and there's no friction there. There's no opposition, there's no criticism. A really high side of this aspect in someone's life can be allowing the energetic information that can be gained from other people, including people's suffering, to really come in and change how one sees the world. Contrasting the trine and the square, the square will always feel pressure and, "You're not doing it right," regarding letting this information in. But the trine is: "You could really take advantage of this information." There's a very different quality in the trine – a supportive, nurturing kind of potential in the dynamic between these two.

The trine does not ask for anyone to change, so it can be very easy just to observe things or to let them be and not really take any information, learn anything and be changed by it. Where the trine can be really juicy in a positive way is to energize us to use both faculties and let them have a conversation going. In the case of Mercury trine Chiron: "Yes, I can see this information, I can feel what's going on for you and, as you speak to me, I can feel the subtext, I can feel the undercurrents of energy that you're experiencing." Depending on my disposition it can be like, "Yes, I can see that information. I don't have to do anything about it," but depending on my interests, depending on where I am with my relationship with my own Chiron wounding, what do I think that energetic information means? You see suffering everywhere, and every time you open your mouth, you're conscious of other people's suffering. But what are you going to use that for, and what does the wounding mean? That can really turn the dialogue around so that this Chironic energetic sensitivity supports the Mercurial mission and vice versa.

Mercury Inconjunct Chiron

With the inconjunct from Mercury to Chiron there's a sense of being knocked off course. Whatever the Mercurial brain-oriented communication mission is, the person can sense by default that allowing sensitivity to come in will totally knock them off their path. You can summarize all of what I've said about Moon and Sun inconjunct Chiron and how to work through that. It's the same exact process. Because I'm talking about energy, I'm not giving you a lot of specifics, because it can manifest in myriad ways. The way through this is to learn to take in that information but not feel subject to it, not feel that you have to be drowning in it. The fear is that, "Not only are you going to knock me off my horse, I'm going to fall in a river of awareness of other people's pain and I'll never get out of it again. I'll never be able to organize my thoughts and communicate to you what's really important to me." Of course that is not true – that is just the fear that can be in place by default, because we're not sure how to experience, in a positive way, this inconjunct.

It's an apparent impossibility. The inconjuncting planets don't know how to be in the same room together. "Both of us can't exist," is the initial feeling. You have to develop some kind of willingness to allow that information in if you have Mercury inconjunct Chiron.

Mercury Opposing Chiron

With the opposition between Mercury and Chiron, whatever information the mind, the conscious communication side of the self, and the senses bring in, seem to keep one from getting his or her mission done. There's the feeling that allowing this information in will prevent the person from being able to get done what he or she needs to get done regarding all things Mercurial. A lot of that will have to deal with what the person has to say, the message a person feels he or she is here to deliver, and the kinds of ways of learning that will all be blocked by the suffering of other people, for example.

Sensitivity to energetic information may be perceived as a threat, but the person has the option to learn about his or her own mind by observing this energetic information. If I observe the suffering of other people and I let it in, that would actually change my Mercurial expression. There's that idea of the gunslingers. If we feel that we can't trust the other person who is opposing us, we'll get defensive. If we can choose to learn what it is that we might be able to learn from that person, we can open up and it doesn't have to be a situation that portend danger or seems to threaten us. That's the real healing offered by this aspect: turning this dynamic around in one's psyche, taking that information in and accepting that the person will be changed by what one learns. The Mercurial expression – that information in and out – will actually change. But it doesn't have to be a negative, as it can feel in the moment of being confronted with change – it can actually be a real gift.

Venus

Venus in a person represents how one goes about creating harmony, fairness, balance, and quality. It also relates to one's self-esteem and what one values about life, his or her value system. In that you can see the duality in the Taurus side of Venus and the Libra side of Venus, as we assign her dual rulership. Venus in the natal chart has to do with somebody's value system but also how one goes about creating fairness and harmony in relationships. You can tie that together by seeing what kinds of people are deemed worthy of relating to, based on your value system.

There's a long thread from self-esteem that traces through resources, money, skills, time – all the way into what kinds of people are deemed important and how fairness and harmony are approached with those people. Adding Chiron, the energetic sensitizer, to Venus therefore has a dual effect and will affect the person's value system. It will make the person very sensitive and will add some level or different kinds of sensitivity to the experience of developing a value system and developing self-worth and choosing, maintaining, and furthering relationships with other people.

Venus Conjunct Chiron

When they are conjunct, there is a merging of these two energies. The person cannot look at other people, cannot look at oneself, without dealing with Chironic sensitivity. One of the big ways that Chiron comes out in rejection. Whenever one looks at one's self-esteem: "What is it that makes me loveable?" Chiron sensitivity is going to be there. There is a lot about being rejected by other people and therefore rejected by the self.

This conjunction also means that if I have this aspect, every time I have a relationship with someone else, it is Chironic in nature. With this, there's a lot of "wounded bird" stuff happening in relationships because the person, depending on where he or she is in relationship to being wounded, will often ask: "Is it true that other people's reactions to me are valid statements about my worth?" We know it's not, but these people are not sure about that, so with the Venus-Chiron conjunction there are a lot of relationships that probably, frankly, should not be happening. There are a lot of boundary problems, a lot of inappropriate attempts to get things healed or to heal other people, whether the Chiron-Venus person is the wounded bird or is the person caring for the wounded bird.

All relationships have the potential to center on healing, and that is an amazing, marvelous function of our love relationships and our friendships. Yet if there is anything that the Chiron-Venus person is not doing for him- or herself and is expecting other people to do for him or her, then you have a problem with the relationships.

This conjunction calls on someone to learn to discern what belongs to one and what doesn't belong to the other person. Basically, being the energetic emotional sponge regarding other people has a deep effect on one's willingness to love him- or herself, to value the self. If other people are always sucking your energy because you're having a Chironic relationship that is inappropriate and unhealthy, then you are not going to necessarily always feel that you deserve to nurture yourself.

Venus Sextile Chiron

The sextile is stimulation, so how I value myself, how I use my resources, how I gather resources and skills and put them to work, and how I use my money are all things affected by the triggering, the stimulation, the poking, and the tickling of my energetic antenna. How I use my money is triggered by my awareness of other people's suffering. How I think about my own self-worth is triggered, is stimulated, is poked, and is tickled by my awareness of other people's energetic realities.

This affects relationships, but not in the same way as the conjunction between Chiron and Venus. How one perceives the usefulness or the appropriateness of Chiron information – sensitivity to the energy within other people – will determine one's response, whether being poked or tickled is a positive experience or a negative one. This can really trigger a person's value system to become shaped, for example, around the awareness of other people's suffering. But it can also be that the person who becomes aware of other people's suffering doesn't want to give because one perceives this awareness of robbing one of something. For example, this can be somebody who gives money to charity because he or she is very aware, "I feel poked in the ribs by those kids suffering, I want to give money to that cause" or "I don't need to be poked in the ribs by this, and so I refuse to give." It can work either way, as with all these aspects.

If the sextile is being triggered, how does a person feel about this energetic sensitivity? How does this person relate to other people as beings who suffer or who also feel energy? That's going to determine the choices and response and therefore the experience of this aspect.

Venus Square Chiron

The aspect of Venus square Chiron is about friction and pressure. The value system, the use of resources, self-worth and how one has relationships and with whom one is choosing to have relationships are all affected by this Chiron sensitivity, by this energetic antenna. The awareness of other people's suffering can push one's value system. Again, that can be perceived as a positive or a negative. When it comes out in self-esteem, it can be that it always represents that something that we don't want to do, until we get "evolved" and recognize the value in learning new things, is difficult. By default, it is pretty safe to assume that this square is something we don't want to do. The Venus is doing what it's doing and this energetic information is squaring, which is coming at it from the side, pushing from the side. It can keep somebody from choosing to be open to experiencing the sensitivity from other people. It can keep you from connecting in deeply human ways with people, because you don't want to be knocked off course, caught off guard and thrown off your horse by other people's pain.

This is a normal response, and we all should have compassion for whatever somebody chooses about this, but with this particular square there is some difficulty in learning how to integrate what one senses in other people and what one finds important regarding resources, money, and people.

Venus Trine Chiron

With the trine from Venus to Chiron, they speak the same kind of language, they have similar kinds of goals but, again, it can come into laziness and complacency. If the person can turn the corner on not letting other people's pain and suffering be a source of pain and suffering, then the person can learn to use the information to positive ends as affects one's own resources, values, what one finds important, how one uses one's money, and how the person relates to other people. With this aspect we could say that what one perceives as fair is always going to have a stream of information affecting it from other people's energy fields.

There is a definite need to have good boundaries, to develop better energetic boundaries in new ways than what most humans have learned to date, in the history of humanity. With this aspect the stream of information is coming in. What does the person do with it? If the person feels powerless in the face of other people's suffering, then this trine will keep the person from doing anything proactive about sensitivity. But if a person can come out of one's own suffering and understand how to turn the corner, then this can be used to positive effect in having compassion for how other people are wired and the experiences that they're having.

Venus Inconjunct Chiron

This is about an uncomfortable relationship between the value system and information from other people – this energetic information from the world around one. This can feel like your value system is going to be absolutely impossible to manifest, create, and achieve if you allow this energetic sensitivity. This is another example of how it can be easy to cut oneself off from energetic sensitivity in order to maintain a course, in order to not have what is important to one seemingly prevented or destroyed because of the intensity of other people's suffering.

The strategy as with all inconjuncts is to learn to open up to this information and to change one's mind about what it means, but to also always come from a grounded, secure place – basically committed to Venus in this case, committed to your value system, committed to what you find important – and then to take that information in from other people and not let that information overpower you or throw you off course. There is a real need to become super grounded in the Venus in order to learn how to take in the information from Chiron.

Venus Opposing Chiron

The last aspect with Venus is the opposition. If it's a standoff, if they're out in the street getting ready to draw on each other, then what one finds important will be opposed by or will seem threatened by the awareness of other people's experience, the awareness of other people as energetic beings, because of being more attuned to sensing other people's suffering. It's really important for people with this opposition to learn to take this in information from Chiron, take the information that comes through other people's suffering, let it change one and let it further the mission by enriching one's own perspective on what is really important.

Most people with this aspect will have the default experience of feeling threatened by other people's suffering. This can come down to the fact that somebody needs attention, somebody needs care. It could be somebody in the family. This is where I've seen it a lot in clients. What somebody finds really important, the Venus has this sense of: "I need to do this. This is who I am." But tending to other people's woundedness keeps the person from doing what is important to them.

I've seen this in a karmic story in several people. Venus is your creativity, your values, what you find important, it is a source of pleasure, something you do to enjoy life, but when it's opposed by Chiron you can be locked into caring for somebody who will never be able to care for him- or herself. That's one of the ways this can come out, especially in a karmic story. It could be like the youngest kid hundreds of years ago who has older parents who have to be cared for, and it's the youngest kid's job automatically to stay home, never get married, never go out and pursue his or her life (especially a girl) on her own and really experience her Venus, her value system, the way that she wants to do, and have the kinds of relationships she wants, because she is locked into caring for other people's suffering. "If I pay attention to your suffering, I'll never get done what's important to me." These people need to learn how to adjust what is important to them by taking in this information, but also having good boundaries and not getting sucked into taking care of other people perennially or perpetually who can't take care of themselves.

Mars

Mars within a person is the action function. This is the part that responds instinctively to events and stimuli. This is the part that acts instinctively, so it responds without thinking. It is a very embodied, physical, immediate response.

Therefore it has to do with assertion and aggression, sexuality, standing up for and defending oneself.

Many times in human history Mars has shown up as war, violence, and aggression, but that's just one side of it. It's also about this instinctual response that includes aggression, assertion, and rescue and defense. The conscious use of one's will comes to focus when we talk about Chiron being in aspect to Mars. As Chiron adds energetic sensitivity to whatever it touches, what Chiron does in aspect to Mars is bring that part that responds immediately with immediacy, unedited. It brings energetic sensitivity into the conversation.

For most people, by default, it will mediate the unmediated response. It will actually slow Mars down because there's this source of information that Mars isn't sure what to do with regarding energetic sensitivity to other people's emotional realities, including their suffering. So Mars-Chiron aspects can bring this sensitivity and therefore generate a woundedness about action, including defense, rescue, self-assertion and sexuality. Mars also relates to desire, so there can be a woundedness about the desire when Mars is in conversation in aspects with Chiron.

Mars Conjunct Chiron

The conjunction of these two bodies merges the will with the energetic antenna. Ultimately, in the long run, when somebody comes out of an unhealthy relationship with a wound, identifying as wounded in some way, it will injure the will. As we trace it back to what the childhood wounding is to do with action, expressing desire and using the body and moving in a very self-directed unmediated way.

The threat of the loss of love was present when the person used his or her Mars energy. If there's an ongoing relationship with the wound, then we're talking about the person's will being hurt. How the person can come out of this is in accepting that other people are going to respond when one uses one's Mars, because when one does it, it sets one apart, it will make one unique. When one does Mars, being self-interested action, it will set him or her apart. So there's a way of accepting this sensitivity as just a basic feature of humanness and not thinking that everyone is going to stop loving you because you are going to express your will and stand out as different. As one is involved with the wound, one will express desire and have that not ever be met well by other people. That's one way the wounding will come out. The sensitivity to energy, instead of being wounded, needs to inform the desires.

The person with Mars conjunct Chiron going for what he or she wants will meet a need that is reflected by the woundedness. If it is instead based in consciousness of energy and energetic sensitivity then the wounding will no longer have to be perpetuated.

Mars Sextile Chiron

With the sextile, there is a triggering effect between Mars, the action function or will, and this energetic sensitivity. The person expressing desires, the person acting unmediated, defending the self, asserting the self, will come up against the information derived from energetic sensitivity to other people's inner workings, pain and their suffering. One nice way this can come out is that one chooses to act in ways that are informed by the suffering of other people. So this can be a conscious response to the suffering of other people. "Where I want my will to go, I can see the suffering of other people, so I definitely want my will to go toward helping people," for example.

Mars Square Chiron

With the square, the tectonic plates in a person are in play. When a person has or expresses desires or uses the will, the energetic sensitivity will come into play as pressure. It can seem to say, "You shouldn't want what you want, because look at how everybody else is suffering." The way to move through this kind of dynamic with the Mars-Chiron square is to choose to open up to the energetic information from other people and allow the will to adjust its expression, what it is that you want. It can seem that the energy and suffering of other people pushes you in such a way that you can't get what you want done. But there's a real opportunity in this. What will resolve the tension is opening up to what that looks like for other people, that your desires seem to grate against their needs. Take in what those needs of other people are and then evaluate how you want your will to adjust.

It doesn't have to feel like you're losing, with this apparent criticism, "You're doing your Mars wrong, because other people are suffering and you have to change how you're doing your Mars." It doesn't have to be that you lose when you give up some of your need to control the outcome. When that information is taken into account and allowed to matter in some way, it can definitely be enriching and will deepen the expression of Mars in the understanding of the will.

Mars Trine Chiron

This is the conscious will and the energetic antenna aligned with each other. They can speak the same language and have similar goals and at least respect each other. It's always good to be conscious of how the complacency and the laziness between bodies in trine could manifest in order to contrast what the opportunity is. It's easy with the trine to settle into some comfortable rhythm even if it doesn't work, hence the complacency and laziness.

Part of the thing that can be unhealthy about this is if all the Mars energy is directed toward alleviating the suffering of other people. Granted, that can feel really good – we each have part of us that is altruistic and wants to help people, but that's not always healthy. It can seem like a great dynamic because the Mars is flowing to the Chiron energy, being informed by it, but there is a need to have really good boundaries and to take care of oneself as well so that one does not become burned out by alleviating the suffering of others.

Mars Inconjunct Chiron

The inconjunct with Mars in Chiron will be a fundamental misunderstanding between the conscious will, assertion, sexuality, and coming up against the suffering, energetic sensitivity, and needs of other people. Mars just naturally moves quickly, moves fast without thinking. If you get knocked off course because of the need to take into account what other people need, that can really make Mars feel handicapped. So there's a survival strategy that comes into play here: doing Mars on an ongoing basis in order to keep out the influence of other people's needs, energetic sensitivity, and suffering and woundedness. It can turn that Mars into a freight train that is unaware because it can't afford to be, because if it is, then it will be totally knocked off course. It will really threaten whatever the Mars desire is, or at least seem that way.

A healthy strategy for this person is to take this information in but be really clear about the Mars and be committed to it, be committed to the desire. Allow the information to come in without knocking one off course totally, and learn to go back and forth between these parts of the self. Be sensitive to energy, but also be in action and be fast and be unattached when you need to be.

Mars Opposing Chiron

With the opposition, the conscious will is opposed by the needs of other people and the sensitivity to the energy of the world around one. It doesn't always have to be other people's suffering – it can be just energy in general, but that's how we usually latch onto it and that's what we make meaningful. We don't want to feel our own suffering, so we don't want to feel other people's suffering, of course.

This opposition says, "What I want to do and what I want to get done cannot happen because you are sitting there whining, because you have a need that you are not meeting." For example, let's say you're my friend, spouse, sibling, family member, etc., and there is something that you need to take care of for yourself – I cannot be dragged down by doing that thing for you. Obviously, of course, some people will tend to the other person and then feel their will, their energy, their Mars get zapped. Other people will not tend to others in this situation in order to maintain the health of their own energy field.

As with all the other oppositions, there is a really important opportunity in opening up to what this information can tell you about how you express your will. It depends on whether or not the two parties trust each other or on how open the native is to taking that information in. There is a great opportunity in enriching the Martian experience – expression of will and inner fire – if that energetic information about other people is taken in and is given some validity. If it is, then the Mars expression will change and the person's life will be enriched.

Jupiter

The Jupiter function within a person is the belief function. It is about hope, faith, and the part of you that is willing to risk and has an intuitive sense of knowing something that it cannot prove. When Chiron is in any aspect to Jupiter this energetic sensitivity and woundedness that can result from that sensitivity comes into conversation with the part of the self that is about belief, risk, faith, optimism, and hope. It can make this belief function and willingness to take risks and have hope very delicate and vulnerable. Taking in this energetic information can really modify Jupiter's bold, passionate, and buoyant energy and the part of you that declares, "I know this because I know this." It can mitigate that side into being apparently a little more fragile, a little less boisterous perhaps.

Jupiter Conjunct Chiron

With this conjunction, the belief function is joined with the energetic antenna. Everything that the person believes is going to be influenced by Chiron one way or another. If the person is naturally optimistic, then that optimism will be deepened and there will be some subtle awareness added by Chiron. If, on the other hand, the person is pessimistic, then Chiron will intensify that by feeding information about people's suffering, which seems to support why one should be pessimistic.

You cannot talk to the part of this person that deals with belief, hope, risk, faith, and optimism without also talking to Chiron. There are lots of variables here. How does the person relate to his or her own wounding? How does the person experience belief? How does that person land on the belief spectrum and how has that person taken the energetic information that the antenna of Chiron offers? How does the person process that? That's going to determine the experience. Bottom line: This person cannot believe or disbelieve something without Chiron being involved.

Jupiter Sextile Chiron

The sextile between Jupiter and Chiron will bring some stimulation from other people's suffering, energy fields, inner energetic workings, and emotional realities to the belief function. How somebody perceives the usefulness of being aware of other people's suffering will determine what the choices are. By default, it can go back and forth between dealing with suffering and having the beliefs modified because of the experience of dealing with suffering. This person with this aspect will need to gain some consciousness of the point of this energy in order not to just feel triggered into silly, useless, or wasted action.

Jupiter Square Chiron

The square causes friction between the belief function and the energetic sensitivity. Basically, what the person believes and the way the person develops faith and takes risks will be pushed out from the side, interfered with, and pressured by what one feels by being energetically sensitive to other people's pain and suffering.

A healthy strategy is to let this information in. The belief system will naturally shift as a result of this. The person with this aspect, thought, might cling to whatever it is that he or she thinks he or she should believe, which is kind of a myopic Jupiterian malfunction that lots of highly Jupiterian people can experience – not being willing to be changed by experience but having a belief and then filtering everything about the world in terms of that belief. These people can be told something, but they'll twist it in their minds to make it fit what they already believed they might be told. That's a Jupiterian malfunction. Chiron comes along and says there is a separate reality happening within other people. There is a reality of emotion, there is a reality of pain and suffering that blows the lid off the person's philosophy and that person is changed by what he or she learns about the reality of people's pain and suffering.

Jupiter Trine Chiron

Jupiter and Chiron speak the same language here, so they support each other. The belief system will be informed in some ways by the experience of being aware of other people's energy fields. As with Mars trine Chiron, all of this Jupiter energy could go toward the Chiron sensitivity. The Jupiter function can be occupied because the information from other people regarding their pain, suffering. and emotional realities is always taken into account in very prominent ways. So, if a person lets the information happen, this can be a real gift that he or she can give other people. Whatever is trining Chiron can be brought into alignment with supporting other people in coming out of suffering, but it can also be draining. It can also not reflect a belief system that is accurate and important. If all of the Jupiter energies, all of the faith, hope, expansion, and risk goes toward alleviating or attempting to alleviate other people's suffering (because they can't do it for themselves), there is an energy expenditure issue and the person might need to rethink that at some point in order to maintain his or her Jupiterian capacity to have hope and faith and belief in something. If you're pouring your energy, your hope, your time, your faith, and your resources into other people's Chirons, because of this idea that you can't fix your own wounding and there's always something that you're going to suffer about, you're actually feeding a bottomless pit.

I hope that these channeled insights about Chiron can help contribute to shifting that a little bit, but if you're pouring all your energy into Chiron issues present-day, chances are – not across the board – but chances are you're throwing your energy into a bottomless pit. It's not bad, because you are helping other people, but the context of what that help really means and what it looks is ready to shift. These trines can actually lead to burnout because we give so much in this direction where nothing can ever seem to change.

Jupiter Inconjunct Chiron

Jupiter inconjunct Chiron is going to be an apparent inability for these two functions to coexist within a person. Whatever the belief is, whatever the person has faith in, however the person needs to develop faith in something seems to be threatened, to be knocked off course irrevocably by this awareness of energy or the sensitivity to other people's pain and suffering. If you're clinging to the belief, if you are set on the belief – which is a very common Jupiterian-focused approach to belief – then you might as a survival strategy not open up to the sensitivity of other people; otherwise, you'd be totally thrown off course.

The solution, as with all inconjuncts, is to open up to each source of information. One party says, "This is what I believe," and the other party says, "Yeah, but I recognize also that there's pain and suffering around me, and I want to have something to do with that because I am human." If you allow that to happen, your belief system will be changed, but you really need to become grounded and to learn that you don't have to give everything up just because you are allowing each of these parts of you to coexist. What's needed is a conscious going-back-and-forth between these two parts of the self. Over time the person will learn to value each and it won't seem like a total threat of being knocked off course irrevocably if Chiron is honored.

Jupiter Opposing Chiron

The last aspect with Jupiter is the opposition. We have a standoff between a person's function of belief, hope, optimism, faith, and risk and their energetic sensitivity. One way that this could come out is that a person's belief system can be shaped in ways that ignore the subtleties of how humans actually experience their inner emotional workings. This can be a belief system that doesn't reflect how humans actually experience life. Depending on how much somebody clings to the stability of his or her own beliefs, it can be that the Chiron sensitivity, this energetic information, would change the beliefs, philosophies, and worldviews of the person if he or she would let it.

The question becomes: How attached is this person to maintaining a belief that is not connected to the reality of humans, including their pain and suffering? For example, perhaps there's a theoretical approach to life that really appeals to the person, but it might be so theoretical as to not ever include how people actually respond to that theory as individuals. Jupiter has to do with launching this arrow. Once you've let loose the bow the arrow is gone and you can't change its course. That can be one way this could manifest, but there is a reality of human experience with the Chiron opposition Jupiter that is calling to be taken into account as well.

Saturn

Saturn is the part of the self that calls for maturity, discipline, and morality, as well as sacrifice. All of these are tools and aspects of working for something over the long term. Saturn always takes a long view, valuing what is forged over time. Saturn is about becoming somebody who is competent at something, someone who does something well but also receives recognition and respect for doing it well.

When Saturn is involved in a conversation within somebody's energy field with Chiron, the energetic sensitivity, needs, and emotional realities of self and other are brought into conversation with the part that is about normalization, the instruction to "grow up already," the "shoulds," the long-term work, and morality. What ends up happening is that the part of the self that says, "This is what maturity looks like and this is what things should be like" is being informed, probably unwillingly, by the energetic sensitivity of other people. Other people's pain and suffering can get in the way of getting long-term work done.

Saturn Conjunct Chiron

The conjunction says that the work, maturity, discipline function in a person is joined at the hip with this sensitivity to energy. That can seem to handicap the Saturn, because every time Saturn says, "This is the way it should be" (in a stern, booming voice), the Chiron reality of individual sensitivity and pain and suffering of other people is right there. That can really mitigate and change the course of whatever Saturn expression is being considered or sought. Consequently, it can appear as if these people don't really want to grow up. The reality is that their Saturn function is being sensitized to the point that they can't help but be sensitive to what's happening deep down in other people. Because they're hypersensitive to the reactions of others regarding their own Saturnian expression, that will naturally change and make more sensitive the Saturn function.

People with this aspect need to become okay with sensing energy and not make meaningful the fact that other people respond to their Saturn functions in the way that they do. What it looks like to the person with Saturn conjunct Chiron is, "I can't get respect. I can't do something really well enough in order to get other people to respect me. I can't really achieve that. I can't really do that." In developing this Saturnian persona that works to achieve something over the long term, the person needs to understand that everybody is sensitive to the reactions of other people – it's just that the Saturn-Chiron person is more sensitive to it. There has to be this acceptance of what this energetic sensitivity brings and that it doesn't have to be meaningful. So when you do Saturn, if you have this aspect, you're doing it differently.

Saturn Sextile Chiron

With the sextile, there is a triggering, a stimulation, a poke in the ribs, or a tickling and the conversation can go back and forth very quickly. We all have had a lot of role models in our lives that embody a hard-edged, uncompassionate way of doing Saturn energy. For this person, though, that can be experienced as a kind of nagging (another manifestation of the sextile), a poking that never stops. It taps you on the shoulder and says, "I want you to be aware of this" and never stops. It can be a back-and-forth between the part that says, "This is how you should grow up, this is who you should be," and the part that says, "Yeah, but I feel very sensitive" it can be a very uncomfortable dynamic.

If the Saturn relationship within the self is operating negatively, then it needs to be changed. It needs to evolve into a compassionate, nurturing inner parent figure. When that happens, that part of the person will be more able to accept the realities of the Chiron situation and the wounding won't seem as flagrant or as big and important, and there can be some self-compassion.

Saturn Square Chiron

Here we have friction between Saturn and Chiron, so the energetic sensitivity is pushing on this idea of "I ought to be doing this" and is trying to get long-term work done. If I have Saturn square Chiron, my awareness of other people's suffering is going to derail me, or at least it will seem to. If I take that information in, it will change me. But I might want to cling to where I am and don't want other people's pain and suffering in my space: "I don't want to feel my own pain and suffering – why would I want to feel other people's?" It's that kind of pressure. There's an opportunity to be changed and enriched by taking that information in, but it will require you to change course.

So you can either feel pressured by the information and hold tension for a long time – or forever – or you can choose to be changed by it and relieve the tension. That's the challenge of the square: to get the Saturnian function of discipline, maturity, authority, and morality function to open and integrate the information from the Chiron energy antenna of other people's emotional realities.

Saturn Trine Chiron

The trine from Chiron to Saturn natally is a supportive aspect. Saturn judges the part that is hurting because of the wound, the part that says, "Gosh, yeah, I deserve that judgment." That's a very stable Saturn-Chiron trine that is actually very unhealthy. What needs to happen is that the energetic information and the sensitivity to energy need to inform what Saturn is doing and why. Yet there always must be more compassion entered into the dialog. That's what Chiron can teach Saturn: to have more compassion, to look at all of the assumptions about how things should be and to moderate them, to change them into something that is more real about the human experience based in an acknowledgement of the realities of being an energetic being sensitive to energy.

Saturn Inconjunct Chiron

Chiron information can seem to knock Saturn off course irrevocably. It can be very traumatic in this kind of scenario with an inconjunct to open up to whatever's coming through about other people's pain and suffering. It can be very, very traumatic and very, very sudden. That's the energy of the inconjunct – to be so sudden that it knocks you off course. You not only didn't expect it, but you had no idea what it would be like when you got there. You didn't even know it existed and, here it is, knocking you off your horse into the river, twisting your ankle, etc.

Each source of information is important. So take the part of the person that says, "This is what I'm going to create over the long term. This is what it takes to achieve success. This is what morality is. This is what maturity looks like. This is what responsibility looks like." This part needs to be solid and yet the person with this aspect needs to learn to open up to and incorporate the Chiron energy anyway. This is due to the fact that, with the inconjunct being always an apparent lack of ability to be in the same room with each other. Saturn and Chiron can exist in the same room, however, if everybody involved in the conversation understands that nobody's going to die – there's room for everybody.

Saturn Opposing Chiron

With the opposition, all of the conceptions of what work is for and how to develop into a mature, responsible self that is competent at something and worthy of respect for being competent at doing it – having a status of respectability – comes in direct conflict with the needs of other people. The energetic sensitivity to what's really going on underneath will be in direct conflict with "shoulds" that Saturn sets.

Here, Saturn says: "This is a project that I'm going to do, and this is what it's going to take. I'm going to map it out, I'm going to make sure I take care of myself, and I'm going to sacrifice some other things in order to it." But the realities of Chiron will be staring you in the face, trying to get you to recognize that your "shoulds" are intellectual ideas, are notions and not reflective of actual human realities.

So Chiron is staring at you from across the room, saying,:"What you think is worth working toward is limited because you are refusing to take in this other perspective." Given all that, a good strategy is to choose to take in the information that Chiron offers. It will enrich things; it will change what you're doing. If you can trust that you might not know everything when you're doing the Saturn work, the Chiron opposition to it can really enrich it by making whatever you're working toward deeper, more meaningful for how humans actually live. Humans as energetic beings are an entire realm of experience that our Saturnian selves with all of their "shoulds" cannot always envision.

So Saturn opposite Chiron would benefit from opening up to the realities of human information even when it comes in the form of suffering. Saturn, when it's very task-oriented, will say, "I can't afford to deal with your whininess." That's the automatic response, but Saturn can be enriched by taking in the perspective of what others who are suffering offer. Again, it's about changing our minds about what suffering is and learning energetic boundaries. We can take that information in without having it derail us because we're being energetic sponges.

Uranus

Uranus in the natal chart represents the part of us that needs to create freedom at all costs. This is the rebel, the revolutionary, the iconoclast, the anarchist. To do a Uranus well, we have to become willing to be free, which means become willing to say no to and leave scenarios that don't work for us, that constrict us or make us feel fenced in or corralled. Part of the Uranian process also involves being willing to conform until you explode into needing to be free. So there is a long spectrum involved. When we live Uranian stories relative to our Uranus natal placement, it can go from extremely bored to absolutely free and unfettered. There is a wide range of possibilities.

When Uranus is aspecting Chiron natally, the conversation between the energetic sensitizer and the need to be free is engaged. I'm going to cover all the aspects, but I'm going to give special emphasis to Uranus opposite Chiron, which is present in the birth charts of just about everybody born between 1951 and 1991.

Uranus Conjunct Chiron

When Uranus is conjunct Chiron, the energetic sensitizer and the emotional antenna for energy is joined with the need to be free. Some people with this aspect will be absolutely unwilling to take on the suffering of other people. That would be true in the case of a very strong Uranus that is not willing to conform or hide. Such people will be very, very sensitive and highly attuned to what's going on with other people and be very clear that it is not for them. A person with this aspect could be a loner or hermit, but really they would simply not be willing to traffic in codependency and take on other people's suffering and pain in unhealthy ways. This is a healthy manifestation: Recognizing that people are suffering, recognizing that all this stuff is happening and not taking it on – choosing to be free.

The other side is that if someone's not willing to be free, not willing to express Uranus and to slough off the chains that bind, then the Uranus energy is more conformist, and it would lead to feeling bored, stifled, and a little deadened. In that case, the person might not feel that he or she has the strength or the right to say, "Oh, your suffering is for you. I'm absolutely detached from that – it has nothing to do with me." So the person might actually take on a lot, depending on varying levels of consciousness. Uranus actually functions as kind of a lightning rod for sudden insights, sudden energetic awareness. It's a little different from Chiron, but it can augment that Chironic sensitivity, especially when conjunct. So any time that you see a chart where Uranus and Chiron are conjunct, you need to understand that that person needs to get free. They need to choose to be free and to evolve that Uranus into saying, "No thank you" when it comes to taking on the suffering of other people.

Uranus Sextile Chiron

The sextile will bring stimulation between this lightening rod, this source of sudden intuitive information and the energetic antenna. The sextile energy is all about triggering, pushing the button, poking you in the ribs until you respond. The real trick is to be conscious of what one needs regarding freedom, what exactly that means, and how to go about doing that in healthy ways. It is also about learning better energetic boundaries and not taking on the suffering of other people. This kind of triggering can result in Chironic sensitivity to energy triggering senseless or careless Uranian action.

If you study astrology, you're probably aware that Uranus is famous for sudden action, sudden breaks, sudden changes, and explosive behavior. This triggering of the sextile can make such changes seem unconscious. Uranus always has this water-behind-the-dam effect. If the water builds up and suddenly you have to burst because you just can't take it anymore, that water would be the whining, suffering, and neediness of other people. When you see this sextile, it's important to understand that the person needs to choose to do each energy consciously so that when Uranus and Chiron do trigger each other and stimulate each other into action, it is for the person's highest good, etc.

Uranus Square Chiron

The square puts Uranus and Chiron in friction with one another. The energetic antenna is in friction with the need to be free. Such a person might say, "I need to be free in this arena of life. I need not to be tied down. I need to have absolute freedom, as much elbow room as I want." And yet the suffering of other people will seem to come in and demand attention and perhaps push this freedom agenda off course.

The best strategy here, as with all squares, is to allow change. Look at what Uranus is trying to do and open up to receive the information from Chiron, from the energetic antenna. Understand in what ways your freedom might challenge some people around you and what they think they need, and what they think you're going to give them. Do your thing anyway, but allow this information to affect you. Even though the squares almost always feels like being pressured to change in ways you don't want to, allow it – it will ultimately serve your growth.

Uranus Trine Chiron

There is a supportive boosting energy with the trine, as Uranus and Chiron speak the same language, roughly. Whatever Uranus is up to, Chiron will support, and vice versa. If Uranus, for example, is saying, "I don't get to be free. I have to deal with this constricting scenario," Chiron will chime in, "Yeah, and look at how everybody else around you is unhappy and why you deserve to suffer." Kind of like misery loves company. If, on the other hand, Uranus says, "Yeah, I'm not going to be stuck with all these other people's issues and problems," Chiron will say, "Oh well, actually, it's their problem, so that's a good idea. Don't get stuck. It doesn't have anything to do with you." So whatever one is doing will affect the level of consciousness of the other and so the person's behaviors and choices will be affected and modulated by the answer to the question: *Is each body empowered?* With Uranus, is the person okay with saying no and "no thanks" to things? And with Chiron is the person willing to say, "Aha, I can see that you're suffering, but it has nothing to do with me"? Depending on where that person is in that level of consciousness with each of those energies within the self will affect the behavior.

Uranus Inconjunct Chiron

With the inconjunct, we have an uncomfortable relationship between the need to be free and the awareness of suffering of other people, or the awareness of energy. Whatever choices are made about becoming free, getting out of constricting scenarios, leaving behind old ways of being and moving into the future, and creating an appropriate kind of exciting situation or life for oneself will become derailed by the suffering of other people. This person can feel totally knocked off course by the information and, if the person feels overpowered by Chironic sensitivity, the Uranus will suffer.

The strategy with the inconjunct is to go back and forth consciously between the two energies. If the Chiron feels overpowered and weak – "I don't get to have boundaries, and I'm just full of this nonsense and I can't get away from it" – then it will suffer because of all the attention on Chiron. It is also possible that there are a lot of sudden outbreaks with the Uranian energy trying to get out of feeling trapped by the Chiron energy. This sextile will push things, the square will push things, but with the inconjunct it's really a hot-button thing being pushed. If someone is not conscious of what's going on with these two energies, then there can be a real explosive thing going back and forth. The key is to learn how to shift between the two energies consciously, to learn better boundaries, and learn how to choose freedom and express originality.

Uranus Opposing Chiron

Most people born from 1951 to 1991 have Uranus in opposition to Chiron. This opposition is really a confrontation between the need to be free and the awareness of other people's energetic business – their emotions, their pain, their suffering – and the energy in the world around one. This can feel as if you cannot create freedom because you're conscious of the effects that your choices will have on other people. Let's say I'm in a social situation and there are friends that I've had for a number of years but right now cannot stand to be around them – if I'm Uranian, I've got to do my own thing. This is a very sudden, unexpected kind of thing. But if I just ignore them one night or cancel plans, part of me might not be willing to be free because I know that that's going to hurt them. There is a lot of inner tension in these 40 years of births. This can manifest in different ways, because there are different levels of consciousness, choices, karma and conditioning, but there is a lot of tension between the urge to be free – which is a valid need – and the urge to consider other people before we do things – which is also a valid need as we are social creatures. This is true especially now as we are learning more about ourselves as energetic beings. We have to learn how to honor each part of ourselves. We need to be Uranian right now. We're just at the beginning of the cusp of the transition to the Aquarian Age, and we need to develop ourselves, our independence, and our individual genius. We also need to honor the reality that other people are affected by our actions without getting caught up in any reactions.

A good strategy for those with Uranus opposing Chiron is to learn to let other people have their reactions. If you need to do Uranus, fine – just don't let your fear of other people's pain from your actions stop you. Understand that their reactions are about them, and not about you. There's no valid statement of worth about your behavior when somebody else is hurt. Everybody is creating their own experience.

Neptune

As we move more deeply into the outer planets, understand that these aspects to Chiron are not common for the people who are alive on Earth. Nevertheless, I will cover all the aspects.

Neptune is the part of us that seeks to connect to other realms. It's also the part of us that is very energetically sensitive. It can be very porous, opening, trying to open to connect with other dimensions, other forms of consciousness, and other realities. When we talk about Neptune, we're talking about manifesting something of the ineffable and divine into our lives, into and through our consciousness. Neptune has to do with mysticism and getting lost in creativity and inspiration, and it's also about escapism, addiction, and just numbing out because you don't want to feel things.

The real thing to focus on with Neptune is this desire, this need – a natural human need – to connect to other forms of consciousness and to adapt and align our consciousness to higher forms of consciousness.

Neptune Conjunct Chiron

This is an aspect that is happening in the sky now, at the time of this writing. When Neptune is conjunct Chiron, it merges the energetic sensitivity with the need to connect to something higher. How this will come out in people is that it can develop into a wound about the spiritual nature, about the connectedness, but the real thing underlying that is the spiritually energetic sensitivity.

I often talk about being spiritual as being sensitive to energy, but this will connect the energetic antenna with the part of the person that connects to other realms. It makes Neptune work a little differently. For people who have this aspect, they're going to be different when they connect to other realms. This can feel strange and foreign, but there's a beautiful uniqueness waiting for these people when they honor this part of themselves.

Neptune Sextile Chiron

With the sextile, this is a trigger happening between Chiron and Neptune. The mystical experience, the escapist experience, will trigger the Chironic wounding, the energetic antenna, and vice versa. If a person with this aspect feels that the suffering of other people is unavoidable and inescapable, he or she might check out, might inadvertently slip out of his or her body, so he or she doesn't have to feel what that Chiron information is offering. So there's a need here to really get grounded in the body, to learn how to say no to certain energies, to learn about how we are energetic beings and be conscious of what Neptune in a person needs and be conscious of what Chiron is about. So when these two bodies trigger each other, it is in the person's best interest to upgrade the level of awareness regarding each body.

Neptune Square Chiron

The square from Neptune to Chiron puts these two in friction. Information from other people and the world around the person, through the Chiron energy antenna, will press on this and make it hard for the person to connect to other realities and to the divine. Again, the information from Chiron can serve to upgrade whatever the Neptune is about, but the person needs to be open, needs to be willing to change, because the information will change the mission.

Let's say someone has a particular spiritual goal, say, start a series of yoga classes. The person has done yoga at home with a video or whatever goes into this class situation. There are eight people in the class, but the energy in the room is so distracting for the Neptune person that it's really hard to focus. That would be an example of being squared by this energy unconsciously. The conscious strategy is to open up to what that energy is about, to be conscious of it and not take it on and say, "Oh, okay, so maybe this will actually help me deepen in that practice." So, in essence, the square is about forcing change – the strategy is that we become willing to change.

Neptune Trine Chiron

With the Neptune trine to Chiron, there is a supportive flow between the way the person connects to other dimensions, other realms – where the person even escapes – and understands him or herself more than just an egoic being. There is a flow of supportive energy between this and the information from other people. If a person is living Neptune through escapism and not being present, healthfully spiritual or spiritually healthy, then the Chiron information – the suffering of other people – will come in and provide reasons that it's a good idea that the person's checked out. If the Chiron is feeling overwhelmed by the suffering of other people, the Neptune will seem to provide this giant funnel of energy in the environment that will just shoot, direct, and channel energy toward Chiron. So it makes the porousness even worse because there is an open channel flowing between these two energies. Each needs to be raised in conscious, and the person needs to learn that you don't have to take on the suffering of other people, but it is important to be conscious of it so you understand what's going on in the world around you and honor that energetic antenna within you.

Neptune Inconjunct Chiron

The inconjunct creates a very uncomfortable relationship between the energetic antenna and the part of the person that needs to connect to other realms or engage in higher ways of experiencing the self, non-linear ways of experiencing the self. This can manifest as a total misunderstanding between these two parts of the self. With inconjuncts we tend to favor one energy over the other. In this case you can imagine which is more difficult: being conscious of other realms or being sensitive to the suffering of other people. This can lead to living with one of these energies really strongly, emphasizing one of them in order to avoid experiencing both. It's going to vary for people who have this aspect, depending on social conditions, family, karma, and conditioning. Depending on which one is the lesser of the two difficulties. The strategy is to do each consciously, to choose to go back and forth in order to let the tension teach you about things. This can actually be very difficult if one of these energies is ignored, due to pain or fear or being overwhelmed by either. Each of these bodies can serve to overwhelm us – Neptune by opening up and making us porous and being absorbent and Chiron having this energetic antenna feeding us all this information.

Neptune Opposing Chiron

The opposition between Neptune and Chiron will present a confrontation. It will seem that, because of the Chiron information coming in through this antenna, this sensitivity to energy and others in the world around one, that the Neptunian process just can't work the way it needs to. In some people this can be a going back and forth, trying to find a balance. The key is to learn the perspective of each and understand in what ways each is valuable and honor them so that they can inform one another.

Pluto

As Pluto is, in evolutionary astrology, the marker of the soul's desires and intentions as well as the soul's deepest wounding and pain, I look at it as the marker of the soul's empowerment mission. We have to overcome our fears from the pain of the past in order to feel the deep sense of grounded strength that Pluto can offer us, to manifest the mission we came here for.

When Chiron is in aspect to Pluto, Chiron is directly involved in the story of a person's karmic history, the many lives that soul is living in the Earth time-space dimension. It means that Chiron is wrapped up in the intentions and desires of the soul as well as the wounding of the soul. It can seem a little tricky because you have two very different kinds of wounding, and how do you tell them apart? How do you distinguish? How do you separate them?

The Chiron wounding is about the sense of rejection for just being who one is as a unique individual. The Pluto wounding is about feeling disempowered, or not feeling strong enough to accomplish something.

With all these Pluto-Chiron aspects empowerment is a big deal, and so we can manifest issues about empowerment through being sensitive. Say, for example, you feel disempowered because you can't shake your awareness of other people's energy, or you've taken on their problems because you want to be helpful, or you think you don't get to have your own energy field. All of these scenarios will derail your mission. There is a theme of being empowered through sensitivity, and that will manifest situations, dynamics, and relationships of various kinds that will seem to threaten one's strength with Chironic wounding in one way or another.

Pluto Conjunct Chiron

When Pluto is conjunct Chiron, the mission of the soul includes to learn about being energetically sensitive. The Plutonian wounding is about being too energetically sensitive or taking on too much energy from other people. Chiron seems to disable the Plutonian strength and, yet again, when the person goes through the process of changing this relationship to Chiron and this energetic sensitivity, the energy antenna that is Chiron can serve to propel the soul's mission and empower the person. So the person is learning at the soul level about difference – how to be different and empowered through being different.

Pluto Sextile Chiron

With the sextile to Pluto, we have that triggering effect, that poking in the ribs or tickling until one of the two archetypes within a person responds. The Pluto wound of disempowerment will be triggered by sensing the energy in other people and around one, often picking up on the negative energy – the sadness or anger or desperation or pain from other people. That triggering will result in action, so the best thing to do is to gain more consciousness of what each needs so that the action can be more self-directed, more conscious in nature.

Pluto Square Chiron

With the square, there is friction between the soul's mission and the energetic sensitivity. In the person's Plutonian mission to become empowered as a human, to learn what that means, there is friction that is received from Chiron, from wounded people and their energy. There is a real sense of, "I can't get my work done if I have to be aware of this energy," so people with Pluto square Chiron will likely have a very difficult relationship to being sensitive to other people's needs, even on that level of, "If I open up to what you need, I might actually open up to the nonsense that you're carrying, what I perceive as nonsense that has nothing to do with me, that I want nothing to do with." So the square is really difficult.

The Plutonian mission can be enhanced by choosing to open up to see what that energy is without getting attached to it. That's the growth process with Pluto square Chiron – empowerment issues in the face of energetic information.

Pluto Trine Chiron

With the trine, Pluto and Chiron are speaking the same language. They're kind of on the same team, so there's going to be a flow. If Chiron feels utterly disempowered, it's going to contribute to disempowering Pluto and vice versa. If the Chiron part of the self feels overwhelmed and full of this information, the Plutonian self will not be able to stand up and say, "I feel really strong," because of this open channel and supportive flow of information between them. The Pluto mission needs to be understood. The Pluto healing needs to be approached and undertaken. And the Chiron, the nature of the wound and energetic sensitivity and the gift that Chiron can bring with maturity needs to be brought into conscious awareness so they can work together and not feel disempowered.

Pluto Inconjunct Chiron

With the inconjunct, the mission of the soul, the goals of the person in various lives, seem to have been absolutely and irrevocably knocked off course by what was experienced by this energetic antenna. Other people's suffering and needs derail the mission in many lives, such that the person probably feels that he or she can't get up and get on with things. It can feel like being knocked over and being unable to get up, because it was sudden and devastating and shocking and traumatic. By default, the person with the aspect is going to really fear taking in this information, because other people's suffering just "ruined everything." Whatever your goal was, with this aspect, you were just absolutely knocked off course. So, with this energy of the inconjunct being traumatic with Pluto, the need is to learn how to take in this information while not being hampered by it.

Pluto Opposing Chiron
In the mid-1960s Chiron was in Pisces with Saturn and Pluto was in Virgo with Uranus. They were actually opposed to each other for several years, so there's a chunk of people born in the mid- to late 1960s who have this opposition active.

With the opposition there's a standoff. The Pluto opposition to Chiron says that an awareness of energetic information has prevented the person from feeling that he or she achieved the mission the soul set out to do. This is essentially being disempowered by the realities that Chiron brings to us. Because it is about Pluto wounding, it has happened in the past and so the person may fear having to deal with it in the future. More consciousness, learning about how the suffering of others and the energetic information from the world around you can teach you about your mission can reflect to you just what it is you're doing, how well you're doing it, and what your true motivations are. Remember, Pluto tends to be unconscious in us. Getting that information and taking it in as an appropriate reflection of what we're up to is the goal here.

The Nodes of the Moon
When you find Chiron in aspect to the nodes, the karmic story tends to be really juicy. It's just as juicy as Chiron in aspect to Pluto regarding unconscious dynamics, repeating patterns and knee-jerk reactions to things. There are two nodes and they are always opposite one another.

The South Node of the Moon is the repository of emotional memories from our past lives. The South Node by house, sign, and aspect tells us about our conditioning environments, and the families that we choose again and again to be born into. As I relay the aspects of Chiron and the nodes, I'm going to focus on it in relation to the South Node because of this karmic conditioning.

Chiron Conjunct the South Node

When Chiron is conjunct the South Node, the person's environment in various lives and the families he or she chooses to be born into are saturated with Chiron energy. For better or for worse, whether it's healthy or unhealthy, healing or destructive or self-destructive, they are saturated with Chiron energy. Because of this saturation, they will understand a lot about Chiron and have the often difficult task of sorting through what does and doesn't work about that energy. The person will be energetically sensitive, will feel the suffering of other people, and may or may not respond as a healer/helper type. The person may respond to this aspect by feeling overwhelmed by the intensity or the sadness of emotions.

The person comes in, so to speak, armed or outfitted with this incredible tool to sense the energy of other people, but if they have not learned about boundaries, if they have not learned how to say "No thank you" to energy that doesn't work for them, they can definitely feel saturated and overwhelmed. So they need to sort out what works and what doesn't. When you work with clients who have this, they will understand everything you say about the positives and how to sort through this. The fact of sorting through is important, but because we're talking about Chiron, it is an emotional process. Thinking about and talking about it for an hour with an astrologer is not going to dissolve the feeling of being overwhelmed. The person needs to go through a transformative emotional process to leave behind what doesn't work, really weeding through the psyche and through the energy field, specifically in regard to relationships.

Because the South Node represents the families we're born into, when someone has Chiron on the South Node, conjunct it, the family is saturated with this energy. Probably the person is trying to come out into some kind of healing mode but is surrounded by suffering, surrounded by people who have no idea how to take care of themselves, how to honor who they are and their own emotional sensitivity. This very early wounding with Chiron conjunct in the South Node can look like this: the parents look in the kid's eyes and see a being who is extremely sensitive, just as sensitive as they are and they can't deal with it.

Chiron Sextile the South Node

The sextile to the South Node says that the environments the person is born into are triggered, are stimulated by Chiron. The buttons are pushed in a very aggressive way here. Again, for better or worse, whether this is about wounding or healing, this person might come from a family that's very responsive to social causes that address people's suffering. Or it may be that the family is deeply affected by self-destructive behaviors that come from an inability to deal with emotional issues, some kind of escapism or addiction that the family has imprinted or driven into action by this. For better or for worse, for positive or negative, this person will be accustomed to being triggered by Chiron energy.

Chiron Square the South Node

With the square to the nodes, there is an unresolved issue in the energy field, in the karmic growth process, of learning how to be human, to learn what the soul came here to do and really do it well. There is confusion about healing, suffering, wounding, giving, energetic boundaries – all of the things that go with this energetic antenna of Chiron. As with all squares to the nodes, there is this habit pattern that needs to be understood, and then the person can learn to make new choices. With Chiron square to the nodes, it can be that the person always gives and never says no and, therefore, ends up in co-dependent situations supporting other people's suffering instead of helping them and teaching them the tools to come out of it. These people can perpetually be in service but be in service for a reason that is not healthy.

Another case is that some people will never open up to the energetic information because they saw that trouble was coming down the pike and were like, "No, forget it. I'm not going to deal with this." That's an unresolved issue and will, over time, cut you off from a portion of your own humanity. Whether you're really open and overdoing the Chironic energy, which would be leaking energy, or whether you're closed off from it because you're afraid of what it might mean to open to it. Those are extremes, but either way, it misses the point of learning about Chiron, which is helping when we can, but also helping consciousness shift into a mode of helping people take care of themselves in better ways, including ourselves.

That square will also have a lot of gray area. Let's say you attract some Chironic people who are very processed in their wounding and very mature energetically and spiritually and you might also attract some wounded birds, because you're learning more about this, and you have to learn to make new choices. People who have Chiron square the nodes have to look at the patterns of their existing opinions, ideas, and habits about responding to other people's pain and suffering and helping other people and nurturing and healing, etc. They need to look at what those patterns are and then understand that expanding their repertoire by making new choices will resolve the tension of this square.

Chiron Trine the South Node

The trine to the South Node says that there is an open channel of information, a flow of energy between Chironic sources and the places and the people this individual comes from – for better or for worse, we don't know. If it is addiction and alcoholism and wounding and abuse or whether it's healing and shamanism and energy work, we don't know, but there's an open flow of information. This person will recognize Chiron openly and have a flowing relationship. Whether that person is doing it for healthy or not healthy reasons will vary.

Chiron Inconjunct the South Node

The inconjunct to the South Node from Chiron indicates that these people and places the person comes from have been derailed by Chironic energy, Chironic sources, Chironic people and situations. This is very difficult. It can be like being shell-shocked by other people's suffering and can really knock things off course. There's a lot of healing and needing to go back and forth between what is comfortable (the South Node), but also opening up to feeling that energy and changing the person's mind about why suffering exists, what it is for – which is essentially learning the key to this course. The key and how to use it is that choosing compassion relieves all suffering within self and others.

Chiron Opposing the South Node

The last aspect with the nodes is the opposition to the South Node, which is the conjunction to the North Node. When you see Chiron conjunct the North Node opposing the South Node, Chiron and all it means is as far away from the person in the karmic past and the present-day family environment as possible. These people often have not been taught how to process emotions. Some of it is grief, some of it is sadness, but they have not been taught how to process this and they don't understand the point of the energetic antenna. They might not ever have been able to develop their own awareness of it, which is to say, their sensitivity to energy. It can be that they come from very practical environments, very surface-oriented environments, where we don't want to stir the pot, we don't want to find out what's under the surface. The environment can manifest as one in which there's a lack of acknowledgement of this normal, natural, human part of ourselves, which is an awareness of ourselves and others as energetic beings. These people need to learn how to interact with the world as an energetic being. They need to feel and they need to learn that the source of information that comes from this energetic antenna in the form of emotions very often is a valid source of information. Some of them will intellectually recognize it as valid and yet not have any idea how to engage with it or how to do it.

Learning how to feel, honor, and process the emotions that one has is really important with this aspect. When that process begins, then these people need to learn how to not take on other people's crap. Some of these people will come from family environments in which energetic boundaries are unlearned and they will be porous or sponge-like and just absorbing all of this energy in people around them. Regarding the fact that they don't know how to process emotions – for some, it's that they're already full of energetic information, but they just don't understand what to do with it.

Doing the Chiron work of sensitizing the self to energy will lead this person to the North Node, which is karmic growth. With the South Node conjunction, they have to sort through what works and what doesn't work. This is a very different scenario with a conjunction to the North Node; they really need to learn how to tap into this, get in touch with it, and honor the validity of emotional information and their own emotions.

Ascendant-Descendant

The Ascendant-Descendant axis in a natal chart represents how a person goes about experiencing the self, showing the self, exhibiting one's own style (the Ascendant) and also how one approaches others (the Descendant). The Ascendant begins the 1st house and the Descendant begins the 7th house. For each of us there is – when healthy – a dynamic tension that exists between the two. It is possible for us to emphasize one sort of expression over the other, and it's important for us always to keep them in balance.

We have this idea of the projection of the 7th house and the Descendant begins that house. There is a question sometimes, "What am I looking for in other people, that they seem to possess and that I don't seem to have, but I would really love to have in my own life?" So that's the Descendant.

When Chiron is in aspect to the Ascendant-Descendant axis, it will sensitize things in a certain way. I'm going to run through the aspects. What house Chiron is in matters because it can be aspecting the Ascendant, for example, from the 12th or the 1st. I'm going to give you a note on each of those differences for this as well as for the Midheaven-Nadir axis.

Chiron Conjunct Ascendant

When Chiron is conjunct the Ascendant (within 8 degrees), Chiron is going to come out in the outward style. If it's in the 1st, it's all about the body, all about that sense of being different. There is a resonance here with Chiron in the 1st house, so refer to that section for more insight. If Chiron is conjunct the Ascendant from the 12th house, the person is actually very, very strong in a certain way. Chiron is just above the horizon, above the Ascendant side of the horizon, showering its light on the person at the moment of birth. That position tends to be one of the strongest positions in the chart. I don't usually rank aspects in the kind of astrology I do, but when something has just risen, it is likely to be a dominant feature of a person's character. In this case it's going to bring some of the 12th house Chiron issues out in the outer personality, but perhaps unconsciously. It will show up in the body and in the style and personality, but perhaps the person won't really understand why or what is happening. Refer to Chiron in the 12th house to understand more about this placement.

Simultaneously, this Chiron is opposed to the Descendant. As the person carries Chironic energy, there will be revelation from other people. Whether it's conjunct the Ascendant from the 1st or the 12th, there can be an unconscious aspect about this placement, until somebody else tells us that we're like such-and-such or reacts to us in a certain way that draws our attention to being that way. You're carrying the Chiron and somebody else reflects it to you. It can be a sense of rejection, or it can be a sense of other people telling you are different. But it's simply a sense of reflection from other people when Chiron is opposing the Descendant.

Chiron Sextile Ascendant

When Chiron sextiles the Ascendant and trines the Descendant, the Ascendant is triggered by Chiron and vice versa. Awareness and sensitivity from other people about energetic information or information from the world around one will trigger the Ascendant, how that person expresses his or her style and how that person uses the body. It's important for the chart holder to be more conscious of what the Ascendant and Chiron are about, what each energy needs, essentially. Being stimulated to color outside the lines with this aspect does not have to haphazard, destructive, or wasteful if the person understands what he or she needs and how this aspect works.

Simultaneously, the trine to the Descendant will call in support from other people, which will actually ease that self-expression. The self gets triggered, and at the same time there's an open channel of information between other people and that Chiron energy. So there can be a flow involving other people, which will help the person learn how to express his or her Ascendant getting triggered in a healthy way.

Chiron Square Ascendant

When Chiron squares the Ascendant-Descendant axis, one tectonic plate is the energetic antenna and another tectonic plate is the sense of self and sense of other. So there is pressure. The awareness of other people's realities, the awareness of this subtle information, the awareness of energetic subtext will drive, will bring friction to how this person has relationships and how this person behaves and operates the self.

With Chiron squaring two chart points that are in opposition to one another, a T-square is formed. It is a real dynamic setup in the psyche that's about taking in the information from other people and being changed by it, and allowing relationships and self-expression always to be open to evolving based on that dynamic, based on that information.

If you're looking at the chart of somebody who has the angles more or less perpendicular to each other, check out if Chiron in square to that axis is also conjunct the Midheaven or Nadir. That's going to add a layer of information. If it's above the horizon, squaring the horizon there will be a more outward way of experiencing Chiron that gives friction to the Ascendant-Descendant, to the self-other axis. When bodies are below the horizon, we traditionally say they're not seen quite as much and operate "more internally," because this is where the Sun travels at night. So when Chiron is below the horizon and not visible in the sky, the energies and pressure will be felt more internally – inner sensitivity to Chiron, inner information, inner energetic awareness will contribute to this ongoing tectonic plate dynamic with the Ascendant-Descendant.

Chiron Trine Ascendant

With the trine, all this energetic information will have an open channel with how that person expresses him- or herself. Simultaneously, that will sextile the Descendant and trigger something about the way the person approaches, has, and maintains relationships. Natally, it will manifest as other people triggering the Chiron. It is similar to but not the same as Venus sextile Chiron. Essentially, how the person approaches relationship and what kind of person is looked for is affected by this triggering by Chiron. Ideally, the Ascendant trine will have the person working in a comfortable relationship with receiving Chiron energy in some way.

On the other hand, it can also be sloppy or lazy and complacent with the energetic sensitivity feeding information to the Ascendant. If there is a self-indulgence and whining happening with the Chiron, that Ascendant isn't going to be better off just because it's trining – it's going to actually that Chiron agenda.

Chiron Opposing Ascendant

When Chiron opposes the Ascendant, it conjuncts the Descendant. I'm going to talk about the Descendant conjunction first.

If it's in the 6th house, it basically puts Chiron front and center whenever the person is dealing with other people. Whether it's in the 6th or the 7th house, this person has got to make a lot of progress with dealing with the Chiron wound in order to progress out of attracting people who will take care of him or her – for instance. displaced Mommy/Daddy crap or drawing people in who need to be taken care of in a Chironic way. Chiron placements in all charts have to do with energetic boundaries, but this is a clear instance of someone needing to learn that energetic boundaries between self and other are absolutely critical.

There is a lot of overlap with the Descendant conjunction, because the Descendant is the beginning of the 7th house. When it's in the 6th conjunct the Descendant, look at the section on Chiron in the 6th house and understand that that gets automatically shuttled or pushed into the dynamic of relating with other people. Is the person in the 6th house with Chiron feeling "less than?" Is that person feeling stepped on, unable to take responsibility for things, shamed for not knowing something, or knowing how to do something well? Those kinds of issues are going to be put front and center in all of the relationship dynamics in the person's life.

As Chiron opposes the Ascendant, something in other people will seem to block the natural expression of that Ascendant. That energy and expression, that bursting on the scene with "Here I am," when confronted with other people's suffering and neediness, gets blocked in a way. If I were to have this, my Ascendant might be saying, "Yeah, I just need to go and do this thing, but when I'm constantly aware of other people's Chirons, that will mitigate my behavior. I will modulate my personal expression if I'm constantly aware of other people's suffering. So that just echoes the dynamic of having Chiron in the 7th, saying, "I really need to learn healthy energetic boundaries and leave you to your crap, leave you to your evolution, to your process. I can help you if I can, but I really need to take care of myself, I need to express myself." What can happen though, because that seems to block the Ascendant expression, is that the person has to deal with all of these energetic boundaries. That whole package of healthy Chironic education has to be worked through before the person will feel really comfortable expressing that Ascendant energy.

Midheaven-Nadir

The other angles to discuss are the Midheaven-Nadir axis, which has to do with the public self and the private self. The Midheaven, the beginning of the 10th house, has to do with the kind of place we want in community or in the world, the kind of role that we have, how we show up in public. It's our public face. At the opposite end, the Nadir is our private face – who we are when no one else is around. We're not putting on a show, we're not having airs, we're not trying to inhabit a role – we just are who we are.

Chiron in natal aspect to this axis is going to, in different ways, push buttons on what is public and what is private. Again, whether Chiron is conjunct the Midheaven from the 9th or 10th is going to make a difference.

Chiron Conjunct Midheaven

Regarding Chiron conjunct the Midheaven in general, Chiron is a part of this person's public persona. Whether he or she likes it or not, unavoidably so, Chiron comes out in public. If it's in the 10th house, refer to the section on Chiron in the 10th. If it's from the 9th house, issues surrounding faith, belief, religion, philosophy, the search for truth – all of that becomes Chironically embodied in the person's public self. It drags, essentially, the 9th house Chiron into the 10th when it's conjunct the Midheaven. I tend to use 3 or 4 degrees as an orb in this situation. When you see it really close like that, just understand that Chiron on the Midheaven is front and center in that person's public life. If the person is not owning that in the persona, then it will be surrounding that person.

When it is conjunct the Midheaven it's also opposing the Nadir, and this has to do with what is experienced in the world regarding Chiron. Whether it's rejection for what one finds important to manifest in the world, a wound to the sense of being ambitious, or an inability to be responsible enough to envision a long-term plan and strategize about how to achieve it – all of that experience will come in and seem to block some aspect of personal expression. For example, if you have Chiron on the Midheaven and you're experiencing rejection at work just for doing what you think is important, that's going to really affect how it is you relate to your inner foundation, especially if you are constantly rejected publicly. Ideally we want your inner foundation to become stronger so that you can learn to not take that rejection personally, but you can see the wide range of possibilities with this. Ultimately, it's going to stimulate and challenge what that person needs on the inside.

Chiron Sextile Midheaven

When the Midheaven sextiles Chiron, the public self is receiving stimulation natally from this energetic antenna. So the public self and the public life is triggered into evolution by the need to have compassion – to respond to life in the world with compassion. You'll find activists with this placement. You'll find people who are very compassionate and looking to help their public selves evolve, but it's being triggered, so there can be a sense of urgency, of seeing that suffering and then responding.

The simultaneous trine to the Nadir is going to feed energetic information in a seemingly supportive way to that inner self. If the sextile is haywire, then this trine from the inner self continues to support it. If somebody is overworked, for example, because they're being triggered into hasty or unplanned action – coloring outside the lines, spilling over, by that sextile to Midheaven – if that person is not honoring his or her inner needs there can be an outflow of energy from that grounded, rooted center. That psychic basement can become depleted through triggering by the Midheaven. This whole dynamic comes into play and needs to be consciously approached.

Chiron Square Midheaven

When the Midheaven-Nadir axis squares Chiron, we have tectonic plate action. One plate is the energetic antenna and the other is this conversation about what's private and what's public. I actually have this placement, and just had to pause for a second to consider whether or not I wanted to share this, but it's a great illustration. I wanted to share something useful about it, but what's public and what's private? My Chiron's right on the Descendant and squares my Midheaven axis. So there's this question about what you can share publicly and what you can't. You're picking up energetic information – from the vantage point of either the Descendant or the Ascendant. On the Descendant it's that you observe, you sense, you feel things in your interactions with other people and find Chiron everywhere around you. If Chiron's conjunct the Ascendant, it's that you find Chiron within you and so that colors how this public-private discussion goes.

With the square, there is a question about, "How much of my sensitivity can come out either in relationship (conjunct the Descendant) or in my own expression (conjunct the Ascendant)? How does that change my public life and my private life and how is that conversation between public and private evolving?" When you have Chiron square the Ascendant-Descendant, there's the sense that this pressure always evolves the conception of self and other. With the Midheaven-Nadir axis involved, this pressure always serves to push that evolution of public and private. "Who am I in the world? Who am I at home? What belongs in my public self? What belongs at home?" There will be some friction, so there will be at times confusion and missteps, but it all serves evolution – letting the Chiron button be pushed by public-private and vice versa.

Chiron Trine Midheaven

The trine of Chiron to the Midheaven coincides with a sextile to the Nadir. Because it's a stimulating triggering, Chiron's sextile to the Nadir can have the inner self be haphazardly or hastily affected by the energetic information, by the Chironic antenna. If a person responds by being in action in order to ground more, this trine to the Midheaven can come out as a lot of energy flowing into the public self. You have this dynamic of being triggered because you can feel this energy and then it comes out in your public self. When you can look at the sextile vs. the trine in tandem, you see a stimulating trigger on one hand and a channel open at a flow on the other hand. That produces the dynamic of having the stimulation feeding something.

Chiron needs to come into focus for these people, and they need to make sure that what's being triggered is actually good, is actually healthy and that what's being trined is not being overdone because the open channel of energy is very receptive.

Chiron Opposing Midheaven

The last aspect to cover here is Chiron opposing the Midheaven and conjunct the Nadir. With the conjunction, the nature of Chiron will be different, depending on the house placement. If Chiron is in the 4th house, refer to that section. If it's conjunct from the 3rd house, that Chironic awareness about the exploring the senses and the environment, and the way the mind works, asks questions and gathers data – that part is going to be dragged a little bit into the 4th house. It's going to bring all those questions and all that doubt about how the mind works into the person's foundation. When you go into that psychic basement, you're finding Chiron, with all the questions starting in the 3rd house.

Generally speaking, for either of these house placements conjunct the Nadir, the basic idea is that in the psychic basement when nobody else is around, that's where we find Chiron. We find sensitivity, we find vulnerability, we find an awareness and sensitivity to energy. With the 4th house placement, I see it as an energetic inheritance that travels through families – even if it's in the 3rd conjunct the Nadir, the family has to do with it as well.

With the simultaneous opposition to the Midheaven, that inner Chiron activity can seem to block public expression – for instance, if you have doubts that you have the right to love yourself or that you have the right to have safety and security. If you doubt that you have the right to have your emotions, then that is really going to shape the kind of public self you create. With this placement, it is necessary to get some education and evolve the Chironic wounding in order to have a solid foundation where you love and accept yourself. Once you are able to accept yourself for all that you are and because you understand yourself, you then take yourself into the public sphere, even though it feels like kind of a risk. As a result, your Midheaven will reflect more of who you really are – more than a lot of people have reflected in their public personas.

Transits to Chiron

Transiting planets ask questions. They stimulate, stir, challenge, or confront the energies within in order to inspire us to figure out answers to those questions. Transits to Chiron ask questions that vary depending upon the transiting planet. All the questions from transiting planets to Chiron center on our relationship to ourselves as sensitive to energy. How will we respond to the pain and suffering within us and outside of us? What will we decide it means that we feel what we *can* feel and what we *do* feel?

When these questions are asked of us by these transiting planets, invariably our past experiences in navigating the energy of Chiron, in living the energy of Chiron, come up for review. Remember that most outer planet transits are slow, so with Uranus, Neptune, and Pluto, it might be a two-and-a-half-year process of confronting a particular situation with Chiron, depending on how it is that we're running that energy. As a consequence, a lot of impactful experiences can build up over that time and we can be stirred to go really, really deep into how it is that we experience our Chirons.

For any outer planet transit our experience is determined by our response to the questions. As Jupiter, Saturn, Uranus, Neptune and Pluto ask their questions, whether it is a positive or a negative experience is determined by our response. Navigating transits to Chiron in a healthy way invariably requires coming out of being wounded, coming out of choosing to perceive ourselves as victims being forced to experience the energy around us.

When we are wounded with Chiron, we tend to remember and pick up on the negative energy. We will feel all of the energy, of course, but what will stick with us and what will get lodged in our consciousness is the pain and suffering because most of us don't know how to deal with that. As these outer planets ask difficult questions and ask us to change our minds about the point of pain and suffering – ultimately to come into being able to experience more of ourselves as energetic beings – it can be very, very difficult to confront our wounding.

One of the underlying ideas with these transits is that through asking these questions, our wounds will be triggered and our Chironic pain will come to the surface. Obviously this is an opportunity to change our minds about and learn to work through the past wounding, but if we're still identifying with that wound, it will just be a repeat of suffering, or it will seem to be more of the same kind of suffering but experienced from different angles and in different ways.

Jupiter

Jupiter transits always ask us to expand, to take some risk, to imagine something better than we've had before. Jupiter questions are like: Have you underestimated yourself? Should you believe in yourself more? Should you do more, risk more, be bigger in some way? We tend to think of Jupiter as this great bringer of luck, a kind of Santa Claus, but what Jupiter really does is bring the opportunity for us to believe in ourselves and to believe that our life can be better and more enjoyable.

When Jupiter transits Chiron, it brings this opportunity, this question about risking more sensitivity. Regardless of the aspect, the questions Jupiter asks Chiron are: "Are you willing to feel more? Are you willing to imagine that what you thought something meant is different that what it actually meant?" It will do this by bringing an abundance of feeling opportunities. For somebody who is really identifying with the wound in Chiron, Jupiter will seem to augment it. Jupiter will seem to bring opportunities surrounding it. Automatically, as soon as you open to that energy of making something bigger, Jupiter brings this energy of abundance to you. If you're feeling the wound and you're not letting it go, then the feeling will intensify and probably will bring new opportunities to feel into what this Chiron natal wound is.

Jupiter transits will present the opportunity to expand if we only allow more energetic sensitivity in or change our minds about what it means. Jupiter by transit can crack open the channel that Chiron energy runs on. It blows the plug or the gum in the system out and really opens us up to feeling. The opportunity is to feel more. Obviously this is very difficult for many, many people, to be more energetically sensitive. The vast majority of us growing up in Western cultures have not been taught how to deal with being energetically sensitive. As we're trained to see the world through our brains, through our minds, eyes, ears, and brains and create the world through our minds, eyes, ears, and brains, we're not taught how to understand ourselves as energetic beings. Jupiter will seem to make things difficult for those of us who don't want to understand this or who are too scared to because it is offering us the opportunity to open.

Jupiter Conjunct Chiron

When Jupiter conjuncts Chiron there's going to be an infusion of energy from the inside out, as though Chiron feels the need to get bigger. If someone is identifying with the wound, it will augment and intensify the wound from within. It could be that the person can no longer hold in the pain, because it's just too big or it can seem too big for the physical body. Maybe that person needs to start emoting about this Chiron wound. Maybe he or she needs to start communicating about it and recognizing that he or she is sensitive to energy and pain and suffering.

When Jupiter comes to make the conjunction with Chiron, whatever box you put your Chiron in, it will destroy that box from the inside out. Your Chiron energy will get very, very big. There is the opportunity here for adjusting to this, for opening to this experience of being more energetically sensitive, but the person will have to change his or her mind about what that means. The energy of Jupiter coming to Chiron is like this sensitivity ripping the lid off the box or disintegrating the box because it's no longer capable of containing the energy, so the person with Jupiter conjunct Chiron can seem to walk around just being emotion. This emotion is simply the result of being sensitive to the energy in his or her environment, but the person will not perceive it that way until he or she gets a little guidance, support, and context to what's happening. The person might seem to be an overflowing barrel of energy, an overflowing container of emotion. It might be about specific emotions, but it could also be a kind of roller coaster, because the person is picking up energy in the environment, which is super-charging the energetic/emotion antenna within the person.

Jupiter Sextile Chiron

The sextile from Jupiter to Chiron will set off Chiron and trigger the Chironic sensitivity. So instead of exploding the box from the inside out, the effect is poking Chiron in the ribs or tickling Chiron so that it can't help but respond. This is the energy of bigness stimulating or triggering this antenna for energy that is Chiron in a person. During this transit there will be a lot of new opportunities to feel. If the person is not comfortable feeling all that his or her human energy antenna can pick up, then there's going to be some "coloring outside the lines," so to speak. It can feel like Chiron being pushed, so there's going to be some spilling – inadvertent spilling.

If the person is identifying with the wound and is not wanting to feel as sensitive as he or she could, then there will be some inadvertent spilling in ways that probably will make the person feel very uncomfortable – sensing energy in new ways, at new levels, and increasing levels of sensitivity to the energy surrounding one. Remember Jupiter is making everything it touches bigger, so it's making the sensitivity bigger. The stimulation from the sextile will push and trigger things, and the person will not be able *not* to respond unless, of course, there's some kind of gargantuan, Herculean effort to build a bigger box for Chiron within the self. Even when that happens the person will still have stuff coming out against their will – stuff they don't want to have come out, but Jupiter is going to trigger it, to make sure that it does.

Jupiter Square Chiron

The square from Jupiter to Chiron will put pressure on the sensitivity in the energetic antenna within a person. This is about opportunity drawing the person to come out of whatever Chiron context he or she has been living. Squares from Jupiter will pressure the Chiron to change, to open up, and it can come in the form of opportunities that are very alluring. There will be an opportunity to go in this new direction, yes ... "But if I do that, I really have to confront this fear I have, this fear of rejection."

Squares do not feel good. Though to be honest, any aspect from a transiting planet to Chiron can feel not good if we're not understanding the opportunity that comes with being as sensitive as we are. The Jupiter square to Chiron will create a lot of discomfort if the person is not willing to face these fears. The idea with the square to Chiron from Jupiter is that opportunities exist, but the person has to – in order to follow them – face and overcome some of the fear of being as energetically sensitive as he or she is.

Jupiter Trine Chiron

We think of trines as supportive and boosting and great. Jupiter is going to support whatever is going on with Chiron and will say, "Hey, I'm on your team. I'm on your side. Whatever you're up to, I've got your back." So if a person is fearful of being sensitive to energy, if the person is holding on to that wounding, taking everything personally and not comfortable as being as energetically or emotionally sensitive as he or she is, then Jupiter will augment this. Jupiter is bringing opportunity, but it will tend to inflate that sense of Chiron sensitivity.

There is also the possibility with this transit that people who are Jupiterian or Chironic show up in one's life and can help the Chiron person navigate these things better. They can be trusting relationships, because we're talking about the energy of a trine. There will be tension focused on Chiron that ends up making its experience or its expression – whether it's healthy or unhealthy – bigger.

Jupiter Inconjunct Chiron

The inconjunct from Jupiter is going to present a really discomfiting energy to Chiron. This is the energy of opportunity, but it will seem that the opportunity is not available, because we're talking about the inconjunct, a perennially uncomfortable relationship between two energies. Here, Jupiter and Chiron don't know how to be in the same room together. In my own experience and in my experience with clients, the best way to use the energy of an inconjunct is to allow the tension to come up, allow this irresolvable and irreconcilable tension to arise, because that inspires us to learn and reveals to us where we stand. Imagine that there's somebody that you just can't get along with – you just can't figure out how to be in the same room together. That person actually teaches you about who you are, because your awareness goes to what is really important to you. What am I willing to budge on, what am I willing to give up, what am I not willing to give up on?

When Jupiter comes to inconjunct Chiron by transit, there is this evaluation that's necessary about what it is about Chiron that's important, because the Jupiter energy is expansion, opportunity, abundance, and increasing something. The best way to use this transit is to allow awareness to be heightened of one's own Chiron issues.

Jupiter Opposition Chiron

The opposition from Jupiter to Chiron by transit is going to show the person in what ways he or she is not open to opportunity, expansion, and abundance because of the Chiron wounding. Oppositions show us something we can't see about ourselves by ourselves. Jupiter here will say, "Hey, you could have this, you could have something wonderful, you could have something great – if you only give up some ideas and change your mind about what you think and how you live."

There will be some fantastic growth opportunities that come during this transit. With all Jupiter transits to Chiron there are such opportunities, but it will be readily apparent with this one because it's "over there," it's opposite the person. It will because readily apparent that: "If I only gave this up, I could have that." The person doesn't really have to give up anything other than their ideas associated with their own Chiron wounding.

So when Jupiter comes to oppose Chiron there are going to be a ton of opportunities to grow out of the wounding by letting go of some of the identity with the wound.

Saturn

When Saturn transits, it asks very different kinds of questions than those of Jupiter. Saturn transits ask, "Are you doing enough? Are you working hard enough? Are you realistic? Are you mature? Are you willing to sacrifice in order to achieve a goal? Are you disciplined? Are you willing to introduce structure into your life?"

When Saturn comes to Chiron, there will be varying levels of questions. "Is it true that you are realistic that this is what suffering is about? Are you being realistic about what you think pain and suffering are for?" Questions will arise regarding structure and discipline and sacrifice – stern Saturnian questions like, "What kind of self–indulgent emotional whininess are you willing to give up in order to achieve a goal?" How a person experiences such questioning is dependent upon his or her response and what the person's experience of Saturn in his or her life has been. If there is a harsh taskmaster inside the person or a lot of judgment and self–recrimination for making mistakes or potentially making mistakes, these transits can be extremely difficult. Even so, there is always the opportunity for that loving, nurturing Saturnian energy – the compassionate, grounded, structured disciplinarian parent – to come through. The nature of these transits will depend on how a person experiences Saturn energy in him- or herself.

Saturn Conjunct Chiron

When Saturn conjuncts Chiron, there will be an infusion of Saturnian energy into the Chiron from the inside out. If the person is not very compassionate with him- or herself, then this can be a very difficult time, with a lot of self-judgment about the sensitive part of the nature, to which will say: "Quit whining, it's time to do something about this." The conjunction can be a very empowering time because the person is inspired to do something about the Chiron. Is the person stuck in an infantile level of consciousness about Chiron? If so, then it might seem that everything gets more difficult surrounding the pain. During this conjunction the person will naturally draw opportunities in life to stand up and do something constructive about the Chiron wounding and be realistic about it.

Saturn here will ask you: "Is that real?" The person having the conjunction will have some opportunities to see into his or her Chironic reactions and perceptions in order to see if those expectations of rejection are founded and based in reality. But of course, they're not. When rejection happens, it is created because the person is expecting it. There is the opportunity here to get realistic and grounded in the sensitivity that Chiron brings, to be constructive about energy management, boundaries, self-care, nurturing inner children – these are ideal things to do under this transit. Hopefully, also the person undergoing this transit will visit their astrology to help get grounded and do some concrete things in order to change their minds about what this wounding is about.

Saturn Sextile Chiron

The sextile from Saturn will stimulate and trigger Chiron, so Saturnian people and circumstances will stimulate the wound. The opportunity is to learn more about the wound through someone Saturnian who probably doesn't experience his or her wound in the exact same way you do. You can get some helpful advice from this person, which is one of the ways that sextiles can come in. They might jab you in such a way as to say, "Hey, you're not doing this right," but with a sextile it's always followed by, "Here's a constructive way to do it." The sextile has a supportive, underlying energy. There can be some spilling over, coloring outside the lines, driving outside the lines, etc., when it comes to emotional expression during this time because the person's Chiron is being stimulated, and that can make the current container (the little box the Chiron has been put in) go nuts, if the person is not willing to feel sensitive. Chiron can go haywire in a sense, from Saturn poking him in the ribs and being pressured until this part of you does something. Chiron can't help but do something in response to all the stimulation.

These transits are often embodied by other people and Saturn transits are embodied by people who are older than we are, who are more experienced, and who seem more competent or are more competent than we are. They can be people who are well-known, people who have a reputation and respect in the community but also parents, judges, police officers, teachers, and authority figures of all kinds. The real idea with this transit is to introduce some structure so that the person can understand more about what the Chiron is doing. The person with this transit, who might not be willing to be so sensitive, might have difficulty catching up to experiencing this energetic sensitivity as a positive in his or her life. That's where the gentle pushing by the Saturnian figure can be immensely helpful.

Saturn Square Chiron

The square from Saturn to Chiron in transit will say, "You're not doing it right. Whatever you're doing with your Chiron, whatever you're feeling, however you're feeling, you're not doing it right. Here are some ways that you need to change in order to make that better." The square is friction and pressure. Whenever something squares something else, there is natural criticism by some outside force, urging you to change.

When the sextile is poking you in the ribs until something happens, what follows is usually an involuntary response. Think about that. When you're poked in the ribs, you respond instinctively – your body jerks. When you're tickled, the same exact thing happens. Those are sextile keywords. With the square, it's just pressing on you until you change something, until you give in, until you change your behavior. The high possibility is that you learn from new input, but the square is naturally something we don't want to give into. So Saturn squaring Chiron says: "You really need to do something about this Chiron. You really need to do something about this sensitivity." Now that can come in the form of very difficult experiences of experiencing Saturnian people and their inner sensitivity, because you'll be receiving energy from their Saturns to your Chiron. You're being pressured by the energy of authority, age, discipline, structure, maturity – even morality can come into play. Are there ways that you respond with your Chiron that don't make you feel good in a moral sense? This square will pressure the person until a different choice is made. If that doesn't happen, as with any square, something has to give. The energy of the square is like the tectonic plates of the Earth pressing against each other. Eventually something has to give, after the pressure builds up enough.

The square from Saturn to Chiron in transit can seem a demand to grow up. Not many of us respond well to that, but there is inherent in the opportunity to give up some of the whininess or victim mentality and begin to do things that are constructive and challenging, in a good way. We might not know how to do that, but we have to open up to this new experience of becoming more grounded, being better at boundaries, and being more authoritative about caring for ourselves and meeting our own needs.

Saturn Trine Chiron

The trine from Saturn to Chiron will bring Saturnian support to whatever Chiron is already up to. There is no pressure to change here. What will happen with the trine is that the person will get support in repeating old patterns of perpetuating the wounding or avoiding energetic sensitivity. Some part of that person, even the subconscious, will say, "Wow, that pattern really isn't healthy, but I get to perpetuate it now." So there's this opportunity by way of support from Saturn to change how that works, but it's not going to feel like pressure to change.

Old habits can be perpetuated very easily during this time. Where there is a fear of rejection or a whininess or immaturity surrounding this person's Chiron, Saturn will bring people who let the person get away with it. This gives the person the opportunity to police him- or herself, to be realistic and honest: "Well, is that really how I want to behave? Is that really how I want to do this Chiron energy?" The person experiencing this transit will have the opportunity to change it; however, they will be supported by Saturnian people and circumstance in perpetuating it, if that's what they want.

Saturn Inconjunct Chiron

The inconjunct between Saturn and Chiron is all about irreconcilable differences. Saturnian people are going to come into the person's life and make it impossible for the Chiron person to be in the same room. The point is to have the person undergoing this transit become more realistic about what the wound is, what the pain does, and what that fear of rejection actually brings him or her. The highest use of the inconjunct is to become aware in what ways the person is not willing to grow up, be realistic and honest, and to do something structured, grounded, and mature about the sense of wounding and rejection.

This transit can bring a lot of conflict with highly Saturnian people, a lot of rubbing up against Saturnian people who are not going to budge. This can very difficult, but it's about increasing awareness of how one runs this Chiron energy at that time.

Saturn Opposing Chiron

The opposition from Saturn to Chiron will shed some light on how the person is not willing to grow up, give up this fear of rejection, or in what way opportunities to become Saturnian are prevented by the person's identification with the wounding. There will be opportunities to gain more respect, to set into motion something over the long term that will result in achievement. There will be the opportunity to become someone competent, whom others respect, as an authority, doing whatever he or she does. The ideal is to gain consciousness of how the Chiron wounding and expectation and fear of rejection get in the way of manifesting something over the long term. The person's natal placement of Saturn as well as how that person's conditioning and karma surrounding Saturn will matter a great deal during this transit. Saturn opposing Chiron might appear as a mentor to teach energetic boundaries and emotional healing or it could an authority figure that is critical of the person for being as sensitive as he or she is. It can go either way, and it really depends on the person's experience with Saturn energy and what's going on in that person's energy field of consciousness regarding Saturn and how Saturn shows up.

During this transit, as with any transit, there will be many possibilities that show up in the person's life in order to learn Saturn's transit lesson but the person will only be attuned to hearing what he or she is ready to hear. This has to do with the conditioning in the past.

Uranus

Uranus's questions are very different from those asked by Jupiter and Saturn. Uranus asks: "Are you free enough? Are you original enough? Are you free of convention, but also free of things that make you feel deadened or stuck in ruts or routine?" Uranus always wants you to break free of whatever is binding you. Uranus transits are famous for inspiring sudden, life-changing action – we suddenly gain consciousness of the fact that the ways in which we are not free and have not been for a long time are suddenly, extremely important. That's the Uranus effect in transit. When it comes around to Chiron, Uranus asks us in what ways our sensitivity binds us. Maybe we give too much to other people energetically, maybe we have porous boundaries and need to adjust them. Maybe we don't give anything to others and feel cut off from people, which is a lack of freedom of energetic movement and connectedness. It could be lots of different things with Chiron, but that's the basic idea; "What is it about how you do your Chiron that is not freeing for your, that does not bring you alive and make you feel like you're soaring through your life?"

Uranus Conjunct Chiron

When Uranus comes to conjunct Chiron, the sense of freedom comes from the inside out. Uranus is boosting, pouring its energy into whatever is happening with Chiron. If a person is identifying with the wound, there can be a sudden capacity to gain insight into what's happening. That can require some reexperiencing of the pain, old scenarios that we remember or new scenarios that seem to echo that Chiron wounding from the past.

One of the gifts that Uranus brings in transit is that sudden awareness, that sudden ability to be objective, to see clearly the snapshot of what's actually happening and what has been building and happening for a very long time. This Uranus conjunction to Chiron can shift perspective very quickly. It can also – in the process or leading up to that process – bring some sudden reactivations of the wound, whatever that wound is. That can, coupled with the objectivity, bring an awareness of the patterns as they have existed, being energetically reactive to the pain, suffering. or anger that the person's Chiron seems attuned to because of his or her own wounding.

149

The person with transiting Uranus conjunct Chiron will have the capacity to shift perspective. I see all Chiron healing as a shifting of energy. I get the image of being on the balls of our feet, and suddenly we're facing a new direction. It just took a tiny little pivot, from facing one direction to another – one idea of what the suffering and pain are about, and shifting very quickly to another perspective. That can happen with Chiron in general, but Uranus conjunct Chiron can really speed the process up and make it instantaneous. You can turn a corner around whatever the wounding is about very quickly.

With all these Uranus transits, we also have to look at what Chiron is doing. If that Chiron sensitivity to other people's suffering has led a person to allow him- or herself to be fenced in by certain relationships, those relationships will need to change during this time or there will be a lot of tension and pressure about that. It will come out differently depending on the aspect transiting Uranus makes to Chiron, but that's something in common for all transits. Whatever the Chiron is doing – if it traps us in a job that doesn't work, if it traps us in a home, certain family dynamics, whatever it is – Uranus will say, "Gotta go! Get rid of it – pronto!" It's this sudden awareness that whatever the wounded part of the person was holding onto is now no longer appropriate.

Uranus Sextile Chiron

With the Chiron conjunction, there was an awareness, objectivity, this sudden ability to see the snapshot of the reality clearly. With the sextile Uranus is going to be pushing at the person in order to get that person to change and shift perspective. This can come in the form of people egging on the wounding, or it can come in the form of people saying, "Hey, look, you seem to operate with this pain. You don't have to do that." And really drawing you out in a friendly way. Sextiles can be very chummy when it comes down to it.

Coloring outside the lines or spilling over the container, inadvertently, can happen with this sextile from Uranus to Chiron as well. This is about developing a new relationship with one's own energetic sensitivity that does not make the person feel handicapped in any way. This can manifest as Uranian others showing up to stimulate you, punch you in the arm and say, "Hey, come on! Get over it already!" Then you can see the wounding, the fear of rejection, the particular idea you have of why you have this energetic sensitivity and what pain and suffering are about. There can be a kind of ease in letting go of some of it because you have the good-natured support of these Uranian others.

Uranus Square Chiron

The square from Uranus is going to put pressure on whatever Chiron is doing. Here, Uranus is telling you that you can be free if you just leave behind the things you're clinging to, if you leave behind the fears and the ideas and identities with the wounding that you cling to. The pressure from Uranus, through sudden events, sudden changes in environment, relationships, home, whatever it is – events that could be perceived as traumatic – will snap you out of perpetuating your wound and maintaining the idea of why painful things happen to you.

Uranus is always this present moment, what's happening right now. Whenever we start to live in the past or the future, which has a lot to with Saturn, Uranus will try to shake us out of it. This square is trying to bring you into more of a sense of presence so that you are freed from the past. The nature of the square is to try to force you out of sticking with the things that you cling to that are not good. It will *not* shake you out of what you cling to that *is* good. The things that are fear-based are what Uranus wants us to get rid of. We're not free when we cling to fear. The keyword to focus on with Uranus square Chiron is pressure – to let go of the wound or to change one's mind about it and to change the life scenarios that support the wound.

During the square, anything not beneficial about one's relationships, structures, jobs, family dynamics will be pressured to change. Uranus has this effect of being like a pressure cooker. This is only because we often don't want to change and don't realize how significant these calls to change can be until the pressure builds. Again, the water behind the dam takes a long time to build up, but eventually, it's just a drop or two that makes it burst. This is the effect of Uranus transits. We become conscious very quickly of a scenario that has already been unfolding for a long time, and it's suddenly not okay to perpetuate it. The square will have us changing things in our lives inadvertently or by choice, and we quickly learn about how we build our lives around the fear of rejection that Chiron represents.

Uranus Trine Chiron

The trine from Uranus to Chiron by transit generates a supportive energy. There will be Uranian people and circumstances that support perpetuating the wound. The person can gain the perspective on whether or not perpetuating the wound is a good thing to keep doing – if a person has identified with the wound. He or she can choose whether or not that kind of perpetuation is actually desired.

Uranus Inconjunct Chiron

When Uranus arrives by transit to an inconjunct with Chiron, there is this feeling that the two cannot be in the same room together. So, the spirit of change, of creating freedom, of expressing individuality and genius cannot be in the same room with how the person is living with Chiron. If the person is deeply identified with the Chiron wounding, then Uranus will seem to rub up against the scenario in an unavoidable, extremely unpleasant way that can seem to threaten to destroy the Chiron person. This energy is absolutely incompatible with what the person's wound is about.

The opportunity is to gain conscious awareness of how one lives with their own Chiron. This is sudden information, sudden change, sudden opportunities, sudden meetings and people that challenge and press up against that Chiron from the inside out. There is that "can't stay in the same room together" idea, and the person might feel that that energetic sensitivity, that wound, might be eradicated. If we're identifying with the wound, this can be extremely difficult.

There is an opportunity to gain such awareness and perspective via this sudden objectivity, when this whole, clear picture snaps into view in an instant about what we're doing with our Chiron and shifting that pivot of how we approach the Chiron. It can happen very quickly, but that depends on how much the person is identifying with the Chiron wound, clinging to the identity of being wounded and expecting rejection.

Uranus Opposing Chiron

The opposition from Uranus to Chiron is going to show in what ways the person could be free if he or she would let go of some of this wounding. With this transit, there will be sudden events and sudden changes in relationships and circumstances that present opportunities to be free. The person will have this confrontation with him- or herself about how much of the wounding he or she should cling to. "How much should I think that this pain and suffering is me? How much should I think that this history of rejection is true and is warranted and that I'm not worthy of love? How much should I really buy into that?" The opposition from Uranus to Chiron will challenge this and present this wonderful opportunity for freedom if the person is willing to adopt this view, make changes, leave some things behind about how he or she identifies with the pain and suffering, and how that person relates to pain and suffering in other people.

Neptune

The questions that Neptune asks in transit are unique from all the others we've talked about so far in this section. Neptune asks, "Are you willing to open to something that's greater than yourself that you will feel surrounded by?" Neptune represents mysticism, escapism, spirituality, meditation, addictions, and any kind of substance abuse. These all relate to the core Neptune experience, which is that we go on these journeys as humans and learn to surrender control to something outside ourselves.

By transit, Neptune asks: "What is it about surrender that you're not doing? What are you not willing to surrender?" Then, for roughly two-and-a-half years, it builds that pressure up and asks that question more and more loudly: "What are you not willing to give up? Why won't you give up?"

Neptune transits are very difficult for many people because we are trained to think that we have to control everything. These transits, though, can be amazingly beneficial and enriching in connecting us to something greater than our egoic, mind-based selves are conscious of let alone create. Neptune transits always seek to open us up energetically. One of the words we talk about with Neptune is "spiritual," which is another way of saying being conscious of energy. Neptune seems to do this by transit and when we play along, we experience ourselves as more than just our minds. Our minds, in fact, become tools to help us understand certain things, but they also recognize that they can't understand everything. Neptune wants to bring to us all the things we can experience that we can't explain. And Neptune transits to Chiron want us to open to surrender to feeling all of the energetic sensitivity that we possess.

As I mentioned, this can be extremely difficult for people. All Neptune transits are challenging but the transits to Chiron are especially challenging because you have to give in, surrender, give up control, stop trying to fashion your reality; and surrender to your pain and suffering. The point isn't to wallow in pain and suffering, which is what part of our minds will say as a criticism. "Well I can't open to that because I would just be self-indulgent and wallowing in whining and suffering." It's not that. It's about truly going into the pain and suffering and gaining an experiential viewpoint about how to change your mind.

Another keyword for Neptune energy is compassion, so Neptune and Chiron are simpatico in many senses. Currently, the two bodies are transiting together in late Aquarius. So I've been telling this story to a lot of clients who come in who are trying to figure out why they are supposed to let go of control and what that means.

Neptune Conjunct Chiron

When Neptune comes to conjunct Chiron, the invitation is to surrender from the inside out. With this transit, all the previously imagined or preestablished boundaries about energetic sensitivity are dissolved from the inside out. This can make someone feel that he or she is melting and that the energy antenna simply needs to be opened wide so that it can experience much more of the totality of possibilities than it has so far. It's difficult on the personality level to be pressured to give up control. One thing about control is that when we think we have it, it's always proven to us that we don't, and the Neptune-Chiron transits are going to be an amazing opportunity for anybody with any of these aspects to understand in what ways they can't control something. But when they give into it, by experiencing it, they can learn that it's not a control but a kind of volition, that there is a different kind of intentionality that goes with it, that actually changes that fear of control.

Neptune always wants us to give up the fear of losing control and its transits to Chiron figure big in our lives in that way. This conjunction states: "You can't do anything *but* give up control. You can't do anything *but* surrender right now to this pain and suffering." Of course, it will be to one's own pain and suffering, but also to the pain and suffering of other people. A lot of these outer planet transits to Chiron can actually inspire a person to need to spend a lot of time alone. There is a sense of just becoming a blob of energetic sensitivity, and it can look like a blob of emotions. People undergoing this transit would do well to go to a good astrologer who can help them ground and get some perspective and help them shift their experience of energetic sensitivity.

Neptune Sextile Chiron

With the sextile, the energy of giving up and surrendering control triggers the energetic sensitivity. This is all about pressing buttons: "Really? You think you can control something? Really? Oh here, no, you can't." It's this perpetual egging on, pushing the person to really open up. That's going to generate frustration and can actually make the person willing to open up and feel all this stuff. Many of us, regarding Chiron, will hold pent-up emotions, and this Neptune sextiling the Chiron will push the button until we finally give in, or until we choose to open up. When we do give in, after all that pressure, it can be a feeling of collapse, but we need to experience all we can experience with Chiron and Neptune here is just trying to inspire that.

Neptune Square Chiron

When Neptune squares Chiron, it's going to be bearing down on that energetic sensitivity. Let's say that the person is identifying deeply and consistently with the wound, and there's that sense of potential rejection out there, so the person engineers his or her life to avoid being hurt in that way. This Neptune will bear down and bring pressure and friction. Remember the image of the tectonic plates that are at angles to each other, pushing on each other and forcing each other to change. When you have Neptune square Chiron, you can choose to change, you can choose to open. Squares tell us to do things differently than we feel we naturally should, so we can cling to our ways of doing it. Neptune will attempt to erode all of the nonsense about this wound, and all of the nonsense about keeping out energy and trying to remain in our heads. We won't be able to stop the emotions coming during this two-and-a-half year transit, as Neptune will be constantly pressuring us to "just *feel* already."

Neptune Trine Chiron

During this transit, there's support for whatever the person is doing regarding his or her Chiron energy from Neptunian sources. This is where things can seem easy but the person will somehow gain an insight. Because it's a gentle and supportive energy that characterizes this transit, the person will gain some perspective and insight on what it is they're doing with their Chiron, in what ways they might not be taking care of themselves energetically, and in what ways they might rely on other people to do certain things for them emotionally or energetically that they don't do for themselves. There will be the opportunity to do some course correction because the person will feel how easy it can be to remain immature and not take care of the self.

Neptune Inconjunct Chiron

The inconjunct is an uncomfortable, discomfiting aspect – Neptune and Chiron are not sure how to be in the same room together. There is going to be a sense that something outside of one's own control prevents the person from being able to sit with the wound. As with all these inconjuncts with these outer planets, the ideal is to gain perspective on what one's doing with Chiron and what's important about that and what's not – what needs go. Neptune transits seek to erode slowly or melt away the boundaries, melt away everything that doesn't work. When you're done with a Neptune transit, what is necessary and essential is what remains. We tend to cling to so many things in our lives – attitudes, identities, and issues – that Neptune tries to erode. This energy of the inconjunct will be a consistent grinding away at whatever is not necessary about this Chiron. Some people will come out at the end of such a Neptune transit to Chiron being more willing to feel and having a different idea of feeling it. For those of us who are identifying with the wound, this can be a particularly difficult transit.

Neptune Opposing Chiron

The opposition to Chiron from Neptune is about seeing in what ways we're not connected to the world around us – in what ways we don't let ourselves experience a greater reality. Neptune wants us to connect with the greater reality surrounding us. In what ways we don't because of our own wounding – because of our idea of why we have experienced pain and suffering, and why it is that we have to feel the pain and suffering of other people – is called into question. This is a time when there are opportunities to do Neptunian stuff that we don't want to do because we might not want to risk opening energetically. Yet during this transit, we end up learning a tremendous amount about the wounded in a confronting way, and it is probably not as threatening as the inconjunct or the square. The opposition shines light on what it is we think pain and suffering are for. An unhealthy response to the transit is simply being confronted by things you can't control and then forming a lot of opinions about what that means about you. The high side of Neptune of this transit is that a person opens up to experience and basically surrenders the identity of being wounded in order to experience this Neptune reality, this other fabric of reality that surrounds the person. That experience will change how that person deals with energy and works his or her energetic/emotional boundaries. That's the ideal.

Pluto

On to our last outer planet transit for this section: Pluto. Pluto asks, "What's not authentic? What's not real? What is it about your life that is surfacey or not deep and not rooted in your own true self?" The Pluto transits always ask us to dig below the surface of our present level of awareness in order to understand more about how we're wired, more about our true natures, more about our true desires and motivations. This Pluto transit can be summed up with the questions: "What is it that you're doing that is not authentic? Who are you really? What do you really want?"

Pluto transits call on us to do shadow work, to look within in order to see what we're afraid of, to see what parts of ourselves we might not want to own and then become friends with those parts of ourselves. Pluto is famous for destroying things it touches, but what it destroys is not real, because it's not based in who you really are. These transits oftentimes force us to look within in order to find out just who that is, just exactly who we are.

Pluto Conjunct Chiron

Pluto coming to Chiron is going to try to get a person to look deeply and feel deeply within that wound. It will try to drag that person down into his or her own psychic basement where shadow sides of pain and suffering are. When Pluto comes to conjunct Chiron there is a need for this sense of authenticity to come up and out from the basement – to bring that authenticity that's inside *out*. Pluto is pouring its energy of penetrating awareness into the part of the self that carries this Chiron wounding. It will ultimately destroy whatever the idea of the wounded self is. That's the best thing that it can do – absolutely eradicate every structure in the psyche and the energy field that are perpetuating the wound or holding onto a sense of woundedness and not open to experiencing energy. This conjunction will do this from the inside out. It will a revamping, a total destruction of the idea of woundedness.

All of this probably sounds pretty dramatic, but this transit tends to feel very dramatic. If a person is not willing to become more energetically sensitive, to feel all he or she can feel and is not willing to let Pluto do what it wants, Pluto will do it anyway and it will do so in a very destructive and perhaps energetically violent way. It doesn't mean violence inevitably happens during a Pluto transit, but the energy is: "This is happening – this is going to happen." It can be very difficult if we avoid looking within ourselves to see what's really there.

These transits are particularly challenging for people who are not willing to open up, people who cannot trust that there might be a different reason than they thought for why they can feel as much as they can feel or why they have hurt in the ways that they have been hurt. In a sense, the Chironic self during this transit becomes Plutonian, so there's a delving deep into the wound. The best thing that can happen is a change in perspective.

Now, i August 2010, Pluto is at about 3 degrees Capricorn. I have a client whose natal Chiron is at 28 Sagittarius, and her ascendant is at 3 Capricorn. So, she had several years of Pluto going over that 12th-house Chiron. She walked into my office and she was a model of open Chironic energy because she had had everything stripped away, which was very, very difficult. All her defenses got stripped away. But she was actually very happy because now she was living a full, much richer life, being aware of energy and being in touch with, in harmony with, the universe and herself as a part of it.

Pluto Sextile Chiron

With Pluto sextile Chiron, things that are outside your control, that are bigger than you and stronger than you will trigger you. This is one of the ways we experience Pluto coming at us in the form of other people or events: Things that are undeniable or unavoidable cause us to confront our fears, so they tend to be things that are scary.

With the sextile, it can be those kinds of things coming to trigger and stimulate the part of us that has a wound. There is the opportunity, as with all sextiles, to come out of it well, but I want to focus on this idea that when we identify with the wound, if we're not willing to give up our identity as wounded, this transit can be very difficult. After all, Pluto, the Lord of the Underworld, the Lord of the Dead, is poking you in the ribs until you do something about your wound. It can be a very intense experience.

Pluto Square Chiron

With the square we have this idea of the tectonic plates, the idea of pressure that builds over time, over the course of this transit, which lasts roughly two-and-a-half years. Pluto is serving to pressure the wound so that the person can see what the wound is made of. Pluto asks: "Is this real. Is this authentic. Is this who you really are?" There is the possibility of feeling pressured by Plutonian circumstances in order to get some perspective on the wound, in order to change what one thinks is happening with the pain and suffering. "Why was I hurt the way I was? Why did that happen? What were these people who hurt me about?"

A lot of times Chiron wounding starts in families so family members tend to get all the blame – it doesn't matter who the family is. There will be pressure against that wound for the person to change how Chiron is done. This will inspire the need to develop better energetic boundaries, because encountering Plutonian people who seem stronger than we are requires just this.

Pluto Trine Chiron

The Pluto trine to Chiron in transit will boost up whatever the person is doing with the Chiron. This transit can seem easy – people don't come in to see a karmic astrologer for a healing session when Pluto's trining Chiron, but the circumstances can let them see how they perpetuate their own wounding and how they want to change their minds about doing it. Some people will feel some guilt about perpetuating that wound and letting that part of themselves remain infantile or very young and immature, but this transit allows one to really foresee how that process works, how that wound is perpetuated.

Pluto Inconjunct Chiron

Inconjuncts are always uncomfortable and discomfiting – here, Pluto and Chiron can't be in the same room together. The same strategy with the inconjunct from a transiting planet applies here – to let the tension of "I can't be in the same room with this situation" teach the person about how he or she lives the Chiron. The purpose of this transit is to make apparent how the person navigates his or her own energetic sensitivity and how that person responds to energetic sensitivity in other people. There will be Plutonian circumstances or people that will seem to grate and grind into the person's wound. There's an opportunity therein to change the person's mind about why this is happening, about why pain exists, about why these people treated him or her the way they did and what the lesson is.

Pluto Opposing Chiron

All Pluto aspects have to do with empowerment. That's one of the invitations – it's the end-game that Pluto offers when you are willing to look at the shadow parts. When you are willing to look at what scares you and what seems like it might overpower you, you take back the energy that you've given to your fear. This is obvious with Pluto opposing Chiron because we will meet Plutonian others who seem to block us from perpetuating our wound, who don't support what it is that we're doing, who aren't understanding, who aren't supportive of us maintaining our crummy boundaries or our ideas of why we are hurt. This is the invitation to see through someone else's perspective – the reflection that the opposition always offers us. This can manifest in two ways, and it can also go back and forth, vacillate, depending on a person's conception of Pluto, strength, and power, and how willing someone is to look at one's fear. It can vacillate between being blocked by strong others, by unyielding others, or situations that prevent the perpetuation of the wound. So a person can feel blocked in a negative way or feel blocked in a positive way where somebody says, "Hey, look at what you're doing – this is a little ridiculous. We have to talk about this," or "I think you need to talk to someone about this, because this is really disempowering you. This wound, this pain, this fear of talking about this issue or experiencing this part of life is really getting in your way."

Receiving such a reflection can be challenging, especially if we find that we don't trust this other person. This can happen under a Pluto transit – depending on our relationship with our own Pluto energy, we can draw people to us whom we don't trust. It can prove to be a difficult experience. Nevertheless, there will be the opportunity to take whatever reflection you receive from this other person and make incredible healing progress.

To recap, transiting planets ask questions, and our experience of the transits is entirely determined by our response to these questions. Are we willing to even hear the questions, let alone answer them? There are different ways to go about it and we all have free will. We don't have to respond, we don't have to take in the perspective of the other, we don't have to change. Some of these questions will force us to change, but the responses to the questions are what are really important.

For each of these delineations, I haven't provided you with all the details I could because I want you to think astrologically about these aspects to Chiron in terms of energy. The really important part when looking at somebody's chart regarding Chiron and the transits to Chiron is to understand what that person's relationship with the wound is in that moment, at that point in his or her life. This will set the stage for that person's response to the questions.

Progressions to Chiron

Secondary progressions – commonly referred to as "progressions" by most astrologers – represent inner change. These inner changes eventually become expressed outwardly, but they are based on ongoing internal changes. During transits, the energy in a person attracts different kinds of people, situations, and experiences in the outside world. With progressions, it works from the inside out – the different parts of you, the different functions represented by the angles and planetary bodies that we progress in charts undergo evolution over time. As you age, as you grow, as you have different experiences, you are adding to your repertory. Progressions, in a way, represent the sum total of all those changes.

During a transit, there is an external opportunity waiting for us to take advantage of in order to learn about ourselves. With progressions, there is an internal need to change our outer behavior as we add this certain understanding to our repertory – we'll notice a change on the inside and feel an urge to do something in a new way or for a new reason.

Progressions to Chiron indicate a need for different parts of us to incorporate and integrate an awareness of energetic sensitivity into our conception of self and the world, and then ultimately to allow that to come out in our behavior. So our lives change from the inside out by adapting to new information and levels of opening to and incorporating the data that our Chironic antenna for energy provides us. Progressions, therefore, do not represent outward events; they represent inner need to change our expression over time. When we add progressed elements to a chart, we look at Sun, Moon, Mercury, Venus, and Mars as well as the angles, Ascendant-Descendant axis and the Midheaven-Nadir axis. The outer planets move too slowly to be considered useful when considering progressions.

Sun

The Sun in a person's chart, in a person's life, psyche, and energy field represents the CEO of the internal meeting that is that person. The Sun is the energy around which the rest of the self should be orbiting. There are some of us who don't express our Suns that much so other parts get emphasized, but the Sun should be the ultimate decision maker.

The Sun should be the biggest part of the self around which everything else revolves. I think of it in terms of a meeting as the CEO, the person who ultimately should be making decisions in a board-room type situation. I look at all these other parts of us as having different voices in this meeting. Moon speaks to feelings, Mercury to logic, Saturn to discipline . . . and, again, the Sun is the one that ultimately makes final decisions. So when the Sun progresses to Chiron, the decision maker needs to experience and open up to new forms of information from Chiron, and also learn to value that information, this energetic sensitivity, in a new way. In a nutshell, the decision maker within a person needs to learn and incorporate a Chironic perspective into the decision-making process.

For somebody who happens to be very Chironic, this might be a very smooth transition. For other people who might identify a lot with the wound and shy away from Chironic sensitivity, it can be very challenging to open up to this energy. You can't keep making decisions without the input of this voice. When people are identified with the wound, it gets very difficult to process this experience. They will begin to recognize more the importance of energetic input, which is to say emotion, and also be challenged to develop in a new way, and to have a new kind of relationship with pain and suffering.

This entire process of the Sun being Chironified or being challenged, regardless of the aspect, is about making the person more sensitive to Chiron, more willing to recognize the importance of this energy.

Progressed Sun Conjunct Chiron

With a conjunction, the energy of Chiron needs to be incorporated from the inside out. The person needs to absorb Chiron centrally, as a central message and add this Chironic sensitivity to the roster of factors when making decisions, when organizing the rest of the self. For the person to continue his or her solar evolution as someone vital, creative, bold, and willing and able to be seen, Chiron's teaching need to be added to the scope of the sense of self. For people who focus on the wound, who identity with the wound, this can make them more wounded. For those who open up to the challenge to rethink what compassion is for, what suffering is for, and why one has experienced pain, this can add a very interesting perspective to the repertory of that inner decision maker. Suddenly, the world can open up in a new way. The person can start to see, for example, through his or her own spiritual eyes, recognizing some of the underlying patterns of energy that manifest as day-to-day decisions and behaviors in self and others. This adds

Chironic sensitivity to the part of the self that holds everything together. This is a real life shift.

All of these progressions of Sun to natal Chiron bring a life shift or, at least, hold the potential to help the person shift in very significant ways. Among all the progressions, perhaps the ones involving the Sun are of some of the most significant. The person who is making the decisions becomes Chironic. That's a major shift, especially because we look at the Sun as being a rational influence. Adding Chiron can – at least until someone stops identifying with the wound – tend to make things not quite as rational because there's so much energetic information being processed. Until the person learns how to have good boundaries and not have meaning associated with all the energies they sense, there can be some big changes waiting for him or her.

Progressed Sun Sextile Chiron

With a sextile from progressed Sun to Chiron, instead of having it be an inundation of Chironic sensitivity from the inside out, this part of the self who's making decisions, the evolving sense of self, the evolving way the person holds everything together into one package, needs to be stimulated by Chiron. That part of the person needs to allow that energetic antenna to affect it in a stimulating way. The sextile stimulates and pokes repeatedly until somebody responds. This is about having that evolving inner decision maker respond to Chiron by being triggered repeatedly by it.

So, with this progression, energetic sensitivity, the emotional sensitivity that already exists in the person, will start to push the buttons, of that evolving decision maker. That evolving Sun, that progressed Sun, needs to open to this information and be triggered, tickled, and poked in the ribs.

Progressed Sun Square Chiron

The square from the progressed Sun is going to feel like pressure and friction from the side. The square is going to say that this information that this function of energetic sensitization that's already happening in the person – this evolving sense of self, this progressed Sun, needs to learn from that Chiron and incorporate its different perspective. Squares always represent two different ways of doing things. And with the progressed Sun coming here, it's time for the person to open up to working with Chironic information in a new way and learning how, essentially by pressure.

Progressed Sun Trine Chiron

The trine represents support. The way the person is evolving the inner decision maker is supporting the Chironic mission and is able to learn in a certain way from that Chiron, which is unprecedented. Bodies in trine to each other tend to speak roughly the same language, so that evolving inner decision maker will be more open to the input from Chiron.

Progressed Sun Inconjunct Chiron

The inconjunct from the progressed Sun to Chiron will have the person learning very difficult lessons about energetic sensitivity. The ideal strategy is to open up, to see this new perspective, to understand how evolving self can learn from the Chiron and peacefully coexist with it.

A very difficult lesson takes place when this progression comes around. The progressed Sun and Chiron can't be in the same room together. There needs to be some opening up in a major way to how Chiron functions. The person with the progressed sign inconjunct to Chiron will have some difficult lessons in learning to incorporate this. It may seem impossible, but there are lessons to be learned from opening to this perspective.

Progressed Sun Opposing Chiron

With the opposition from progressed Sun to natal Chiron, the inner decision maker is going to be confronted head-on with energetic sensitivity. The information that already comes through via the natal Chiron is going to confront how that person is evolving. This can be an inner standoff, where the person who's making the decisions, this Sun, sees fully how that energetic antenna works and has to make decisions about how much input to take from it, how to value it and how to factor in what it says – what does this energetic sensitivity have to say in the spirit of this evolution? Because the potential outcome is that the person sees things better. The opportunity to advance how one uses Chironic information is great.

Moon

The Moon in the natal chart represents what we need, what we enjoy, what makes us happy, what we need to do to feed ourselves emotionally. The progressed Moon, then, represents the evolving ways that we meet those needs and how we seek happiness. As it progresses around the wheel, which will take 27 to 28 years roughly, it goes through every sign and house, each roughly two-and-a-half years there is a shift in emphasis of the need of the moment.

Some people will experience that as what makes them happy gradually shifts over time. Other people experience it more markedly: "For some reason I need to work on boundaries right now, whereas two years ago, I really needed to get specific about my health" (through the 7th and 6th houses, respectively). And you can trace that progression all the way around the wheel regarding these emotional-need priorities.

When the progressed Moon contacts Chiron there is a need for the emotional nature, for the feeling nature, to open to this energetic sensitivity and the information there. As I observe it in clients and myself, there is a need to process the Chiron wound at that time. The need of the moment is to process Chironic feelings, to become more present on a day-to-day basis to whatever that Chiron is doing. Ideally, if something needs to be healed, then that's what should happen, but the real need is to have this energetic sensitivity come more into conscious feeling on a regular basis.

Progressed Moon Conjunct Chiron

The conjunction will be experienced by many people as a call to directly experience the wound. Most people don't like this, as they find it very difficult. They find themselves weepy or suddenly feeling very vulnerable and emotional because that conscious awareness of emotions suddenly gets turned on to the wound and to that energetic antenna.

The progressed Moon conjunct the Chiron is tied to becoming aware of this energetic sensitivity and integrating that sensitivity at the same time. The progression serves to change our minds about why we've suffered pain. Changing our minds about this Chironic childhood wound and how to meet our own needs by constructing better energetic boundaries. It is time to turn a corner now regarding all this.

Progressed Moon Sextile Chiron

With this progression, it is time for that evolving feeling nature to be triggered by the Chiron sensitivity. Now, the evolving Moon needs to be stimulated, to be pushed to act, to be stirred to draw or drive outside the lines in order to be in action about whatever the Chiron sensitivity is about. The need of the moment is to be triggered into action by energetic sensitivity to learn more about it and also learn to relate to that part of the self on a deeper, more conscious level.

The Moon represents our conscious feelings. When the progressed Moon sweeps around the chart every 27 or 28 years, it brings into consciousness each section of the wheel in turn. When it comes to Chiron, there's this need to have come into consciousness the energetic antenna, the point of pain and suffering, and why we have experienced what we have. Oftentimes when a person experiences this aspect by progression, they can feel unlovable, but of course that's not the case. The point of this is time is to feel your feelings consciously and openly. What can result is a reality check once those feelings are opened to, welcomed, and experienced in the moment.

Progressed Moon Square Chiron

When the progressed Moon squares Chiron there is tectonic-plate pressure and slow pushing until something changes. This is information from Chiron that would not be otherwise integrated by the progressed Moon – now, it needs to be integrated. The progressed Moon has a different agenda than natal Chiron here. Squares always represent different ways doing things and, in this case, it's time for that progressed Moon to integrate, even though it is very difficult what that energetic sensitivity has to say.

Progressed Moon Trine Chiron

The trine will seem to be a more comfortable relationship. People don't come in for counseling and astrology readings when progressed Moon is trine Chiron. It tends to put some light on the Chiron, but it doesn't always seem like it's a serious problem, even if the person is identifying with the wound to some degree. What it does is greases the wheels of the moment to experience that energetic sensitivity. As with trines from the outer planets to Chiron in the previous section, there is the possibility that things about perpetuating the wound seem simple and easy, and a person experiencing it can then notice that pattern and make changes with more conscious awareness.

Progressed Moon Inconjunct Chiron

The inconjunct will challenge a person to incorporate something about the energetic sensitivity that seems impossible to incorporate. The progressed Moon and Chiron can't be in the same room together. One very high potential with this progression is to become conscious of extremely deep levels of the pain and suffering that one feels or that others feel. This impossible lack of resolution, the impossible situation can cause a person to recognize his or her own energetic sensitivity and what can and can't be done about it. This recognition can often come out in the context of relationships, because if we have a default mode of using Chiron to support other people's pain and suffering or in some way enable or allow other people to perpetuate their Chironic wounds, this progression will make that impossible. We will not be able to perpetuate that pattern. This can contribute to a deep level of awareness – sometimes not even a conscious awareness. During this progression, the person might simply feel the need to pull away from situations that have crappy energetic boundaries, in which they give too much or let their energy be leaked.

Progressed Moon Opposing Chiron

The opposition from progressed Moon to natal Chiron is going to put perspective on whatever is going on with Chiron. If the person is identifying with the wounded part of themselves and in a mode of suffering, this progressed Moon will offer perspective on how to change how the situation works. Depending upon how the person feels about change and being confronted with this challenge to evolve – to gain perspective on and not perpetuate the wound – and how invested he or she is in the victim consciousness that can come with the natal Chiron placement, they might not make different choices. The conscious feelings, the need of the moment to this progressed Moon is in conflict with the wound. The progressed Moon is saying, "Actually this is not true about the wound. This is not true about this sense of rejection." With this progression, there's the opportunity to gain some perspective in a very clear-cut, immediate way if the person is not married to the identity of being wounded.

Mercury

Mercury in the natal chart represents perception, mind, communication, curiosity, and general interests. Progressed Mercury represents all of these things in an evolving state: the evolving interests, the evolving communication style, the evolving perception style and learning abilities.

Progressed Mercury coming to Chiron is about Chiron coming into more left-brain consciousness. With each progression it's not so much about feeling, as with the Moon, but about understanding rationally what Chiron is bringing. Mercury will bring more mental clarity to how someone perceives life and him- or herself, the style of communication, the interests, and how the person fits into the greater scheme of life.

To me, this is a very interesting progression because most of us are trained to rely extremely heavily on Mercury: the left brain, rational thought, reason, the powers of the conscious mind. When Mercury comes under the influence of

Chiron, it's very interesting to see the alchemical process the conscious mind will take in the direction of letting in more information from Chiron. The rational mind does not normally recognize Chiron as a valid source of information. When progressed Mercury makes contact to Chiron, that has the opportunity to change.

Progressed Mercury Conjunct Chiron

With the conjunction of progressed Mercury to Chiron, inner evolving mind is filled with Chiron from the inside out. The mind and the interests are going to be affected by Chiron in a very direct, merging way. The person will end up becoming more interested in some Chiron idea or way of thinking or living. That could be being more sensitive to energy, being more consciously sensitive. It could be talking about literal senses. It could be seeing energy, seeing auras. It could be hearing things that other people can't hear – not being imbalanced or sick, but different ways of experiencing energy, because Chiron will "alternify" such things. As somebody opens up to that energy that Mercury normally doesn't recognize as valid, the mind will get influenced very directly and very immediately by Chiron.

The person's senses will probably become more sensitive to loud noises and bright lights, and more sensitive to touch, depending on the person's natal Mercury placement. For instance, is natal Mercury in a water sign or an Earth sign? That kind of thing will matter. The idea is that the mind and what's connected to the mind, including the senses and the nervous system to some degree, will also be affected by getting more Chironic, getting more sensitive to energy. Also, the wound itself needs to be brought directly into consciousness during this progression. Metaphorically, the finger needs to be put directly on what that wound is. The person undergoing this will need to talk about his or her wound and understand the importance of energetic sensitivity. He or she must being willing to begin communicating about it. It will be important to talk about feelings, talk about energy, perhaps say things like, "While the words you're using my brain understands, the energy you're throwing at me is difficult to process, and this is why."

So, the key is to become aware of the different ways one is sensing energy and then be able to communicate about it. People who are not used to these new ways of sensing energy might feel like they're getting curve balls thrown at them, but that's the point: To become more sensitive to energy, to become more conscious of the value of such input regarding how the mind runs the person's life.

Progressed Mercury Sextile Chiron

The sextile will have something in common with the conjunction because the mind and senses will be triggered by energy. All progressed Mercury aspects to natal Chiron could sensitize the senses, the eyes, the ears, to the point that there are new faculties, new levels of awareness of energy. With the sextile it will come via stimulation, triggering, having a button pushed until somebody responds. It won't necessarily be dramatic – just a persistent nudging until somebody responds.

Progressed Mercury Square Chiron

With the square from progressed Mercury, there will be pressure in the form of Chironic information that the person does not want. The person with the progressed Mercury will have a goal, a certain way that the mind works. The square will say, "Here, do it this way instead." So the square will have to do with the natal Chiron function needing to be incorporated in a new way, even though it's very challenging for this progressed mind.

Progressed Mercury Trine Chiron

The trine from progressed Mercury will bring Chironic information to the evolving mind. It will also shift in a nonthreatening way ideas of how this information is useful and how to actually experience energy through the senses and in the person's environment. This is probably the aspect among these six in which it is the easiest for the person undergoing the progression to talk about energy, to begin talking about what energy is about.

Progressed Mercury Inconjunct Chiron

The inconjunct from progressed Mercury, on the other hand, will bring Chironic information into the mind in a very uncomfortable way. It can be difficult for the person experiencing this progression to figure out what to do with this information. This is the aspect that says, "Not sure how we can be in the same room together." The person's energetic antenna, this energetic sensitivity represented by Chiron, will be in a very difficult relationship with the evolving perception, communication, and interests of the person. Ideally, this discomfort can allow the person to bring into consciousness a tremendous amount of information and experiential contact with Chiron. Chiron will show up as thing that you can't avoid, you can't escape and you can't make it leave the room. You have to be conscious of this friction, of this grinding against you. This is a real opportunity to gain awareness about one's own Chiron wounding, about energetic

169

sensitivity, and also what one thinks about the suffering of self, the suffering of others and what the point of pain is.

For any contact with Chiron by transit or progression, the value of compassion should not be underestimated. Becoming more conscious of the value of compassion is important with the progressed Mercury contacts here. And with the inconjunct, especially, it will be very difficult to process this need.

Progressed Mercury Opposing Chiron

With the opposition from progressed Mercury, the evolving conscious mind, interests, perceptive faculties, and methods of communication are going to be confronted by this energetic sensitivity. This can seem like a standoff where two opposing forces have differing ideals and they might want to eradicate each other if they feel threatened. But the perceptive mind, the left brain, the rational mind now has the capacity to see in full view, under the full light of day, what is going on with Chiron. If the person can have compassion for him- or herself as well as for others who exhibit Chironic sensitivity and who feel some kind of sense of wounding, then this is an amazing opportunity to gain consciousness – direct, immediate, clear, clearly focused awareness of the wound, of the value of compassion, and why it's important to open the heart. Literally, this progression can be a real eye-opener to energy and how we live. This person needs to come out of identifying with the wound in some way and to begin rethinking the value of this energy. This is work that needs to be done from the inside out, so the opposition will not manifest Chironic others. The person having this experience will see Chiron in the self and, as a result, will see others in a different light.

Venus

In the natal chart Venus has to do with one's value system, self-worth, how one creates fairness and harmony with others, and how one creates or seeks balance, equality, and justice. When progressed Venus comes to Chiron, Chiron will influence what the person finds important, how the person relates to others, and/or how one deals with money. We tend to think of Venus as love, associated with the 4th chakra, the heart center. With Chiron, we learn about the value in compassion and choosing compassion, so when these two get together, there can be a real sensitization to the heart. There can be a heart opening that's possible. Also just as with progressed Mercury to Chiron, there could be a real mind opening. We associate Moon with the feelings, the emotional nature, but Venus has to do a lot with our sensitivity and conscious awareness of what's happening with other people. This progressed Venus to Chiron can Chironify that Venus. Venus adds Chiron understanding and tools to its repertory and can help open up the heart by teaching people how to be compassionate toward self and others.

Progressed Venus Conjunct Chiron

When progressed Venus conjuncts Chiron, it is time for the person's value system and how that person goes about creating quality and fairness to become Chironic from the inside out. For this period of time, the person's relationships will become more Chironic. There is going to be much more sensitivity to other people, their reactions, along with the energetic waves and currents that flow though other people. There is also going to be the capacity – if the person is wounded – to identify with the natal Chiron wound. People who will be attracted to the person undergoing this progression are going to be some kind of healer or some kind of wounded bird, and it will put a lot of attention on that Chiron – what it does and how it is. This person will respond more to Venus situations with a Chiron consciousness. If that is as the wounded then that will be heightened and if that is as a wounded healer, that will be heightened. If the person is someone who really understands Chironic energy, it can simply just sensitize him or her to Chironic issues in general regarding Venus and how everybody is vulnerable. This is a time when the person can make some progress with working with his or her own vulnerability and sensitivity to energy and emotion.

Progressed Venus Sextile Chiron

The sextile from progressed Venus to Chiron will bring stimulation. This person's evolving value system and the evolving ways of relating to others and self will need to because more Chironic. Chiron here will be pushing a button, triggering, tickling, poking the person in the ribs – again and again and again until the person makes some new choices and integrates some of what Chiron has to say into these Venusian processes.

Progressed Venus Square Chiron

The square from progressed Venus to Chiron introduces that tectonic plate pressure idea, the person's value system in relationships. The input from Chiron's energetic antenna will be difficult to integrate because it will cause the person's evolving value system to change. Imagine somebody who is pretty confident about what he or she values. Then enter Chiron sensitivity to energy of some situation, an energy which needs to be or is undeniable needs to be taken into account. It might go against that person's plan. And that's the energy of the square – to alter the preset plan. Opening to that is very important, but it can also cause one to feel as if they're taken off track. The ideal, the point of this aspect by progression, is to learn about one's own evolving values by being pressured to change by Chiron sensitivity.

Progressed Venus Trine Chiron

The trine from progressed Venus to Chiron will bring opportunities for these two planetary bodies to speak some of the same language. There can be an easy – or, at least, perhaps somewhat painless – incorporation of some of the information that Chiron brings, affecting the person's relationship with money, self-worth, and relationships.

Progressed Venus Inconjunct Chiron

With the inconjunct, it will be difficult for the person to figure out how to integrate things that seem like oil and water, that just can't mix. The ways that he or she will want to relate to others will seem to be derailed by the energetic sensitivity. Progressed Venus and Chiron here seem to be saying to one another: "I can see what you're saying, but I'm feeling something different." The discrepancy between the appearance of what's going on in the relationship and the energetic subtext will be very, very difficult for the person to integrate. With the inconjunct by progression, there is a need to open up to the information and do what one can to stay open to various ways this can be useful. Even though this might bring about a situation or situations that seem impossible to resolve, there is a great opportunity to gain awareness of what the natal Chiron has to say.

Progressed Venus Opposing Chiron

This progression is going to invite the person, via his or her evolving value system and evolving sense of self-worth, to open to Chiron input in a new way. This is the opposition which says, "I can see you in a way you can't see yourself." The inner evolving value system, what is important to the person – including how relationships, money, and resources are used – will confront this Chironic sensitivity.

The ideal is that the person undergoing this aspect by progression allows this input, allows this energetic sensitivity, this awareness and consciousness of emotions and energy to alter, inform, and help the person guide the development of his or her evolving value systems. All of this is rooted in the person's own internal evolving sense of developing that value system.

Mars

Mars in the natal chart represents our will, our assertion, our drive, our get-up-and-go function. Progressed Mars represents the evolving way that part of us develops. We add to our repertory over time and we explore new ways of developing will, of asserting ourselves, of developing healthy boundaries of taking action, and to responding to the world around us in instinctive ways.

When progressed Mars comes into contact with Chiron, this evolving will and way of being in action and expressing desire comes into a situation where it needs to take more information in from Chiron. Whatever the person's natal Chiron is doing, progressed Mars now needs to take information from that. Depending upon the aspect, it needs to begin to respond to the external stimulus around the person with information from that Chiron in mind.

In many people, this will be a time to do something about the Chiron wound or about the way energetic boundaries are managed, because specifically Mars represents defense and rescue. When progressed Mars comes into contact with Chiron, we might realize that we've been giving way too much, we've been leaking too much energy and/or we've been nurturing others in their suffering and not feeling that we get to do what we need to do.

Progressed Mars Conjunct Chiron

When progressed Mars conjuncts Chiron, a person's inner need to act in new ways will take the lead in incorporating what Chiron is about. Progressions always work from the inside out, so there will likely be a call from the inside out to do something proactive and perhaps even rescue and defense about that wound. Perhaps it is taking care of the self better. It could be beginning to say no to people that we serve too much at the expense of our own energetic and emotional health. Or it could be a part of the person rising up and saying, "You know, I'm kind of done whining about this; I'm just going to learn how to move on." There can be a lot of different kinds of responses, but this energy will be from the inside out. Chiron needs to be informing the person's evolving sense of will, assertion, aggression and being in action, in general.

Progressed Mars Sextile Chiron

When progressed Mars sextiles Chiron, the information from the Chironic energetic antenna – including the repository of history, opinions, and beliefs about what wounding, suffering, service, healing, and what this experience of being an energetic being is all about – will be triggered by this evolving sense of will. The action one takes, the self-assertion, and the aggression that one displays will somehow trigger the Chiron wound in the self. Ideally, the person can gain more consciousness about the Chiron wounding, because the action is triggering it. The person's actions will expose the wound in order for the person to understand more about that wounding. The part that says, "I need to go do this now, I didn't feel this way five years ago, but I need to act this way now …" – that part will be exposing the wound. The ideal is for the person to gain consciousness and learn how to process and move on.

Progressed Mars Square Chiron

When progressed Mars squares natal Chiron, what needs to be done now, what needs to be acted upon, will give friction to the wound. "I need to go do this thing, and yet if I do that, it really lays bare my experience of the Chiron situation, of the Chiron energetic wounding." It may not feel like a do-or-die situation, but it will definitely feel: "I have to do this, even if it hurts." Because our lives are holographic, we can look at the outside and understand that what is going on around us is a reflection of our inside, our own energy fields. In this case, when progressed Mars is square natal Chiron, the action that needs to be taken will seem to stir up or bring on wounding that's difficult to deal with, that we don't even want to deal with. We have to understand that that reflects our own relationship with Chiron energy inside us, so there's an opportunity to learn more about this energy, to process it and find a way to generate healthy, self-interested action. This is a great way to think about progressed Mars here – it drives us to learn more about, and ultimately heal, process, and release this Chiron wounding and really shift our understanding of what Chiron is all about.

Progressed Mars Trine Chiron

The trine from progressed Mars to natal Chiron will bring up all this action. The person's self-interested action, self-assertion, and sense of developing and expressing will and boundaries will come into a supportive relationship with Chiron. We've been told that trines are easy, and we've been led to believe that they're lucky or something. What really goes on with a trine, though, is that whatever one planetary body is doing, the other one will support. In this case, the evolving Mars – the way that somebody goes about doing something and acts on desire – will have an energy flow to the Chiron. What is taken action on will naturally support what is going on with the Chiron. The trick here is to become more conscious of that Chiron. When you see what needs to be understood more about that Chiron, understand that the progressed Mars is right there to take self-interested action, and this can actually support healing the Chiron wounding and moving into experiencing oneself as an energetic being and being able to choose compassion more. This is self-interested action coming into contact with the part of us that can learn the importance of always choosing compassion in the face of suffering.

Progressed Mars Inconjunct Chiron

With the inconjunct, the progressed Mars – the thing the person needs to do now, the way the person needs to develop boundaries, and the way the person needs to act and behave in a self-interested, assertive way – will come into a lot of uncomfortable friction with the natal wounding. If somebody is guarding the Chiron, guarding the energetic sensitivity, harboring a wound, or not coming out of woundedness, this aspect can be challenging because the person will feel an inner guidance to do the Mars in a way that brings up the wounding. The person experiencing this progression is going to need a lot of information about how to cut through all the Chiron nonsense – nurturing the wound from infancy, whining, and feeling that he or she needs protection – and move more into a conscious way of living with Chiron.

Progressed Mars Opposing Chiron

When progressed Mars comes into opposition with Chiron, this self-interested action, the evolving way that someone takes action comes into opposition with the wound. This is a really great way – if not the best way – to gain consciousness of what the Chironic wounding is all about. The person will be naturally and internally guided to do things that keep exhibiting the wound, that keep revealing to oneself and others the wound. There is no denying the wound when it is in a showdown with you, staring at you from across the room. This is a fantastic healing opportunity for the person who has this progressed aspect who is willing to look at and experience the wounding in order to move beyond it.

Ascendant-Descendant

Next, we look at the horizon, which is the Ascendant-Descendant axis. Because it's an axis, having two ends, whenever one point contacts a body by progression, the opposite point is simultaneously aspecting it. I will cover all possibilities here.

The natal Ascendant represents how we show ourselves, our style and our first impressions, and also how we relate to and use our bodies. The progressed Ascendant is the evolving way that we show ourselves, our evolving style, what parts of us need to come out. The natal Descendant is what we look for in others and how we approach others in relationship. The progressed Descendant has to do with our evolving strategies in relationship and our evolving ways of opening up to others and seeking connection. Naturally, what we look for in others changes over time.

Progressed Ascendant Conjunct Chiron

When progressed Ascendant conjuncts Chiron, the Descendant is automatically, simultaneously opposing Chiron. When the progressed Ascendant conjuncts Chiron, the Chiron needs to come out in the outward behavior. If the person has been nursing a wound, harboring it, hiding it, this is going to lay bare the emotional sensitivity and all the cache of emotions that have been hidden, stored away, shoved in the basement, or shoved to the back of that crowded closet. This is going to be an unavoidable expression of Chiron. It can't be hidden anymore – it has to come out from the inside out.

When the Descendant opposes Chiron, other people will reflect to us – and we will see in the people that we attract to us – more about our Chirons. If the Chiron is hiding, this will be difficult. If, in these simultaneous dual aspects Chiron is *not* hiding, it can be a really great way to nudge Chiron to come out more consciously in the open.

If someone is having his or her progressed Ascendant hitting Chiron, that means their natal Chiron will be in the 1st, 2nd or 3rd house. So, if you refer to the sections on the houses and look at the nature of the wounding in each, the story will become clearer. Chiron in the 1st brings body issues; Chiron in the 2nd, the self-esteem issues, Chiron in the 3rd, the questions, the mind, and the curiosity. And now, with the progressed Ascendant conjunct Chiron, it all needs to come out.

Because of the Descendant opposing it, there's also the idea that when the person expresses the Chiron in whatever way he or she does with the progression of the Ascendant to the Chiron, other people will respond. The relationships will change. Other people will say, "Wow, you're kind of whiney," or "Hey, you've really reached a milestone with how you deal with your emotions. That's great. I like you." One way or another, interactions and relationships with others will change.

Progressed Ascendant Sextiling Chiron

When the progressed Ascendant sextiles Chiron, there will be stimulation. The way that the style and self-presentation are evolving and unfolding over time is now being triggered by the Chiron wounding, the Chironic sensitivity to energy. This is a time when the person's style is going to adapt and respond to this poke in the ribs by the information from the energetic antenna of Chiron.

The simultaneous trine from the progressed Descendant will connect a person with others who are drawn to or resonate with what the person is experiencing, or other people will be able to give constructive advice or criticism about how that sextile is working between the Ascendant and Chiron. This can be a fabulous way to get some tutoring on Chiron wounding and healing at the same time as it gets put into play in relationships. And, because it is sextile the Ascendant, the beginning of the 1st house, it can really connect us organically, viscerally to the information that Chiron offers.

Progressed Ascendant Square Chiron

When the progressed horizon is square Chiron, it will bring friction from this energetic antenna to the evolving way the person expresses the self simultaneously with the evolving way the person approaches and seek others. All of these aspects come into focus over time. The progressed Ascendant- Descendant axis does not move very quickly, but with this idea of the square involving tectonic plates – the tectonic plates here are how the person who has this progressed aspect conceives of self and other. "What am I responsible for? What are these other people responsible for? What kind of friends, what kind of relationships do I expect to have? What am I willing to do within them? How can I present myself in order to attract these relationships?" So this square introduces friction about self and other, about fairness and who gets to have what when.

The whole axis is now one tectonic plate, and the person's evolved way of approaching these things is now one of these two tectonic plates. The second tectonic plate is the energetic antenna. The person will, in the body, feel more energetic information and will receive from other people more energetic information. The squares always drive change, so the best strategy is let this information change: a) how one does the Chiron, and b) how one thinks of self and other and who is responsible for what.

This can be a great time to clean up any boundary issues one might have in his or her relationships. The person could still be waiting for a parent to do something that the parent just isn't going to do. That will be a reflection of the inner wounded infant still waiting to get love. When this aspect comes up with the progressed Ascendant-Descendant, it can really come out in relationships and how one behaves and treats the body and treats other people. There is a great learning opportunity there.

Progressed Ascendant Trine Chiron

When the progressed Ascendant trines natal Chiron and the Descendant sextiles it, it is different from when the progressed Ascendant sextiles and the Descendant trines, because now the stimulation is coming from other people. The triggering, the poke in the ribs, is coming from others – not from the body and how energy is sensed in the body, like with the other aspect.

Ideally, as this information comes in from other people, one's relationships have the opportunity to change. With the trine to the progressed Ascendant, relationships with others, with one's body and the information that comes through the energetic antenna can really help the person evolve the way he or she relates. This is a great opportunity for growth in opening up to this information and letting it change how one is evolving the self-other axis.

Progressed Ascendant Opposing Chiron

When the progressed Ascendant opposes natal Chiron the progressed Descendant conjuncts it. I'm going to start with the Descendant.

When the progressed Descendant conjuncts Chiron, the Chironic energetic sensitivity needs to come out in the way the person is evolving a sense of fairness, harmony, and balance in general as well as in their relationships. The energetic antenna needs to be a major source of information for the path this person is on regarding relationships. As that person opens up to this information in other people and their energetic sensitivities are reflected, their wounding, their history, their emotions, their needs, their suffering will be felt more acutely.

One way this can happen by default is that the person just starts absorbing things left and right and then feels drained. This doesn't happen overnight, but this influence can build up over time and challenge the person's emotional, energetic, and even physical health. The person undergoing this aspect needs to recognize this energy and say, "Aha, yes. That's not mine. I can't take on your suffering. If I can help you I will. But there are lots of cases where I have to say 'no thanks' and wish you well or point you in a direction that I think will help you, without me being your nursemaid."

At the same time, the Chiron opposes the progressed Ascendant so for the person pressed to speak up in relationship as mentioned, this will serve the evolution of the person as far as he or she presents him- or herself. When the Descendant hits the Chiron, the person might also feel surrounded by suffering: "Wow, everyone's suffering and whining – I shouldn't have to deal with this."

When the person instead says "no thanks" and focuses attention on taking care of him- or herself, that will serve the evolution of the progressed Ascendant.

Midheaven-Nadir

Natally, the Midheaven-Nadir axis deals with the public and private parts of the self – what should happen in a person's public world and what should happen in a person's private world. When we are talking about the progressed axis, this has to do with the evolving way one needs to be in the world, and the evolving way one needs to take care of the self and have a private life. When the axis comes into contact with Chiron, the energetic sensitivity, the energetic antenna, needs to come into play in order to affect how one does one's work in the community and how one relates to family and history.

Progressed Midheaven Conjunct Chiron

The progressed Midheaven conjuncting Chiron says that the person's public self needs to incorporate more of what Chiron is about. Chiron might already be in the 10th house natally, but this progressed Midheaven coming to it would just say that Chiron needs to be the focus. This is what the person is majoring in, this is what the person is focusing on for as long as that progression occurs, in order to really bring that Chironic self out.

For people who are hiding the wound, maybe that shows up as having some woundedness issues come out at work, which of course can be very difficult. If that happens the person needs to turn the corner on the wound. The simultaneous opposition of the Nadir, the bottom of the chart, to Chiron will say that whatever you're seeing come out publicly should tell you more about what you need as far as your inner world goes.

A specific example of woundedness coming out at work: "Well, you need to learn how to take better care of yourself. You need to go home and nurture yourself." That will take away the need for this to come out publicly. It might not actually totally alleviate the need, because the Chiron is still up there with the progressed Midheaven on it, but it will reflect to the person how to take better care of the self.

Progressed Midheaven Sextile Chiron

When the progressed Midheaven sextiles Chiron, the evolving public self needs to be stimulated by whatever the Chiron is doing, by the energetic information. The simultaneous trine to the Nadir will reveal some inner support for processing whatever the Chiron is about. While the public self gets stimulated, the private self can take some cues about how to take better care. With the trine of the Nadir to natal Chiron, it's a real challenge. It can be accompanied by the feeling that you have to get off your butt and start taking care of sometime at home. This serves to facilitate better balance and flow so the person can take some cues about his or her history, how to take better care of oneself, relationships to family, etc.

Progressed Midheaven Square Chiron

When this axis squares Chiron, again, there is tectonic plate activity. One tectonic plate is the evolving relationship between the public self and the private self. This aspect by progression will have the person asking questions like: "What's public? What's private? What's mine? What am I comfortable sharing with my colleague, a grocery store clerk? What do I keep private?" This progression aids the person in learning more about that balance and how that person evolves that balance over time.

The other tectonic plate is the person's energetic sensitivity. This aspect will trigger the wound and sensitivity in both arenas of life – inner (home, family, private self) and outer (public self, community standing, social status). That can seem like a lot of pressure building up but some key information from Chiron can come through now. Because we're talking about the Midheaven-Nadir axis – it could have to do with a kind of respect and respectability that we want regarding the kinds of people and places from which we come. It can be about relationships with family, our history, and ancestry, for example, and how we think of those things affect our public life. The square, like all squares, offers up a wonderful opportunity to grow if we accept that we have to change.

Progressed Midheaven Trine Chiron

With the progressed Midheaven trine Chiron, the flow is going to be with the public self and the stimulation is going to be with the private self. The stimulation with the sextile to the IC to Chiron is going to drive an inner knowing. It will push buttons and poke the person in the ribs until he or she responds by taking better care of the self. This progression will help the person see in what ways Chironic information is detrimental and is misunderstood and in what ways it can be beneficial. That kind of triggering will simultaneously flow with the development of the public self.

Progressed MC Opposing Chiron

The last aspect by progression is the progressed Midheaven opposing Chiron and the progressed Nadir conjuncting it. Starting with the Nadir conjuncting Chiron: This is the inner self, the evolving way somebody experiences a private life and develops and maintains relationships with family and home life, etc., that is coming to Chiron. This is a time when that inner landscape needs to be influenced directly and infused by Chiron. The energetic sensitivity needs to be recognized in private from the inside out. So it's about getting in touch with feelings, getting in touch with woundedness. There will come an understanding about the ways our parents did the best they could for us, but how we have to parent ourselves.

With the simultaneous opposition from the progressed Midheaven, everything that you're learning about with the Nadir's conjunction to Chiron is teaching you about who you really are. And that, in turn, can change who you are in the world. You might be somehow holding back, going after a certain job or promotion, a certain kind of public accomplishment or recognition because a parent or an uncle told you that you would never amount to anything. With this progression, you can get to know the dynamic behind that history in a new way. You have the opportunity to change your mind about that history. You have the chance to feel those feelings, process them and move on. In the end, you're in a better position to create the kind of public self that you really want to have.

Chiron Transits

Chiron in transit serves as an energetic sensitizer. When Chiron transits in the sky and touches the different planets and angles and points in our natal chart, it offers the opportunity for us – in new ways and for reasons we never would have encountered or would have imagined before – to experience energetic information. Again, how we typically receive that information is in the form of emotions. Chiron in transit will bring us opportunities to open, to feel, relative to the planet it is aspecting and the outcome, of course, depends on the whole natal configuration. As it travels, Chiron will seek to open that part of the person, that part of the energy field, that part of the psyche, to the input of energetic information.

Chiron's transits will serve to make us question how it is that we typically function in relationship to Chiron. They will stir the natal Chiron wounding or actually open up the natal Chiron proclivity, tendency, or inclination to respond to energetic information in one way or another. Our experience with Chiron will be determined by our choices in response to the external stimuli. And our choices are based in our beliefs about this energy. When you are still wallowing in the wound and feeling overpowered by the energetic antenna and energetic/emotional information from other people, then these transits have the potential to be more difficult than if you have started to process the wounding and have learned the benefit of Chironic sensitivity. If you don't understand the value in choosing compassion and that compassion is a balm that heals all wounds, then the challenges that come with a Chiron square, for example, will just look like another difficult thing you don't know how to deal with.

If, on the other hand, you're processing the wound, and instead of thinking, "This happens to me," you're contemplating, "Oh, I can see that I kind of create this stuff. Why am I so sensitive? What should I do with this pain? How can I understand my emotional history and what it is that I carry around in my heart? What's mine? What isn't mine?" – then Chiron transits can offer an opportunity to gain more consciousness.

This energetic information that arrives by transit could be in the form of other people who are suffering or other people who are having issues and trouble.

Remember, transits are outward events that come to us, outer energies that are attracted to our energy. We need this energy to come to us and so it does. So again, it can often come in the form of other people, it can come in the form of situations and scenarios –the bottom line is that it is something outside you that shows up to reflect your need to learn more about this energy.

For somebody who is processing their wound and is practiced in dealing with suffering and responding with compassion, nurturing self and others in healthy ways that reflect a good understanding and strong foundation in energetic boundaries, then Chiron transits will serve to deepen the connection this person has with the world around him or her as well as the people in it. If you're already choosing the compassionate route when Chiron transits something in your chart, you are going to be invited to just simply practice Chiron a little more, experience the energy a little more. By that point, it is not a burden to experience this energetic reality in the world around you – you just accept that this is part of your human education to learn more about it through experience, very often with other people.

This section will be a bit different. As I talk about the planetary bodies, I'm going to spend more time on Chiron transiting that body, and then I will give some level of detail but not as much as in the previous sections because I want you to understand the energy involved. You can plug in how each aspect would modify this relationship – it'll tell you about the question that Chiron asks as it transits and how the different parts of us, the different planets, and the angles are affected or are faced with making these decisions.

The core questions for all of these transits and their relative aspects are: "Are you open to energy? Are you open to the information in the world around you that you perhaps cannot see, cannot quantify and have not as yet experienced? Are you open to your own energetic information and to being changed by this new energetic information?" Many times, the answer will be: "Well I never thought about it that way," or "That never crossed my mind."

As we, as a collective, learn more about this energy of sensitivity, learn more about ourselves as energetic beings, capable of being sensitive to other people, the answer will shift over time to, "Oh, well, okay, I'm supposed to learn this lesson," or "Gosh, that's difficult. I'm going to try to figure that out." For many of us, the answer so far has been, "Yeah, I don't even know what to do with that. It just looks like that dude is whining over there. I can't deal with that."

With all of these transits, the healthy proactive strategy and response would be to take the information in, to let your consciousness be changed, to let this part of you be changed by what is experienced and what is learned.

Sun

As the Sun is the person's inner CEO, Chiron transits of the Sun will ask the question: "Are you sensitive enough? Are you conscious enough of energy? Are you aware enough that you are not just a machine but actually an energetic being having a physical experience?" Chiron will also ask: "Are you willing to take this information in to factor into your decisions? Are you willing to become well-rounded? Are you willing to open up to acknowledge this?"

The Sun is part of our natural sense of confidence when healthy. Chiron's transit to the Sun will bring up energy about and sensitivity to things that, frankly, are not healthy. This is a time when there could be some questioning about a person's vitality, health, and sanity, because this other information is coming in, begging the question: "What am I supposed to do with this information?" This new information doesn't have to threaten a person's health, but it can seem to threaten the apparent stability that the Sun ensures within the rest of the person's being.

So, ideally, the Sun takes this information in. Ideally, the part of the self inside making the decisions, the CEO in the psychic boardroom, would take in this information and recognize it as a valid source of information.

With the conjunction, it's going to be from the inside out. With the sextile, it's going to be triggering and stimulating. With the square, it's going to be friction and pressure. With the trine, it's going to be speaking the same language and trying to open up a channel of positive sharing. With the inconjunct, it's going to be seeming irreconcilable differences, seeming caught off-guard, perhaps a little traumatic in one way. And the opposition will be a challenge.

None of these transits are necessarily easy and none of these transits are necessarily difficult. It all depends on the person's response to the energetic information and to this challenge to open up.

Moon

The Moon is the marker of a person's emotional side. It is what a person needs to do to make the self happy. It also has to do with safety, security, and nesting, as the Moon relates to home and family. In transit to the Moon, Chiron's question, "Are you open to energetic information?" will come in the form of: "Are you willing to feel more? Are you willing to feel all that you can feel?" If the person undergoing this transit has the Moon conjunct Chiron natally, he or she might respond in a different way than somebody who doesn't.

Generally, this transit will bring opportunities to connect with people in new ways. Chiron and Moon both have to do with connecting with people, but in different ways. The ideal is that a person becomes or chooses to become more vulnerable and yet, as I've explored elsewhere in this course, we live in this very Saturn society where people are afraid of being vulnerable. People are afraid of letting emotions run in healthy ways. Most of us have not always been taught how to express emotion healthily, so we have a fear that we'll gush all over the floor if we actually open up. The Chiron transits to the Moon may seem to challenge people in this manner and it doesn't matter which aspect it is. Chiron comes knocking. The energetic antenna, the sensitivity – which is to say, an awareness of other people's emotions – comes knocking.

The outcomes of these transits depend on how the person functions with Chiron natally and responds to that energy. You have to look to what's going on in the person's history and family and how that person has responded to the particular wound that he or she developed when very young. This Chiron transit to the Moon will want to open the door to the heart, will want to open the floodgates of emotion so that the person can become willing to feel all that he or she can feel. Because that can feel threatening, Chiron-Moon transits can be very difficult for people who are, for example, holding a job, having and taking care of kids and families and paying a mortgage (which accounts for the majority of the population, actually), is required to balance all those responsibilities with the necessity to often just sit and be with their feelings. This is one of the great strategies of this transit, of any of these transits: to sit and feel. Not staring at the wall, depressed, or weeping all the time, but really become more consciously in touch with all the emotions that one can feel.

With the conjunction, this is going to be from the inside out. This is going to infuse Moon with Chiron energy. This question will come from the inside out, moving the person to open up and bubble up in order to really get him or her to feel.

The sextile will trigger, stimulate, tickle, and poke the person in the ribs to get something to happen: "Here's this information, here's this information." This will often come in the form of other people's suffering and other people's neediness. The person will need to respond to this information somehow, emotionally.

The square will be pressure and friction. As with all squares, we don't want to give up what we're doing and hear, "You're doing it wrong." But transiting Chiron will ask, "Are you willing to be sensitive? Are you willing to open up to this information, Moon?" And Chiron will really push on the Moon until something gives. The person will need to learn to choose to open up in order to relieve the tension consciously. Otherwise, it can come out as real emotional outbursts.

The trine will bring energetic information in a seemingly supportive way. This energy, this information, this relationship with other people, it might seem like good thing, might seem appropriate and healthy. Whatever the Moon is doing, Chiron will try to support it. If a person has poor energetic or emotional boundaries, Chiron trine the Moon will actually augment that. Ideally, hopefully, the person can figure out how to have some better boundaries and say no to some things, so that what he or she says yes to can actually function better.

The inconjunct is going to be difficult. It will feel like being caught off-guard, knocked off course perhaps, by the reality of energetic information in the world around a person. It can really serve to shake up whatever that Moon is doing. Ideally, this transit will enable the person to be more on his or her toes and respond better to energy.

The opposition will be a confrontation that seems to say, "You know what? Whatever you need to feel here … feel this instead." It wants to get that person to open up and be willing to experience the new information. This transit truly will tell the person more about his or her needs, represented by the Moon. It will teach the person more about boundaries, nesting, their nurturing instincts, etc. The challenge is to not feel threatened, blocked, or confounded by the Chiron information, which will usually come in the form of other people's neediness or suffering.

Mercury

When Chiron transits Mercury – which rules the perceptive faculty, communication and a person's interests – it will ask the left brain if it can open up. As it is, most of us perceive ourselves as our left brains. This is the way we've been trained to understand ourselves: as minds. When Chiron comes here, the person will be opening up to different sources of energetic information. Chiron will ask: "Can you recognize that the feeling that you have is just as valid as what you're thinking about and your idea of the world?"

The reality of energetic information, including other people's inner worlds and their needs, suffering, and sense of uniqueness will, during these transits, ideally change the person's mind about something. Whatever opinion they hold, whatever idea they have, whatever idea they expect to find in the world, is up for change. These transits could also open up a person to become curious about different ways of exploring how it is one knows what he or she knows. So there can be a sort of analytical, epistemological shift from how we know something to the reality of the information in the world around us.

With the conjunction, it's going to happen from the inside out. The mind itself will be Chironified from the inside out. This will impact the person's interests and their communication style – he or she will be a little more vulnerable in listening, a little more sensitive to light, something like this. The senses and the mind and speech organs will be affected.

The sextile will trigger information from Chironic sources, will poke the person in the ribs. until some Mercurial response is had. The response could be learning. The response could be communicating, speaking. The response could even be speaking up and saying, "Hey stop that." But there needs to be a response, and the Chiron energy will trigger the person's mind until something happens.

The square will present friction, saying: "Whatever you're thinking here, there is actually a different take on it that you could really do well for yourself by opening up to." And that's going to require the mind to change and for the person's ideas to be pushed from the side. Using the metaphor of tectonic plates, one tectonic plate is the mind, the attachment to ideas, communication, and the person's interests. Chiron, the other tectonic plate, will come in and say, "Hey, there's this other source of information. Open up to it."

The trine will bring energetic information that can support and boost what the person is interested in and how that person thinks. If the person is actually Mercurially engaged, if the mind is active, if the person is communicating, this can bring in the energy of boosting and supporting how that person takes in energetic information in a nonthreatening way.

With the inconjunct, the person can be caught off guard and be pushed in uncomfortable ways by energetic information. The person's goals can get totally obliterated by somebody else's needs. The ideal is to take the information in and then get one's footing again once the person has learned what is needed to be learned from this new source of information.

The opposition will be a confrontation. Chiron will come around and say, "Look, this is who you think you are, but there is actually another way to look at yourself, and it actually can serve to make you more complete as a human." It can show up as a confrontation with the gunslingers in the street or as people who at least respect each other but don't necessarily get along: "I can see this thing about you that you cannot see." The information from Chiron will come in and reveal more about how this person's thought process works and what he or she is really interested in.

Venus

Venus represents what is important to us, our value system, how we relate to others, and how we relate things to themselves in creativity and art and music – harmony, balance, fairness, equality. When Chiron transits Venus, how one relates to other people and what one finds important needs to be Chironified. It could be the Chiron people come in. Either Chironified people or situations enter the person's life and press the person's creative buttons. This energy comes in to change and augment what this person finds important, how that person expresses the value system and skills, and the approach to resources and relationships.

As Chiron always indicates difference, the Venusian value system can be opened up to incorporate more perspectives based on difference. We can be very black-and-white about what is important to us and the Chiron transit to Venus can ask the person to be more sensitive to the human realities that don't fit according to such terms, that actually destroy the black-and-white system if you give them any attention and credence.

When it comes to relationships, Chironic people will come in and the Venus person experiencing this transit will have to make a decision on what's going to be given to these people. "How am I supposed to think of these people? What am I going to give to them? They're suffering and I can see that. They might even be asking me for some kind of support." Venus as related to the 7th house is the house where we ask other people for help. The person undergoing this transit will have to make decisions. Maybe he or she will attract whiney people or people who have issues with one of their parents. Perhaps it shows up in their dating life, for instance, a woman attracting men who have Mommy issues, and she sees it right away. Chironifying the way one relates to somebody can bring in people who are not actually healthy for one to be around, so this person is going to have to learn how to say, "Aha, right. No thanks. That's not where I am. I'm not going to be your mommy, etc." It can work the same way with men attracting women with Daddy issues. Because it's Chiron, it can have a lot to do with the childhood wounding.

With the conjunction, it's going to be from the inside out. The person's Venus – the way a person approaches somebody else, the way he or she expresses his or her value system and understands what's important – will get sensitized from the inside out. This energetic antenna, temporarily passing by, gets plugged straight into Venus. So the person will have to respond differently to things.

With the sextile, there will be new information coming in from Chiron, as well as people with Chironic issues of one kind or another coming into the person's life. Chironic people don't always show up as wounded, either; they can be healer types, shaman types, or unique, alternative types – people who are fine being different and who have processed their own stuff. So with the sextile, the information from Chiron is going to be triggering the person, and this is where some tension can come in. If you're attracting negative people or wounded people, that can feel very negative, especially if you have poor energetic boundaries. If you're not sure what to give and what not to give, this transit is going to be an invitation for you to figure that out.

With the square you're going to draw people who are at odds with you, people who have different agendas, who are giving you friction, who are pressuring you to do something for them, to give them something, or to be willing to experience something with them. This is a real test of the boundaries, because you're being pressed and you have to get really clear on what you are and are not willing to do.

With the trine, it might seem like it's a good situation, but you have to be clear on boundaries and be really accepting that you can't always do something for somebody, even if you can see how to do it, and you would like that person not to suffer anymore.

The inconjunct to Venus will knock the value system or the relating function off course for a bit. This seemingly irresolvable tension seems to say Chiron and Venus can't be in the same room together. You're going to attract Chiron people with this transit who embody that and you have to figure out how to be grounded, be stable, take in the information as far as recognizing what it is and be clear that you are or not going to work with it.

The opposition will involve Chironic people coming to you who oppose you somehow. So you're saying, "I have Value System A and this what I'm going to be doing. This is what's important to me." Then the Chironic influence comes to you and says, "You really need to do Z." You respond with, "That's all the way over there. That's not what I'm up to." So you get reflection from the Chironic person who might need something or want something. If you attract a wounded person, it is likely that that person will expect you to do something that you don't want to do or that you're not going to do. This is all to teach you more about your value system, and the challenge is to learn how to respond with good energetic boundaries.

Mars

When Chiron comes to Mars, the will, the assertion function, the get-up-and-go, the fire in the belly or fire in the loins need to get more sensitive to Chironic

189

information. For you to take action during a Chiron-Mars transit, you first have to take in subtle information that you can't necessarily prove. Mars is already instinctual and the energy from Chiron wants it to open up its channels, to open up to take in this subtle information that's below the surface, behind the scenes – the real subtext of whatever is going on.

Because Mars is instinctive and we tend to react with our Mars without thinking, this transit can be a little weird. You either shift your footing and change gears, understanding that there's some other information that you're supposed to be taking in … or you don't, it gets a little clunky, and you might trip over yourself a little bit. The ideal strategy is to look at where you're headed, look at your goals, look at what you are really desirous about, and allow that to open up to this other source of information.

Chiron in transit coming to natal Mars can seem to thwart the will, because all of a sudden you have this needy person standing in front of you, needing something from you. So you have to make a decision about what you will and won't do for other people. It echoes the boundary issue that can accompany Chiron-Venus transits.

With the conjunction, the part of the self that is action-oriented needs to become more sensitive to energy. Again, this is Chiron working from the inside out, infusing energetic information into the part that acts. As with all transits from Chiron to Mars, it might cause you to slow down and become more conscious of how you behave and cause you to become less instinctual, less automatically reactive.

The sextile is going to be triggering. It is going to press on that Mars until you do something about the energetic information. If you have this transit or you're working with people who have it, help them weed out the whininess and the neediness that comes from other people and help them understand that the reason Chiron's coming to them in that form has to do with their relationship with their own wounding.

The square is going to bring friction because other people need certain things, and you can't really just go about your business doing what you're doing.

The trine will seem supportive. Again, it *seems* supportive. It might seem that you can do something for somebody who needs something, and yet you have to be really clear about what the true motivations are and what you are and are not willing to do.

The inconjunct will seem to throw things off course, push things from the side and you can really feel like you're just going to get knocked off the rails and never get back on. There is a need to check in with what the will is trying to do, because if it can get knocked off course like this, you have to look at how much of it is really stable and secure. How much of it is real? How much of it is really authentic? These are questions to ask when working with this transit.

The opposition can come in the form of blocking. It can seem that Chironic others are blocking you from what you're trying to get done. There's a need to take the reflection of what it is that's important to you: Why are you doing this? What are you getting out of it? That kind of thing. Mars is not necessarily unconscious; it's really about instinctual reaction. When Chiron opposes Mars, it can slow us down to help us learn more about how we use our wills and why.

Jupiter

Jupiter is the belief function in a person. It is the part of the self that can hold a vision, get in touch with imagination, and believes in things. Jupiter is the part of us that develops an overarching principle on how and why to live.

When Chiron comes to Jupiter by transit, Chiron attempts to sensitize the input of energetic information. Jupiter can go along happy-go-lucky, not taking in details, and not being sensitive to the realities around it. Jupiter is famous for having blinders on, and because it can hold a vision and is the belief function, sometimes the details of day-to-day living get left out. As a result, the entire world can be experienced in terms of what the person has already believed or expected to find.

Again, when Chiron comes to Jupiter, things have to get sensitized. This is a time when human reality can shake up the belief system. If the person is willing to take on the energy that Chiron brings, usually in the form of other people's pain and suffering, it can enhance how the person develops belief.

Jupiter also represents the right brain, imagination, intuition, gut instinct, and any feeling that you can't prove. When Chiron interacts with Jupiter, the kind of information that comes in can trigger that sense of knowing something without being able to explain why. It can shift how the imagination works. And it can shift the kind of vision the person finds worthy of holding and developing.

With the conjunction, Jupiter will be sensitized from the inside out. This energetic antenna gets plugged right into the belief function. Just as with the transits to Mars, with Chiron slowing Mars down a little bit, it can also slow down Jupiter. Jupiter can be kind of, "This is the vision I hold. Full steam ahead!" So when Chiron comes to it, it can definitely soften a person's confidence. With all of this energetic information and suffering coming in, Jupiter has to slow down and figure out how to respond.

The sextile will usually brings in information from Chironic others or situations that trigger the person's belief system to either stir into action or to change. It's like that poke in the ribs, "This is true. This is true. This is real." And the person's belief function will need to make a different kind of decision because of it.

The square feel threatening. "You're supposed to do this a different way. Here's this new reality. You can't continue as you have been. You just can't function the way that you prefer." That square is going to push from the side and try to get that person to open up the belief system to include, or at least to reflect, the consideration of the reality of energetic information, including other people's emotions, needs, and suffering.

The trine will bring information to the Jupiter that supports whatever the belief function is doing, whatever the imagination is doing. This can be a really great time for developing the imagination by tapping into the realities of people around you.

The inconjunct can seem to throw somebody off. Jupiter says: "This is what I believe. This is what I know is true. Even if I can't explain it to you, I know it's true." Then Chiron comes in with new energetic information, a person who needs something, a person who is injured, a person who is immature or cannot take care of him- or herself comes in, etc. If the Jupiter person actually responds to these situations and these people, it can really seem to undermine, in a real fundamental way, what that person believes. It's very sudden and the person can feel as if they are caught off guard and knocked off course.

With the opposition, you are going to be confronted with something real about what's going on inside another person. You might feel stopped in your Jupiter belief function tracks by the human reality that somebody brings to you, that somebody reveals to you. If you open up to this information, it can show you about your belief system, that there is something limited about how you see the world and how you expect and require the world to be. This transit can open you up – if you're willing to take in that information – and help you fashion a belief system, an overarching guiding principle by which to live your life that reflects more truly the human reality that exists in the world, and in yourself.

Saturn

Saturn has a normative influence on us. It's the part that says, "You should be doing this. You should be doing it that way." It is always trying to fashion every single thing into a bell curve so we can understand how to serve the greatest good for the greatest number of people. Chiron, on the other hand, always makes things unique. Chiron wants us to open up to difference and sensitivity, and the realities of what sensitive people as energetic beings are experiencing.

Chiron, in transit to Saturn, can have this element of: "Oh really? You think this is what's happening? Here's what's *really* happening. Here's what you would like to think is happening, but *this* is the reality." It's like a reality check for the reality checker. Chiron is saying, "This is what human experience is about." And Saturn often can say, "Well this is how I prefer things to be." Then Chiron is still saying (depending on the aspect): "this reality isn't going away just because you would like the world to be different than it really is."

This can come in the form of other people who don't fit in with the steel or iron or concrete worldview that Saturn develops. Saturn says, "I really need to develop stability so I can achieve this long-term goal." Chiron says, "Here's this unique detail. Here's this person, full of uniqueness." The nature of the aspect in question will determine how that comes through.

With the conjunction it's going to come from the inside out. Chironic people who understand the person's Saturn function might show up and say, "I understand this is how you're trying to create the world around you, but this is the reality. This is the energetic emotional reality that doesn't fit with that." The ideal is that this sensitizes that Saturn to take in more information about the realities of human experience rather than just working towards *shoulds*: "People should be like this. People should be like that."

The sextile will show up as stimulation and poking. If the person is really uptight with Saturn energy, it could be a wounded person who nags, who tugs on your jacket or on the sleeve of your shirt until you respond. The real need is to respond to the suffering, but to do it in a healthy way. The person with this transit has to figure out the mature way to respond, rather than just, "Get this thing out of my way."

The square will present friction. It will seem to threaten to push a person over on his or her side. He or she might feel like: "I have to do this thing, and these people who want something very different are telling me I'm doing it wrong and I have to change." That can be very difficult for a person who's running that Saturn energy in a strong way. Whether it's healthy or not, Saturn can still come off like a freight train. Once it gets going, it has the capacity to never stop. This Chironic information, this sensitivity to energy coming in from the side, can seem threatening. The person has to remain grounded and choose to open up to receive this information, because it will change how that Saturn functions. It's important not to be totally attached to the identity of that Saturn energy, because it needs to be changed by what it learns through this friction with Chiron.

The trine is going to seem to present opportunities to help, but you have to decide on good boundaries. You have to decide on what you are willing to do. That's going to be a Saturnian response to unhealthy Chiron: "I shouldn't do this, because it's immature." The response can be, "Okay great. Thanks for the opportunity to evaluate where I am with what I'm going to give and what I'm not."

The inconjunct will seem to threaten Saturn's mission. The strategy is to open up to this Chiron information. "What is that thing really doing? That will teach me more about why it is really important for me not to let it in. When I observe it and see what it really is and see what it really says about the human condition and not feel threatened and destroyed by it, it can teach me."

The opposition will come in the form of Chironic others, Chironic situations, and Chironic dynamics that come to us and say, "How you're doing your Saturn energy, how you do this inner judge, or this maturity or this morality – well, there's this other thing, this other reality that other people live." It can seem threatening, like that standoff with the gunslingers in the street, because Saturn, of course, does not want to change in this scenario. It's really important for the person to learn about his or her Saturn function by observing the Chironic people and circumstances that come to him or her.

Uranus

The Chiron transits to Uranus are going to try to sensitize the inner anarchist or genius or freedom fighter, the inner innovator or inventor. Uranus represents the part of the person that says, "This is what freedom is. This is how I'm going to achieve it." There is a wide variety, a wide range of possibilities with the Uranian archetype – from totally bored to totally iconoclastic and anarchist and free so I'm going to talk strictly about the energies here.

Uranus wants to be free of what confines. When Chiron comes around and somebody is experiencing wounded others or other situations that bring Chiron energy, the Uranus instinct – if healthy – is in part to observe it with detachment and then not be around it, saying, "Okay, no thanks. That does not make me feel free." There is also the humanitarian side of Uranus, which makes us want to help people and build toward the future. In that reality, when Chiron comes around by transit, that humanitarian self, that person who wants to create a better future, can get activated as well. There's a tremendous amount of variety.

With the conjunction, that inner innovator and freedom fighter needs to become more sensitive from the inside out. Chiron is going to be pouring buckets of energetic information into a person's life. How does he or she respond? "This does not make me feel free, so I should reject it." Or, "Does this make me more sensitive to the realities of human experience? Because, since I'm Uranus, I'm actually a little detached and I can view things objectively and dispassionately." This Chiron transit to Uranus can serve to really wake up Uranus, if it's detached, to the realities of individuals, the experiences of individuals, and the overall emotional human energetic experience of souls having these physical experiences.

The sextile will trigger and push a person's buttons until he or she does something in response. The square is going to bring friction of the two tectonic plates, again. The Chiron information will bear down on the Uranian part of the self, and something will shift. Whether that shift is conscious or not will depend on the person's awareness and circumstances. The trine will bring in information that seems non-threatening. It can be helpful if the person consciously applies energy toward it.

The inconjunct is going to be difficult – the person can feel knocked off course by the reality of this new Chironic information. It can definitely make the Uranian part of the person feel not free and subject to this confining scenario, perhaps feeling knocked over and not being able to stand up for a little bit.

The opposition will bring Chironic sources who say, "Look at how you create freedom. Look at what you think freedom is. Look at where you are in your Uranian process." And the Chiron figures will reflect this to the person.

Since most births from 1951 to 1991 have Uranus opposing Chiron natally, when this transit happens, it will mark Chiron return for these people. This opposition is really important to explore in general, so I will address it in a separate section called The Chiron Return, which follows these sections.

Neptune

Neptune has a technology that we use to connect to other parts of ourselves. It is the part of ourselves that needs to connect to other realities, understanding ourselves as more than the egoic, earthbound selves that we are.

When Chiron transits Neptune, it wants to open up this part of the self to receiving new sources of information. Neptune is like a station on the radio dial. And Chiron is a different station on that dial. So when Chiron comes to transit Neptune, whatever is happening with Neptune – in the spirit of getting Chironified, getting more sensitive to energy – it can actually focus the wide satellite dish of Neptune into a very small dish aimed at one particular person in order to learn more about the human experience. Even if you're focused on the grander reality with Neptune (which is healthy – connecting to something higher), Chiron can serve to focus it because it's a different frequency that has to do with uniqueness – individual uniqueness.

With the conjunction, Chiron will do this directly. It will just come in and sit on Neptune and want to open it up from the inside out. Neptune is already sensitive to energy, but Chiron wants to further sensitize that sensitivity function and to do that in a way so that it blossoms.

The sextile will have Chiron triggering the Neptune function in a person. If someone's unconsciously living Neptune, this can result in coloring outside the lines in very messy ways. The person has checked out or is trying to numb out from being sensitive to energy in the first place. So the sextile can be difficult because it's going to cause the person to act. The more conscious a person is of what Neptune's about and why this Chiron information is pressing the person's buttons is important.

With the square, the person is going to have to change somehow. He or she is going to have to give in to the challenge posed by Chiron to do something differently that he or she does not want to do regarding Neptune.

The trine is going to bring in information. If the person's Neptunian channel is wide open, it can bring in a ton of information about other people, about their suffering, about their uniqueness and difficulties in healing their wounds – the realities of human experience, in general. Some people who live Neptune stories have a compassionate story already. In this case, with the trine, there can be a real opportunity to help people in important ways.

With the inconjunct, depending on how the person lives out their Neptune, it can be really jarring, shake the person out of routine, and cause him or her to have to evaluate what Neptune's about. Chiron will throw seemingly incompatible, incongruous sets of information at the person during this time.

The opposition by transiting Chiron to natal Neptune is going to confront the person's Neptune function with energetic information that it might not want to experience. The person might not want to take this in, might not want to see this, but it's going to confront him or her with this information so that they might teach an insight about their own Neptunian function.

Pluto

Pluto is the marker of the soul's journey, the soul's empowerment journey. It is the marker of how the soul empowers itself as a human, ultimately to remember what real power is and that it is divine. Pluto represents the wounding of the soul as well as the desires and intentions of the soul. How a person is going to be empowered is the intention and when it goes wrong and it hurts, that's the wounding. Chiron coming to Pluto will sensitize this power function, which lies just below the surface like an atomic energy power plant. It will seek to sensitize this part of the self to what can look like weakness, but Chiron here is really looking to teach this Pluto – the empowerment part of the self – the soul empowerment journey. It is attempting to enrich Pluto by sensitizing it to the realities of individual human experience and really seeking to open the Pluto up to reconceiving what strength is. This is the kernel, the core of it: to reconsider what strength is given this energetic information – given that this is what people feel.

Pluto represents our unconscious and, depending on where Pluto is in the natal chart, it already picks up on under-the-surface information related to the 8th house and Scorpio, and other people's psychological motivations. So Chiron coming to Pluto by transit will open up that inner natural psychologist, even if the person is not consciously aware that that function exists within him- or herself.

The conjunction can seem to drop the bottom out of whatever strength the person thought was important and real because it will be pouring buckets of Chironic information and sensitivity, including the suffering of other people. The person's going to feel it, even if just under the surface, and it will really affect this person's foundation.

The sextile will trigger and push on the person until he or she responds, until the inner Pluto responds. What does the person think power and strength are? Whether the person is conscious of the answer or not is irrelevant. However he or she conceives unconsciously or consciously of strength and power, Chiron will push the button to make the person respond in Plutonian ways, hopefully taking in the information and learning something about the self.

With the square, there will be pressure and friction. If the Plutonian desires and fears are unconscious, it can serve to stir them up. And it will stir them up into consciousness because the person will hear this critic saying, "Oh, that's how you do your Pluto? You're actually doing it wrong and this is why." Chiron can open up a floodgate of emotional information that seems to threaten to knock one off course.

With the trine, the Chironic information can seem to support the individual's and the soul's mission. Whatever a person thinks power is, Chironic others are going to come in and support that, and feed that whatever that conception is.

The inconjunct can be a dose of Chironic reality that knocks a person off course and makes him or her feel he or she can't get up again. It will be a difficult experience of other people's pain and suffering that can seem to derail the mission. Because it's a transit, though, it's a temporary situation, so I advise people to get more conscious of what that Pluto really needs and then to reestablish firmer foundations once this difficult time is over.

With the opposition, the Chiron sensitivity and energetic reality that humans carry about their emotions is going to challenge, confront, and oppose the person's Plutonian sense of strength, whatever that is. If the person is unconscious about their inner Pluto and how they feel deep down about power and strength, then the Chiron sources that now come to the person can seem to block it critically and say, "This is not how you do it." They will threaten to stop the person from achieving what he or she wants to do.

Because Pluto can be unconscious and Chiron (sensitivity to energy) is not often talked about, all of these Pluto transits can be very strange to experience. The person might not have a frame of reference for being challenged with energetic information. This is true for all of these transits. We don't know how to talk about energy. We're just at the beginning of the transition to the Aquarian Age. We will, in several hundred years, be conceiving of ourselves as energetic beings having human experiences. So this is new for us.

The Nodes of the Moon

When Chiron is conjunct the South Node, it will deepen the person's emotional experience regarding the karmic baggage of emotional memories from other lives. It will seek to sensitize that by perhaps digging things up from the past in order for the person to become willing – or to learn how and to then become willing – to process emotions and stuff from the past that doesn't serve him or her anymore. It can also activate a unique gift carried in the person's South Node of which he or she has not yet been aware.

When Chiron comes to square the nodes, it is going to try to dig the person out of some pattern form the past that doesn't work and say, "Look, getting more sensitive to energy is going to change how your life works." There will be a real invitation or call to step out of some pattern from the past by choosing to take Chironic information in and letting it change the person. Naturally speaking, when we have a transit or square to the nodes, when we respond to the invitation of the pressure of that square, which wants to pull us out of our comfort zone (a key phrase for the South Node), our lives change. We are often enabled to move toward the North Node in a more smooth or facile way, because we have had that experience of saying, "Aha! Right. My old pattern doesn't work. Let me try something new."

When Chiron opposes the South Node by transit, it also will be conjunct the North Node. Chiron here will bring energetic information, sensitivity, and awareness of difference and uniqueness that challenges some of those old habit patterns. If a person responds to this Chiron transit, then old patterns are seen to be obviously not serving the person. Obviously, because Chiron will be near or conjunct the North Node, it will it take that person into the North Node and that can be very, very freeing, though – of course – very, very frightening at the same time. The North Node represents what in our various lives as humans we have not done that much of. So the Chiron call there is a major growth opportunity to stretch into that new territory, to learn what we have simply left out of our experience thus far as humans.

Ascendant-Descendant

The Ascendant-Descendent axis represents the way the person relates to self and other. It is how you show yourself to others and how you seek others. When Chiron comes here, it can feel that the person is on a high wire. The way the person balances self and other gets affected by Chiron. Chiron coming to the Ascendant will challenge a person, invite the person, and pour Chiron energy into the person, to make the person experience Chiron and express that outwardly. Because this is the Ascendant, a person's body will experience these Chironic effects, too. But the person will need to choose to allow this energetic antenna to be highlighted within the body of the self.

At the same time, Chiron opposes the Descendant and that is going to affect how the person's relationships are going, what it is he or she is looking for. Chiron coming to the Ascendant will change a person's mien, how that person experiences the self, so the relationships will naturally become edited through the opposition of Chiron to the Descendant. This opposition can come in the form of a standoff: "Why are you changing like this?" When someone becomes more Chironic, it can be difficult for others to deal with, depending on where they are, what they're doing with their own energetic antenna, the state of their wounding from infancy, and their relationship with their Chiron wounding.

When transiting Chiron sextiles the Ascendant, there is this triggering of the style, triggering of the self. This information comes in to push the person's buttons and poke her in the ribs until he or she responds. The simultaneous trine to the Descendant can reveal more about the person's relationships and how the person seeks to relate to others, which can – by becoming more Chironic – be benefited. So the trine can bring information to the person simultaneously as it triggers the person to behave in a certain way, to act or respond with Chironic energy in a certain way personally. That will affect how the relationships are run and what kind of person is sought to relate to, whether it's business or personal – friendship, romance, lover, spouse, etc.

When Chiron is square this axis, Chironic situations, dynamics, and people will press against what that person thinks is fair and what the person thinks he or she responsible for and what others are responsible for. This is really going to call up "self and other" in probably an uncomfortable way. Again, with squares, there's a tremendous growth opportunity, but feeling challenged with a square means you have to give up your position. You have to change. How one presents his or her body, the style, how one speaks up for him- or herself, and how one moves are going to be affected by Chiron, at the same time that relationships will be tested by Chironic realities.

When Chiron trines the Ascendant and sextiles the Descendant, it is a bit different. This will stimulate the person's response to other people while it sends information in the stream to the self. It will also serve to change relationships, but it puts more of an emphasis on responding to the other. Chiron energy makes the person respond to the other as opposed to having the person respond when Chiron is sextiling the Ascendant.

When transiting Chiron conjuncts the Descendant and opposes the Ascendant, relationships get "Chironified." Chronic others will come into the picture. And then of course, the person has to make a decision about if this is good or not. "How do I deal with this energy? How do I deal with these people? Do I have good boundaries? Am I going to be a giver, a nurse maid? Am I someone's Mommy?" All this will come up for a person.

With Chiron's opposition to the Ascendant, the person will be asked, "How are you going to be Chironic with other people?" That will naturally shape how the person behaves. What the person is learning from experiencing Chiron in other people will help the person adjust his or her own expression and style.

Midheaven-Nadir

The Midheaven-Nadir axis is the realm of the public and the private. The Midheaven is who we are in the world; the Nadir is who we are at home – who we're willing to be seen as in the public sphere versus who we are when no one's around and the lights are off and we're by ourselves.

When Chiron conjuncts the Midheaven, it's time for the person's public role to get Chironified. This can come in the form of drawing opportunities to do different kinds of work, because Chiron will always bring uniqueness, even in transit. It can also make what doesn't work in that person's public persona really sensitive to the energies of other people. If the person's job is no longer right for them, Chironic sensitivity will come in and reveal things about the job that don't work. The sensitivity will come to the part of the self that develops the public persona. The simultaneous opposition to the Nadir will put someone more in touch with what he or she needs deep down, on the inside, in private, when nobody else is around.

When transiting Chiron sextiles the Midheaven, this public self, this public persona, is being triggered by Chironic information. Who one is in public and how one wants to be perceived in public is probably going to change. During this transit, a person will need to respond to Chironic others, to take in this information and do something – hopefully something positive and not a knee-jerk reaction. With the simultaneous trine to the Nadir, this could reveal who the person is on the inside. It could reveal more information about how that person experiences the private self. If you're being poked in the ribs for your public self to respond to something, your inner needs will speak up. The energies of a trine can offer to teach you something about this in a nonthreatening way.

With the square to the Midheaven-Nadir axis, the inner and outer balance, the public and private balance that the person has worked their entire life to develop, needs to take in and be challenged by Chironic information and Chironic others. When Chiron squares the Midheaven, very often it's going to be somewhere in the vicinity of either the 1st house or the 7th house, so it's going to be other people or the needs of the self that are driving forces in changing how that person relates to public and private, how the person conceives of having a public self, and what role that person wishes to have in the world. So if a person responds openly to the Chiron energy, there can be an honest, compassionate response in how inner and outer are managed. There can be a real shift about who that person thinks he or she is, both publicly and privately. That's the square, the tectonic plates in action. One of them is Chiron – the energetic sensitivity, the needs of others, awareness of energetic information – and the is the balance between public and private, work and home, etc.

When transits Chiron trines the Midheaven, energetic information and Chironic people will come in and provide some kind of support for the development of the person's public role. If the public role, however, is not compassionate, this can become a problem. The trine will seem supportive, but the person has to be really clear about how he or she responds to Chironic sources of information.

When Chiron opposes the Midheaven and conjuncts the Nadir, the inner self needs to get Chironified. When nobody else is around, when nobody's home, the person needs to spend some private time in that psychic basement with the energetic antenna. All of these aspects depend on how the person relates natally to Chiron and to having access to the information, the subtle energies and being an energetic being. Does the person flip up into the head, into the brain, into the mind, in order to continue to have the illusion that he or she is in control of this? If that kind of scenario is in play, then Chiron hitting the Nadir will sensitize the person's foundation. It will be undeniable that this information is real. It's coming to the house of the Moon, so the feelings can get opened up. The inner psychic basement gets Chironified. This can be really unnerving for people who are brainiac-trained, who are control freaks, obsessed with calendars, timing, and progress, etc. In some cultures on Earth it can be very difficult. This transit is a call to open up, feel all one can feel, and have that inner self be recognized and honored in a new way.

The simultaneous opposition to the Midheaven is about when that inner reality is opened up to – when that part of the self is given special attention – the outer self needs to change. If you undergo an alchemical inner process, which is one of the possibilities with Chiron conjuncting the Nadir, your outer self cannot help but change. The look on your face, the general spark in your eyes – or lack thereof – will change. You will not be able to hide that your inner foundation has been Chironified, so the public role is likely to change. It could just be that others are recognizing the difference, but it also could be that, literally, because of this new orientation, direction, and willingness to the sensitive to energy, the person's work, career, or role in the community could change.

The Chiron Return

The Chiron return happens right around age 50. Every return represents a chapter in our experience of an energy. When we talk about a solar return, we're talking about a chapter of experience relative to the Sun, a chapter of experience of the energy of the Sun. When we talk about a Chiron return, this 50-year cycle involves learning about suffering, pain, dealing with the emotions of self and others, as well as learning about dealing with our own energetic sensitivity. It is a 50-year cycle of learning about ourselves as energetic beings. Some people experience two Chiron returns in their lifetime, but most of us experience just one.

As long as people are caught up in experiencing Chiron as a wound, the Chiron cycle can be a 50-year process of experiencing all different kinds of ways that the wound can get activated and expressed. If we're in that mode of suffering, not understanding the role of compassion and how it can bring us out of suffering and victimhood and help us mature spiritually, then the Chiron cycle as a whole can be an experience of repeated suffering.

I want to say that the Chiron return brings wonderful, magical things but it depends on how the person runs the energy. The truth is, there is no magical, alchemical shift or transformation that occurs at this time, but if a person is willing to experience the energy in a different way, to experience the self, there definitely can be magic. Nothing is guaranteed, though. Just like everybody's solar return isn't all sunny and happy. It's the same thing. How does a person run the Sun? Is that person depressed, is that person not vital? Well, it could be another year of *that*.

When we look at Chiron, we see that it's about learning how to take responsibility for your circumstances, learning how to mature spiritually, and learning how to take care of your needs rather than waiting for someone else to do it for you. The whole point of this process is to raise consciousness about Chiron's energy so that people who experience their Chiron returns can shift more easily into that alchemical realization of what the point of pain and suffering is.

When people hit age 50 and have their Chiron returns, their experiences depends on their karma and their intention regarding their own personal evolution and spiritual growth. It depends on how much they're open to

203

experiencing change. Some of those people will suddenly get to a place where they are able to be detached from the wound. Some will hit this point and be able to put the childhood wounding to rest, even if they don't experience something magical, alchemical, and transformational, as is possible. This is a major step for those who are able to do that. Others who hit the Chiron return will instead experience a deepening of the wound that they may never come out of again. Some of them actually can retreat back into a sense of helplessness, because when Chiron meets Chiron –transiting Chiron infusing Chironic energy into one's own natal Chiron – it boosts whatever that natal Chiron is already up to. If the wound is latent, if the wound is buried but not processed, then it's a possibility that a person can feel that wound much more deeply.

At the return, Chiron has completed its orbit around the Sun. It has therefore made all the possible aspects to a person's natal placements that it could over that 50-year period. It has gone through every sign, every house, it has conjuncted every planet in the chart, every angle, it has sextiled everything, it has squared everything, etc. The ideal with the Chiron return is to learn these lessons about energy, to be able to take a step back and say, "Yeah, I experienced this, I experienced that. I've basically been around the Chironic block and my next phase, my second Chironic chapter on Earth is going to be about something new. I've experienced that wound, I've experienced that pain, I've encountered other people's suffering and this is the kind of responses I've made." Usually, over time, we will have varied responses – it depends on the people and circumstances, etc.

At this time, one gets to decide if those attitudes, those responses, those ways of dealing with the intricacies of sensing subtext, sensing energy, and picking up on information that one cannot quantify, explain, prove, or justify – one gets to decide if all those things worked. At the return the person has the opportunity to go a different route. If the person is opened up to it, there could be an energetic shift regarding these matters.

When you're dealing with clients who are near their Chiron return, say up to a year before, look at how that person experiences Chiron. Realistically gauge how that person deals with energy, how that person deals with his or her own sensitivity, his or her own suffering. Where is that person in processing the wound? Is that person no longer holding parents responsible for meeting a need in that person? Or is that person waiting for someone to do something for him or her?

One of the most important things I want to impart to you as I wrap up relaying and sharing this view of Chiron, as channeled from the Ascended Masters, is this:

Be compassionate, and do not judge where someone is in their own Chironic healing process.

So now you might look at a client who comes in, armed with this information about Chiron, armed with this different perspective about how Chiron can help us get to the Aquarian Age by shifting our perspective and shifting our choices about how we view or experience ourselves as energetic beings. And you might then sit down with the client and want to say something, or relay something that you learned here that maybe inspired you a little bit. And that person might not be open to it. He or she might be in a stage of his or her emotional evolution and unfolding when most of this Chiron stuff will sound like baloney or they just won't be able to understand anything you're talking about.

Because this is new information that is seeding new levels of conscious, it might not fit in with everybody's worldview. So try to look at each person as an individual case and gauge where that person is in consciousness with Chiron energy. Again, know that you might say some things that just don't make sense to them. Some people I've done Chiron work with, say, "What are you talking about? There's a wound from when I was a baby? That doesn't make any sense to me. Here I am, I'm a 60-year old guy. What are you talking about?" Still, others welcome it and run with the new perspective, changing something major in their lives right off the bat.

So gauge how you can approach the person best. Obviously, if you're doing this work you already have a sense of that, but this new way of looking at Chiron calls for this especially – to not judge where people are in their process. You might offer a lot of information that that person wouldn't benefit from now, but it could very well kick into their consciousness somewhere down the road. You can throw it out there, suggest things, do whatever you feel is best.

Also understand or keep in mind what I spoke of in the introduction – about 2012 and where we are now – a lot of people might not shift, or a lot of people might shift but not consciously and allow themselves to be dragged along. How we work with people relative to this Chiron teaching is important, and I think it's emphasized with the Chiron return because of the incredible opportunity that does exist for those who want to shift – for those who want to experience themselves on deeper layers and in more conscious ways of how they are energetic beings having human experiences.

So, regarding the Chiron return, the opportunity is in shifting perspective and transforming out of any kind of wound or relationship to the wound. The opportunity is in advancing into feeling the energy, feeling the self as an energetic antenna and learning to manage the energy. This is about learning to say, "This relationship doesn't work. This dynamic doesn't work. This is where I'm leaking energy." This is about choosing to take better care of the self. In the process of healing the wound, whether that happens at the Chiron return or when someone is 10 or when someone's 95, it is necessary to become more self-nurturing. Some people will experience a deep need to nurture themselves if they haven't done it already. Some will already have mastered self-nurturing and now they want to nurture others in a new way – in an empowered, spiritual way. The possibilities are varied.

Conclusion

Thank you so much for your interest in learning more about Chiron and the potent healing opportunity it offers us at this time in our lives. I know that the Ascended Masters I work with are thrilled that there are so many people who are into this teaching, I guess that's why they encouraged me to get my act in gear! I encourage you to go out in the world and share these new insights about Chiron. Share these new perspectives. This teaching is a key to the next stage in human evolution – understanding ourselves as energetic beings having physical experiences.

About the Author

Tom Jacobs is an evolutionary astrologer, medium, and channel with an active private practice with clients around the globe. A member of Evolutionary Astrologer Steven Forrest's Apprenticeship Program since 2004, his work supports people to uncover and connect deeply with what their souls are here to do.

Tom holds a bachelor's degree in philosophy from The College of Wooster (Wooster, OH). He is the author or channel of nine books on astrology and metaphysics. Tom's writings on astrology and spirituality have appeared in Dell Horoscope Magazine, Aspects Magazine, and InnerChange Magazine.

Tom's original work on the Lilith archetype and emotional healing are reflected in two original natal reports available via his website, *The True Black Moon Lilith Natal Report* and *Living in the Present Tense: A Personalized Astrological 2012 Prep Course*, available via his website. He teaches karmic astrology and intuitive skills development both privately and to groups. He also holds a special interest in how health is affected by karma, including how karma shows up in birth charts and how we can improve our health by healing karma.

Contact Tom via his website, www.tdjacobs.com.

Printed in Great Britain
by Amazon

85127349R00120